STALKING JUSTICE

Also by Paul Mones

When a Child Kills

STALKING JUSTICE

PAUL MONES

POCKET BOOKS

New York   London   Toronto   Sydney   Tokyo   Singapore

POCKET BOOKS, a division of Simon & Schuster Inc.
1230 Avenue of the Americas, New York, NY 10020

Mones, Paul A.
  Stalking justice / Paul Mones.
    p.   cm.
  ISBN: 0-671-70348-X
  1. Spencer, Timothy Wilson, d. 1994.   2. Horgas, Joe.   3. Serial murders—
Virginia—Arlington County—Case studies.   4. Violent crimes—Virginia—
Arlington County—Case studies.   5. Homicide investigation—Virginia—
Arlington County—Case studies.   6. DNA fingerprinting—Virginia—Arlington
County—Case studies.
I Title.
HV6533.V8M65   1994
364.1'523'09755295—dc20   94-46923
                                                            CIP

First Pocket Books hardcover printing July 1995

10   9   8   7   6   5   4   3   2   1

POCKET and colophon are registered trademarks of
Simon & Schuster Inc.

Printed in the U.S.A.

Dedicated to the memory of
Carolyn Hamm, Debbie Dudley Davis,
Susan Hellams, Diane Cho
and
Susan Tucker

ACKNOWLEDGMENTS

I am very grateful to my friend David Burke, who freely gave me his time, energy, and wisdom when I needed it most. My friends Craig Bolotin, Eben Rawls, Don Dutton, and Skip Reeder were there the whole way with great support and encouragement.

I continue to be eternally grateful to my attorney and friend Susan Grode for her unwavering support and guidance.

My deep appreciation goes to my editor, Claire Zion, who patiently plodded through all the drafts and helped reshape my vision.

The sustenance to work through the almost four years it took to bring this book to fruition came from my wife, Nicole. In addition to indispensable moral support, she was instrumental in editing and rewriting this book. Her tireless labor was of inestimable help. I am a lucky man to have her as a partner.

AUTHOR'S NOTE

I shall be forever indebted to all those individuals who generously gave me their time and insights. This book would never have been possible without them.

I am especially grateful to Detective Joe Horgas for allowing me to recount the story of his remarkable investigation. I am also very thankful to his wife, Teresa, and their children, David and Katie, for allowing me into their home for long hours of interviews.

I deeply appreciate the assistance and cooperation of the Arlington County Police Department and Chief William "Smokey" Stover. Chief Stover and his staff were immensely helpful and gracious.

I am similarly indebted to the commonwealth attorney's offices in Arlington for their assistance and cooperation.

The Richmond Bureau of Police and the Chesterfield County Police Department as well as the commonwealth attorney's offices in these jurisdictions were also generous with their time and assistance.

While these law enforcement agencies were of immeasurable help, I would like to acknowledge specifically the tremendous contribution of the following persons in these agencies who sat for long hours patiently answering my questions and giving me their critical insights: Arlington County Police Department (ACPD) Corporal Mike Hill and ACPD Robbery-Homicide Detectives Bob Carrig, Chuck Shelton, and Steve Carter (retired).

Lieutenant Ken Madden, Sergeant Ed Gabrielson, Public Information Officer Tom Bell, and Deputy Chief Arthur Christiansen (retired) were also of great help, particularly in explaining the department's history and procedure.

I also would like to acknowledge the unselfish contributions of other ACPD detectives and supervisory personnel, both present and former: Detective Richard Spalding, Corporal Ed Chapman, Detective John Coale, Detective Rick Schoembs, Corporal William Griffith, Sergeant Richard Alt, Detective Cindy Brenneman, Sergeant Ray Harp, Detective Ray Spivey, Sergeant Henry Trumble, Detective Noel Hanrahan, Detective Pete Tyler, Detective Amon Rusty Comfort, Detective Mike Kyle, and Lieutenant Robert Minnich (retired).

In addition to Arlington County's police officers, the following lawyers and judges were crucial to this effort: former Arlington County Commonwealth Attorney and now U.S. Attorney for the Eastern District of Virginia Helen Fahey, Assistant Arlington County Commonwealth Attorney Arthur Karp, former Commonwealth Attorney Henry Hudson (now in private practice), former assistant Commonwealth Attorney Liam O'Grady (now in private practice), defense attorneys Rich McCue, Phil Hirschkopf, Tom Kelley, and Carl Womack. I am also grateful to Arlington County Circuit Court Judge Benjamin Kendrick for taking time from his busy docket to speak with me.

At the Richmond Police Bureau, I am very thankful to Detective Ray Williams, who spent long hours with me describing both his efforts and those of his now deceased partner Detective Glenn Williams. According to his family, his partner, fellow officers, and others, Glenn Williams was a dedicated police officer and a fine human being. I am sorry I never met him. I know many people miss him.

I also want to acknowledge the contribution of these other

members of the Richmond Police Bureau: Major Stuart Cook (retired), Captain Robert Childress, Lieutenant Larry Beadles, Sergeant Norm Harding (retired), and Captain A. Christine Bailor (retired). At the Chesterfield County Police Department, I extend my thanks to Lieutenant H. M. Shelton, Detective Ernie Hazard, and Detective W. F. Showalter for their contributions.

The following members of the Richmond and Chesterfield legal community also were of very meaningful assistance: former Richmond Commonwealth Attorney A. Aubrey Davis (now assistant Commonwealth Attorney in Chesterfield county); former assistant Richmond Commonwealth Attorney Jack Driscoll (now in private practice), Assistant Chesterfield County Commonwealth Attorney Warren Von Schuch, and Assistant Virginia Attorney General Donald Curry. I am similarly indebted to Richmond defense attorneys Jeffery Everhart, David Johnson, Christopher Collins, William Linka, and Barry Weinstein. Richmond Circuit Court Judge James Wilkerson's contribution is also gratefully acknowledged.

I acknowledge with deep appreciation the significant assistance of the FBI's Investigative Support Unit, especially Supervisory Special Agent R. Stephen Mardigian. Supervisory Special Agent Judson Ray as well as Supervisory Agent Jon Douglas were also of important assistance.

One of the most difficult tasks for me was understanding the intricacies of forensic testing, especially DNA fingerprinting. My grateful thanks to Deanne Dabbs and Paul Ferrara, director of the Virginia Bureau of Forensic Science. Dr. Michael Baird, Dr. Kevin McElfresh, and Lisa Bennett of Lifecodes, Inc., were equally helpful in guiding me through the complicated terrain of DNA fingerprinting.

Finally, I also acknowledge the contribution of the following persons: Fred Pang, Frank Rush, Lorna Wycoff, Eileen Williams, Pauline Mitchell, Betty Miller, Jim Dorton, Drew Gillespie, Mary Jane Burton, and Washington, D.C., Channel 9 television reporter Gary Riels.

This is a true story. Aside from several instances in which fictional names were necessary to protect an individual's privacy, all names and descriptions of people are real.

Certain scenes were re-created based upon accounts of reliable witnesses to those events.

The information in this book is derived from face-to-face and telephonic interviews, court and interview transcripts, defense and prosecution briefs and pleadings, police and coroner photos and reports, television and press reports, and historical books and references.

PREFACE

In the closing moments of the twentieth century, with the Cold War over, no Americans dying on foreign soil, and peace, in fact, breaking out all over the world, Americans should feel safe and secure. But they don't.

The people of the United States are now more frightened and distressed about violence than at any other time in history. In the national political debate, crime of all kinds—from vicious drive-by shootings and rapes to brutal child abuse and spousal battery—has taken the front seat, while foreign policy, the environment, and even the economy have taken the backseat.

All over our nation, from the big cities to the tiny hamlets and everywhere in between, there has been a frightening and unprecedented rise in violent crime. Simultaneously, handgun ownership is at an all-time high. This reflects more than the public's growing fear of crime; it also reveals the collective perception that the police are no longer able to ensure the public's safety. Confidence in and respect for law enforcement is at an all-time low.

The last twenty-five years have seen a rising tide of

police brutality and misconduct, culminating in 1991 with the videotaped beating of Rodney King by members of the Los Angeles Police Department. The grainy image of Rodney King hunched over on the pavement in a haze of frantic kicks and baton swings was burned into the national consciousness. It was an image that somehow brought all the other recent incidents—the beating death of a motorist by a Miami police officer, a homicide perpetrated by police in Detroit, and the constant cases of graft and corruption among narcotics officers in New York—into sharper focus.

As a defense attorney, I have been especially outraged over these blatant and outrageous violations of individual civil rights and the public's sacred trust. I have spent a good part of my career arguing to juries, judges, and legislative committees about the behavior of police. As a children's rights advocate, I have publicly criticized the law enforcement community for failing to protect abused and neglected children and for unfairly treating delinquent teenagers. On several occasions I have even sued various law enforcement officers and agencies for violating the rights of my clients.

In all the years I have spoken against the misdeeds of police officers, I rarely paused to think of the immense complexity of their work. Like many members of the public, especially members of my profession, I was quick to blame all of them for the wrongdoings of a few. I saw only one shade of blue.

Writing this book fundamentally changed my perceptions of the police and their role in the justice system.

During the four years I researched this book, I spent hundreds of hours with detectives, supervisory officers, and street patrol officers from four different police agencies. I sat with them in their offices, drove with them on calls, drank with them at the Fraternal Order of Police, and had dinner with them in their homes. What I saw and heard expanded my understanding and cracked my long-held prejudices about cops.

Above all, I learned that the enforcement of the law is a

highly individualized process guided not only by an officer's experience and intelligence but by his or her compassion and, most important, moral fiber.

The police officer does much more than merely enforce the law by arresting those who transgress. The officer is the quintessential public servant, on call to the American people twenty-four hours a day, seven days a week—long after the politicians and civil servants in city hall, the statehouse, and Congress have gone home.

From the mundane world of traffic control to the gory cosmos of homicide investigation, the police officer is called upon to deal with virtually every single personal and social problem. He mediates disputes between husbands and wives, coaxes suicidal souls off high ledges, rescues abused children from their parents, gives mouth-to-mouth resuscitation to the drowning victim, and has the awful task of informing family members of the accidents, injuries, and deaths of their loved ones.

It is also his duty to chastise his fellow citizens for the most mundane of transgressions: don't speed, don't jay-walk, turn down the music, keep your dog quiet, and on and on.

Aside from these massive obligations, a police officer has a much more subtle responsibility, one rarely recognized by the general public but one which is perhaps the most important—guarding the gates of justice. As schoolchildren we learn that legislators write our laws in the hallowed chambers of our statehouses and judges interpret them from atop their mahogany benches. But day to day, it is the police officer who actually writes and interprets the law, through the constant process of enforcing it.

The average beginning salary for the nation's half million police officers is just $25,000. For this sum, the officer confronts and solves problems that no one else in society wants to have anything to do with. When those problems worsen—when crime rises, when the streets become less safe—the police officers are the first to be blamed. Yet without them, society as we know it would not function.

After twenty-five years police officers retire, often without ever having received one word of thanks from any member of the public. And almost to a man and woman, they carry out their critical duties without expectations of gratitude or praise.

This is the story of one of those silent heroes.

No greater honor will ever be bestowed on an officer or a more profound duty imposed upon him than when he is entrusted with the investigation of the death of a human being. It is his duty to find the facts regardless of color or creed without prejudice, and to let no power on earth deter him from presenting these facts to the court without regard to personality.

—"The Homicide Investigator," by James J. Cadden, retired Detective-Captain, Baltimore City Police Department

The position of a policeman is not an easy one to fill as the thoughtless might suppose. It is trying, vexatious and hard. The capable and useful officer must combine a variety of qualities such as fit him for discharging the most delicate task as well as ferreting out the most mysterious crime. . . . It is as essential for the ideal guardian of the peace to be conservative, gentle, accommodating and courteous as it is for him to be courageous and brave. . . . Our policemen are good men and true and well deserve the place which they hold in the affections of the community. They merit and have our confidence, our esteem and our best wishes.

—"Richmond Police Manual," 1895

STALKING JUSTICE

PROLOGUE

JANUARY 1984

SHE DIDN'T COME TO WORK TUESDAY, NOR DID SHE CALL IN. SHE missed three appointments. It just wasn't like her. Her secretary had learned over the last five years that her boss, a lawyer specializing in architectural preservation, always called ahead even if she was going to arrive only five minutes late.

Still, the secretary hesitated to call her. She knew Carolyn was preparing to leave for an extended trip to Peru—Carolyn was just busy, she told herself. Yet her boss failed to show up Wednesday morning too, even though she had a ten o'clock appointment. The secretary called her home. No answer. She dialed the number five more times over the next two hours and still no one picked up.

Now she was worried. She called Carolyn's closest friend, Darla Henry, and asked her to go to Carolyn's house in Arlington to see if everything was okay.

Darla had just been with Carolyn two nights earlier at the Capitol Hill Squash Club. She did not share the secretary's concern; her thirty-two-year-old friend was probably rushing around to get ready for her trip abroad. Still, hearing the distress in the secretary's voice, Darla agreed to stop by Carolyn's house during lunch.

Turning on to South Twenty-third Street in Arlington, Virginia, on that cold January day in 1984, Darla noticed Carolyn's blue Plymouth parked in the driveway of the two-story white frame home. Betty knew that Carolyn's second car, a Fiat, was not working. That meant Carolyn was home. Everything was fine, she thought. But then Darla saw the front door. It was slightly ajar and at least an inch of snow had drifted into the doorway.

Darla climbed the porch and peered through the open door. She could see mail scattered on the floor of the vestibule. For the first time fear gnawed at her. Maybe she should not go in alone. At the far end of the street a neighbor was pulling out of his driveway. She waved and asked the young man to accompany her into the house.

With Larry Ranser right behind her, Darla pushed open the front door.

"Carolyn! Carolyn. It's Darla. Are you here?" Her voice echoed through the house. "Carolyn! Hey, Carolyn, are you all right?" Darla yelled with a nervous catch in her voice.

No reply.

As she turned in to the kitchen to make a cup of late-night tea, he stepped from the shadows and thrust the stainless steel blade within a hair of her windpipe.

"Scream and I'll cut your face, bitch. All we want is money and we're outta here."

Over the years, hundreds of times, she had thought about what she would do if she were assaulted in some deserted parking lot or on a downtown street—scream, kick him in the balls, and run. Now all her planning was useless; she stood frozen in her nightgown, in her own kitchen. The knife grazed her throat gently. Okay. Do what he says.

"I won't scream. Just please don't hurt me." Had she calculated correctly? Yes. He pulled the knife slowly from her throat. She exhaled in relief.

"Where's your pocketbook? We just want money," he said.

His voice was calmer now, almost polite. "It's upstairs,"
she stammered.

Why did he keep saying "we"? Was there somebody else
in the house? He used the razor-sharp steel blade to prod
her to the second floor where her brown purse dangled from
the banister.

He rummaged through her wallet and his face contorted
in fury. "Is this all you got?" He thrust eighteen dollars in
her face. "Is this all you fucking got!"

Stepping into the vestibule, they noticed the house was a
mess, but that wasn't unusual. Carolyn was highly intelligent
and had earned several advanced degrees, but housekeeping
was not among her many talents. Still, there was something
unnerving about the disarray. It was too chaotic, even for
Carolyn.

Thinking her friend might be hurt or seriously ill, Darla
went upstairs. Papers and books were strewn over the steps
and banister, but this was normal—Carolyn commonly used
the staircase as a giant shelf. Darla gasped however when she
saw her friend's brown leather purse splayed open on the
landing, with eye shadow, checkbook, coins, aspirin, driver's
license, business cards scattered around it. Darla picked up
the pocketbook, then immediately replaced it; somehow she
knew nothing should be disturbed.

A quick look into the upstairs bedrooms revealed nothing
unusual, except that all of Carolyn's bureau drawers were
open, their contents spilling out. Carolyn's glasses sat on the
edge of her bathroom sink. The workout clothes in which
she had played squash with Darla two nights earlier were
wadded on the tile floor. Back downstairs, they saw Carolyn's
dark blue terry-cloth bathrobe crumpled on the living room
rug.

"Let's see what else you got here!" her attacker shrieked
as he pushed her down the steps. A minute ago he had
seemed mild, organized, intelligent, but now he appeared to
be out of control. Pointing to her living room sofa he yelled,

lie

"Take off your robe and go ~~lay~~ down. Face the goddamn wall! I'm gonna have your pussy."

He'll just do it and leave, she thought, trying to stop herself from shaking as she eased onto the couch. I can get through it.

He entered her brutally, and she turned her face away. "Don't look at me, bitch," he hissed. Then: "Come! Come or I'll cut you!" She lay still. When he came, very quickly, she relaxed a little.

Calm, she thought, stay calm. Now he's got everything he came for. He'll be out of here. He'll be gone, and then I can pretend it never happened, I don't even have to tell anybody. I can—

"Now turn around and suck it, bitch."

Everything in the adjoining dining room and kitchen seemed to be in place. But there was a length of stereo speaker wire hanging on the back of a folding chair and a piece of venetian blind cord ~~laying~~ near the rear wall.

lying

"Please. Aren't you done?"

"Shut the fuck up," he roared. "Suck it or we'll slash you."

After a few minutes, he yanked his penis from her mouth and ordered her into the dining room. She started to shake, uncontrollably now, as she saw him unwind a long white cord.

"What are you going to do?"

"I gotta tie you up, but don't worry. I ain't gonna hurt you. Just turn around." Now he was composed again. The rage had evaporated.

He's done with the rape, she reasoned, and now he's really getting the hell out of here. Keep control. Do what he says.

She offered him her wrists.

Cautiously, with Ranser right behind her, Darla began her descent to the basement. Halfway down she was hit with a blast of cold air coming from her immediate right. The ventilator hose from the dryer had been removed from the laundry room window.

4

Darla's gaze then fell on a rolled-up carpet, the one Carolyn had taken up from the living room floor when she moved in two years earlier. It was tied with a thick hemp rope, most of which had been unwound and was lying bunched up on the floor. On top of the carpet was a six-inch steak knife with a light brown wooden handle.

It was the chalk white soles of her feet she saw first. Carolyn was facedown, naked, her ashen body lying in the doorway between the basement and the garage. Her wrists were bound behind her with what looked like miles of venetian blind cord. A section of the rope from the carpet was tied in a noose around her neck. The rope was tautly extended straight up and over a water pipe, then down, into the garage, and tied to the bumper of her blue Fiat.

Except for the way her shoulder-length chestnut hair was tangled in a fist-size knot of rope, they saw no visible signs of injury. No blood or bruises were obvious anywhere on her body.

Neither had ever seen a dead body before. There was a strange calmness to the violence of the scene; in fact, with her eyes closed, her right cheek pressed against the dull gray cement floor, Carolyn looked as if she ~~had~~ might have fallen asleep on the cold concrete floor.

He stopped running when he reached the empty lot far from her house. His heart still pounded: exhilaration, fear. Oh, he thought, we're good. We're so good. He walked through the tall grass, and as he walked he held his hand to his nose, smelling, with great gratification, the last moments of her life on his fingers.

5

JANUARY 1984

JOE HORGAS, A SIXTEEN-YEAR VETERAN OF THE ARLINGTON COUNTY Police Department, popped open the dark green champagne bottle and poured full glasses all around his in-laws' living room in Nanty Glo, Pennsylvania. It was the in-laws' fiftieth wedding anniversary. All of Teresa's brothers and sisters were there, with their children, plus uncles and aunts and cousins he hadn't seen in years. It was a great feeling, having everybody together. He and Teresa and their four-year-old son, David, didn't get back very often these days. "A toast," he said, and raised his glass.

"Joe," whispered a cousin from behind him. "It's the phone for you. Sounds urgent."

Joe's congenial smile faded as he paced down the hall to the phone, his 250-pound frame quick as a cat. Urgent, in his line of work, meant only one thing. Murder. They had a body, someone who'd been killed, and at last it was his turn again. Joe loved homicide investigation. It was the best thing about being a cop. And it had been two long years since he'd had a murder. Not that this was surprising: Arlington County,

Virginia, was a relatively quiet place. Despite its proximity to one of America's murder capitals—Washington, D.C.—there were only a few killings every year in the county, four or five, and with eight guys in the robbery-homicide unit, that meant they mostly worked robberies. It was Joe's turn, though: next up in the barrel. Had to be a murder. They wouldn't call him for anything else.

Excitement was vibrating through him by the time he caught the dangling receiver in his strong hand and shoved it between his bulldog neck and shoulder. "Horgas."

"Joe." It was Sergeant Hawkins. "We have one. A woman."

There was something in the way Hawkins said it that made Horgas think it was really bad, done-by-a-stranger bad, not the usual scene you see of a man with a gun crying beside his dead wife. "I'll be there in four hours," he breathed, calculating a hard ride.

"Joe," Hawkins said firmly. "I know you been waiting. But we can't hold off on this. It's too serious. I'm giving it to Carrig."

"Sir—"

"No, Joe. We've got to move now."

'I'll be there anyway, fast as I can."

"Don't hurry," Hawkins advised. "I had to call you, Joe. Had to tell you. Stay and enjoy the celebration. We got all the manpower we need on this one."

Right, Horgas thought, all except me. He signed off and slumped the receiver back on its cradle. He told himself he would put it from his mind, and he tried to—all through the toasts, the dinner, and the parties that went on through the weekend. But all that time he kept hearing the taut mobilization in Hawkins's voice, the ring of alert that meant the perpetrator was someone they had to find right away.

The following Wednesday morning, seven-thirty, Joe reported back to work. The squad room was a storm of activity. Bob Carrig was heading up the murder, with Chuck Shelton assisting him, and the five remaining detectives were constantly bursting in, racing out, checking out one lead after another. They hadn't made an arrest yet—which was worrisome, considering that more than four days had elapsed since

Carolyn Hamm's body had been discovered. They had a line on somebody, though, somebody they were pretty sure of, and an arrest was not far off. They were closing in on the guy and the tight, urgent knots of conversation in the squad room meant his capture was imminent.

Joe was not a part of it, though, so he turned his attention back to his job. In addition to robberies, he had to deal with attempted murders, assaults with deadly weapons, suicides, drug overdoses, and even routine investigations of natural deaths in the home. He picked up the stack of hot sheets covering crimes of the last few days, the days he had been away, and read through them. Top of the list, of course, was the "suspicious death" at 4921 South Twenty-third—the murder of Carolyn Hamm. Yet there were two other break-ins that caught his eye. These had occurred at Dinwiddie and Columbus, just blocks from the homicide in south Arlington. He took in the details. At the Dinwiddie Street address someone had broken in through a basement window but had left before the woman returned home; she walked upstairs to find pornographic magazines and a length of venetian blind cord on her bed. Hadn't Hamm been strangled with venetian blind cord, and hadn't her home been entered through a basement window? He checked the sheet again. Yes. He turned to the second break-in, and his eyes widened. A woman named Marcie Sanders. Suspect broke in through a rear window, threatened her with a knife, sexually assaulted her, and demanded money. She fought back and screamed: he slashed her pretty bad and fled. This was a perpetrator Joe knew well, a rapist the sex crimes unit was very anxious to catch—the black masked rapist. The guy had been assaulting women around Arlington for the last seven months, since June '83. It was always the same guy, an athletic young black man, wearing a mask. Definitely the one who assaulted Sanders. He checked the last line of the Sanders advisory. Yes: "Look out for a b/m, 5'10", thin build, plaid cloth over face with eye slits in it, wearing gloves and ski cap." I knew it, thought Horgas. Same guy.

Naturally they would check this guy out in connection with the Hamm murder. He flipped on through the pages.

Staring up at him, dated the day before, January 31, 1984, was a request from Sergeant Hawkins.

> The homicide robbery unit would like to be contacted immediately if any sexual assaults are reported in which a suspect broke into the victim's residence, and/or sections of rope cord are located pre-cut. Point of entry is by way of window; victim is a white female living alone or was alone at time. This request is in addition to normal notification.

Why didn't the notice say there was a chance the suspect might be a black male, five-foot-ten, and so on? His eyebrows cramped together as he rifled through the rest of the pages. Nothing.

"Sarge." He leaned in the Sergeant's office door. "Talk to you?"

"Sure, Joe." Hawkins took off his glasses and put down the paper he was studying. He gave a thin, cordial smile but Joe saw the deep lines of exhaustion meshed around his eyes. Caged frustration rushed over Joe again, squeezing hard in his chest: it should have been his, this case! He shouldn't be asking questions like an outsider.

"About this Hamm case." He watched his sergeant. "Don't you think that it's a hell of a coincidence that this masked rapist is working the same area as the murderer? Look at this case on January fourteenth where this masked guy came through a basement window just a couple of blocks from Hamm. God knows what would have happened if the girl's roommate hadn't walked in and scared him away. And look at the Sanders case the same day that Hamm was found. . . ."

"Joe!" Hawkins said irritably. "We have a task force working on this and they are familiar with everything." Hawkins paused to let his words sink in. "Don't you have some robberies that need to be worked on?"

Rape and robbery, Joe thought bitterly. Rape and robbery. That's why his squad hadn't seen more of the cases—because when they were combined with rapes they went to the sex crimes squad. There had been one, though, an attempted robbery out on Columbia Pike. A masked black man attacked a white woman in a parking lot. That case had gone to Joe because there hadn't been a rape, but after interviewing the woman, Horgas was positive the man had intended to rape her. He had forced her at knifepoint into her car and grabbed for her purse. A passerby happened along and the assailant bolted from the car. Joe had never developed one good lead on him, but the crime caught his attention.

"The reason we put out the January thirty-first advisory," Hawkins was saying, "was the Dinwiddie break-in, not the attack on Sanders. At Dinwiddie the guy left a cut length of venetian blind cord on the bed—exactly the same type of rope that was used to tie up Hamm. Woman named Thoreau lived there. What we think, he just got tired of waiting. If Thoreau had come home sooner she'd be as dead as Hamm. She's lucky, that's all."

Horgas nodded in agreement and turned to leave.

"I know how you feel, Joe," Hawkins said. "First murder we've had like this in I can't remember when, but you weren't around."

Hawkins sighed, and for a moment the exhaustion flooded out again. "Didn't that woman who was attacked in her basement see a car parked outside her house?" Hawkins inquired.

"Yeah," Joe shot back. "She reported she saw a black guy sitting in the front seat. It was a beige Pontiac or Buick."

"Well, seeing how strongly you feel about this, go ahead and send a teletype. Maybe some other PD will be familiar with the car being involved in some burglaries."

"Thanks," Joe said with a slight smile as he closed Hawkins's door.

Hawkins was all right, Joe thought, as he hurried back to his desk: their tactical and spiritual leader, father figure, all rolled into one. Hawkins knew Joe's idea was crazy; hell, Joe knew it was crazy too. But it was stuck in his craw like a fish bone, and he couldn't let it go. He maneuvered his bulk smoothly into the chair and tapped out the teletype.

REQUEST REGIONAL BROADCAST
TO: NORTHERN VIRGINIA, WASHINGTON, D.C., MARYLAND
FROM: ARLINGTON COUNTY PD, VIRGINIA

BELOW SUSPECTS AND VEHICLE ARE WANTED FOR
A BURGLARY/ARMED ROBBERY WHICH OCCURRED ON
1-14-84 AT 2255 HOURS IN ARLINGTON, VIRGINIA.

1. BM, 21–23, 5'10", 165 LBS.
   WEARING CREAM CANVAS JACKET, HOMEMADE
   DARK COLORED MASK WITH 2 EYEHOLES, GLOVES
   *ARMED WITH KNIFE

2. BM NFD
   VEHICLE: 1976–1979 BEIGE, 2 DOOR PONTIAC OR
   BUICK WITH LIGHT BROWN VINYL ROOF

IMMED. ADVICE REQUESTED
THKS.
R/H DETECTIVE JOE HORGAS

There was nothing to do then but wait, and tackle his robberies . . . and kick himself over and over for not being in
Arlington at the time of Hamm's murder. Even though it
wasn't his case, Horgas visited the Hamm scene to look it
over for any clues that might hint at the killer's identity. He
rushed to the teletype machine every morning, first thing,
and sifted through the messages; then he found reasons to
stop by and check the machine every few hours during the
day too. Nothing. Apparently the masked rapist was not operating in any other cities. He tried to keep his mind off the
Hamm case, tried to concentrate on his own work, because
just below his control level there was always the anger at
not having the Hamm case for himself. And of course he
couldn't forget it, not entirely, because the other guys were
in and out of the squad room all day, huddling, talking hard,
poring together over papers, photos, and file folders. There
was Carrig, giving orders. Joe tried not to watch. But it was
not a big place: eight metal desks, in two rows, banks of file
cabinets on either side, stacks of papers and looseleaf binders
on every surface. The room was crowded, and no place was
private; the linoleum floor and cinder-block walls seemed to
magnify every sound, every voice.
On February 6, Carrig and Shelton arrested the killer. He

confessed. Twenty-eight-year-old David Vasquez lived just around the corner from Hamm. He had a borderline intelligence but nevertheless had usually managed to hold a menial labor job. Several people had noticed him loitering suspiciously around Hamm's home before her body was found. After being interrogated by Carrig and Shelton, Vasquez confessed.

Despite his confession there was still some feeling among the investigators that Vasquez might have had a partner—it was an intelligent murder, after all, and he himself was none too swift. But he wouldn't give the partner up, no matter how many times they asked him the question.

With the arrest of Vasquez, Joe was finally able to put the murder, and his frustration about not getting it, behind him. They had caught the guy—before he killed again. That was the main thing. Maybe Joe couldn't have even done it any better.

David Vasquez pleaded guilty to second-degree murder and was sentenced to thirty-five years in prison. Arlington County relaxed.

It did not take long for the rhythm of the squad room to return to normal. There was a constant stream of crimes to solve. Some of these were unusual, due to the massive government nexus nearby. The three hundred men and women of the Arlington County PD were constantly, in law enforcement parlance, "interfacing" with the Secret Service, FBI, DEA, INS, U.S. Park Police, Military Police, and other federal agencies. This led to the frequent assignment of officers to nontraditional policing responsibilities—especially in the 1960s and 1970s, when the community was a convenient staging ground for protesters seeking to enter Washington either over the Fourteenth Street Bridge or Key Bridge. The patrolmen also had to cope regularly with the spillover crowds of antiwar protestors who congregated at the Pentagon.

Even in times of social rest, the men and women of the department were required to perform some rather unique tasks—from providing security to the foreign leader who delivered a key address at a local hotel to coordinating protection for a president when he came over the bridge to eat dinner at a favorite Arlington restaurant.

Most of the work, though, when all was said and done, was robberies. Washington, with its chain of federal bureaucracies, attracted a massive horde of yuppies from all over the nation, and many of them chose to reside in Arlington County—from which they departed, five mornings a week, to cross the Potomac and go to work. All the wealth that flowed into the county made it an ideal place for purse snatchings, bank robberies, and late-night holdups of convenience stores. And Joe spent most of the years that followed the Hamm murder chasing down the petty thieves and drug addicts who committed these robberies. When a murder did occur, there was usually a smoking gun nearby: an obvious perpetrator and a quick arrest.

In 1985, for example, the dead body of a thirty-year-old woman was found just off Interstate 66. She had no identification except a Wakefield High School class ring. After checking yearbooks at the high school, Horgas was able to positively identify the woman. Though the school had no current address for her, they had her mother's name and address. The mother informed Horgas that her daughter had had two children and had lived with a man near the spot where the body was discovered. Upon learning that the daughter and her boyfriend were having problems, Horgas and his partner raced over to the apartment. As he approached the building a man was walking out.

"Hi, I'm Detective Horgas from the Arlington police department. What's your name?"

"Vernon Clark," the man replied.

"Vernon Clark, you're under arrest." Clark, Horgas had earlier learned, was the victim's boyfriend. As soon as Clark identified himself, Horgas noticed that the man had a fine splattering of blood all over his hands and forearms. Horgas immediately knew it was the girlfriend's blood. Clark was convicted of the murder.

In the four years following the discovery of Hamm's body, Joe investigated three homicides altogether, the last one being

14

in May of 1986. An elderly woman was killed during a robbery. Her assailant was captured three weeks after the attack and promptly confessed.

It was December 1, 1987, eight-thirty in the evening, when Joe got the phone call that turned his routine upside down.

Teresa Horgas, a tall, slender woman with high cheekbones and dark brown hair, lifted the receiver and winced when she heard Bob Carrig's somber request to speak with Joe. They'd been getting late-night calls for twelve of the fourteen years she and Joe had been married and Teresa knew that now her husband would have to cut short his wrestling match with their seven-year-old son, David. She understood such intrusions, but she never got used to them. It was especially hard to take tonight, because Joe had just walked in the door after being away since early morning.

After finishing his 7 A.M. to 3 P.M. shift, Horgas had gone directly to the home of fellow detective Mike Hill, where he was using his old drywall skills to help finish Hill's basement. A perturbed Teresa had called Joe at seven-thirty demanding that he come home to spend some time with his son. Joe had been home no more than fifteen minutes when Carrig's call came in.

She extended the receiver silently to Joe. "Horgas!" he barked, and the next thing he heard was Carrig's voice, all flattened out and hollow. "We got a dead woman," Carrig said. "It's your ticket." Horgas could hear Carrig swallowing hard, as if it hurt to push the words out.

As Teresa had silently predicted, Joe vanished into the night after scribbling down a nearby address. Yet another wrestling match was put on hold.

Horgas didn't relish racing off at all hours, never knowing when he'd return. There was little he could do about it, though; people did not kill at convenient times. As he quickly slipped into the driver's seat, he felt the familiar pangs of guilt—David was not old enough to understand why Daddy had to leave right in the middle of one of their favorite games, and the pain on his child's face was always so hard for him to walk away from.

These feelings of guilt were, however, short-lived. Within the moments it took to reach South Walter Reed Drive, where he placed the blue bubble light on his dashboard, his entire focus shifted to what he had just heard.

"We got a dead woman." There had been something in Carrig's voice that told Joe this was different. Different and bad.

Carrig's words echoed in the darkness of Joe's gray Ford Crown Victoria. As he sped through the quiet residential neighborhoods, he became increasingly exhilarated. It was not that he looked forward to getting news of a murder. But these investigations, despite the long wait between each of them, were his love, his addiction. Lots of policemen who shared this obsession had had childhood dreams about meting out justice, or had come from a long line of men in blue. Not Joe. He had come to police work almost by accident. All he had known growing up in Morann—a small town in the soft coal fields of central Pennsylvania—was that he didn't want to end up like everyone else in town.

His own father, John Horgas, whose parents had emigrated from Hungary, had been born in a house directly across from the entrance to the Brookwood Shaft. He'd gone to work digging coal by hand in this mine before he was ten years old. After being injured in a mining accident, a fate that befell many in his day, he faced a difficult recovery period in which he raised chickens as a way of supplementing the family income. He and his wife, Mary, had nine children. Joe, the oldest boy, had to spend two days a week at the age of eleven peddling eggs with his father. Joe's father, after recovering from the back injury, went to work as a dragline operator in an open pit mine. It was a hard life.

By the time Joe reached high school, many of his friends looked forward to following their fathers into the mines or striking out for the sprawling steel mills of Pittsburgh or Bethlehem. Joe steadfastly refused these possibilities. Still, he wasn't sure what he *did* want.

Next to the picture of the broad-shouldered boy with light brown, closely cropped, wavy hair, deep-set hazel eyes behind thick black-rimmed glasses, and a cavernous chin cleft, the 1963 Knights yearbook staff wrote, "Neither worries or hurries . . . a great tackle on the football field when not reading library books . . . a whiz at math." The description sounded contradictory. Yet each Saturday, after a hard practice on the football field, Joe had been in the library solving a tricky algebra equation or reading a passage from some obscure Latin text.

To look at him driving to the crime scene this night, his bull neck, bulky hands and forearms, one might think it was football that got him into Penn State. In truth it was his grades, his analytical skills, his strong talent for deductive reasoning, and—most of all—his overpowering drive to compete. It was such an honor for one of the family to be accepted to a university that Joe's father sold the family cow to pay for the first semester's room and board. While the small-town boy was captivated by campus life, he felt embarrassed, as he later said, "to be bumming off his parents."

When Joe returned for Christmas break after the first semester, he saw firsthand how difficult it was for his family. "Mom and Dad had eight other kids to feed," he later commented. "Now that the cow was gone there wasn't much else left to sell." It also didn't help his adolescent ego that his best friend from high school had money and a set of keys to a brand-new car in his pocket.

Instead of returning for the spring semester, he went to work in a junkyard run by his uncle. Six months later, in the summer of 1964, word came to the small Pennsylvania town that anyone with a strong back who wanted to make good money should head down to Arlington, Virginia, where there was a booming market for construction workers. All Joe needed to hear was that the starting salary was an astonishing $3.50 an hour.

Horgas eventually found his niche as a drywaller but had a difficult time making friends in the big city. After two years of living in a succession of bachelor apartments, Horgas moved in with a fellow Pennsylvanian, Mike Saupp, who had recently joined the Arlington County Police Department. Joe quickly found that he liked being around Saupp and other rookies who came by the apartment to watch football or play cards. He admired their camaraderie, and especially enjoyed listening to their war stories about life on the beat.

It might sound better to say that Joe joined the force because he believed that defending and protecting the public was a higher calling than cutting and taping drywall. It was something infinitely more mundane, however, that led him in August of 1968 to take the Arlington police department entrance exam.

"Though I was making a lot better money working construction than my buddies in the PD," he later reflected, "they had security, something to look forward to in the future. I didn't. If I got sick, I didn't get paid; if I went hunting or home for Christmas I might not have a job when I returned. I didn't know what cops really did. To me it was just a job. I felt honored I was selected, but I didn't know what the hell police work was all about."

Within a few short years, however, especially after he became a detective, Joe quickly discovered how much he loved his new job. It was more than just helping people. To him detective work was the ultimate, high-stakes competition: Joe against the criminal. And the more heinous the crime, the more he was driven.

The excitement of leading an investigation coursed through Horgas as he made his right turn going up the hill into the Fairlington complex. He leaned over the steering wheel. He was the type who always jumped over the line before the whistle blew, always charged through the door the instant it was cracked. Almost there! He felt himself driving the pedal to the floor. The crime scene was just ahead.

To his shock, as he pulled up to the scene, he saw fellow detectives Carrig and Steve Carter standing idly outside. Why weren't they in the house? They were bent over a fistful of Polaroids. Joe's car screeched to a halt and he leaped out on the curb. "Whatta we got here?" he yelled. "Who found her?"

Carrig and Carter filled him in. The body had been found by Arlington County patrol officers William Griffith and Dan Borelli. At around 7 P.M. that evening, they had received a radio call to "check on the welfare" of the resident who lived

at 4801 South Twenty-seventh Road in the Fairlington section of Arlington. Neighbors had become alarmed when the
woman at 4801 South Twenty-seventh neither emerged from
her house nor answered her phone, no matter what hour they
tried to call her. All the 911 dispatcher reported to Griffith
and Borelli was: "Suspicious circumstances: woman at address not seen for several days."

As Griffith entered the call into his logbook before driving
to the scene his first thought was that if anything serious had
happened to the resident, it was most likely the result of an
accident. These calls usually involved an elderly person who
had suffered a heart attack or had slipped while getting out
of the bathtub. Fairlington was a solidly middle-income
neighborhood filled with retired persons and childless cou-
ples; it was known as a very safe place, even for peaceful
Arlington County. The police received auto theft reports from
Fairlington, but not much else.

Thirteen minutes after the neighbor's call came in to 911,
William Griffith, followed by fellow officer Dan Borelli,
pulled up in front of the Tucker home. Like other houses in
the neighborhood, it was a simple two-story redbrick dwelling with black shutters and a wrought-iron balcony off the
back door. Fairlington had a parklike quality with its tower-
ing hardwoods, plentiful evergreen bushes, and gently rolling
lawns. Susan Tucker lived in an attached two-family dwelling adjacent to a large, sloping field bordered by a small
forest of elm and oak. Though one could see the twinkling
lights from the surrounding malls and hear the steady roar
of cars from South Walter Reed Drive below, the immediate
area around the house retained a pristine charm.

Because the front door was locked, Griffith and Borelli
went around to the rear and hoisted themselves onto the back
porch. The back door was unlocked but opened only a few
inches because a chair had been wedged upright under the
knob. Peering into the darkened house, Griffith saw the beam
of his flashlight fall on a purse with its scattered contents
lying inside the doorway. Both men unsnapped the hammer
guards on their holsters.

As Borelli shoved the door open with his shoulder, he

screamed, "Police officers! We are entering with our weapons drawn. If anyone is present, make your presence known immediately!"

Silence.

As soon as they stepped through the door, both men were hit by an odor they knew meant only one thing. The stench emitted by a decomposing human body is one that invades your sinuses and sticks to your clothes. One veteran detective described it as akin to the fetid scent that emanates from an unwashed public urinal brimming with stale cigarette butts.

As Griffith crossed through the dining area into the living room and studied the light brown leather shoulder bag splayed open on the floor, he knew his initial assessment had been wrong. Whatever happened to the resident of 4801 South Twenty-seventh Road had *not* been the result of any accident.

Carefully stepping over a red comb, a bus schedule, lipstick, and the other contents of the purse, Borelli went up the stairs; Griffith stayed at the bottom to cover his partner's back. Though they felt fairly sure no one was in the house, neither was taking any chances. At the top, Borelli silently signaled Griffith to join him.

As Griffith climbed the stairs the smell became so strong he had difficulty breathing through his nose. Just as he reached the top step, the living room phone rang. Both men froze. Their job was only to secure the scene. The ringing continued until Griffith joined Borelli at the top.

With Griffith at his back, Borelli opened the door immediately to the left of the landing. Empty. Griffith then turned and walked down the short hallway to the half-opened doorway of another bedroom.

The flashlight beam caught her before he even stepped into the room. They entered—but not to check her vital signs. There was no need for that. They just had to confirm that no one was in the closet or under the bed. As Borelli and Griffith came back down the stairs the phone rang again, this time much longer than before. When the ringing ceased Griffith called into headquarters on his walkie-talkie. In the sixteen short minutes since he had received the call, his simple "check on the welfare" call had become a very gruesome homicide.

Within moments of Griffith's call to headquarters, waves of police cars screamed up to South Twenty-seventh Road. The first officers to arrive were crime scene agents John Coale and Rick Schoembs, driving the crime scene van, referred to in the department as Agent 50. Coale and Schoembs were forensic specialists, officers whose job it was to secure the scene, photograph it, measure it, and gather initial physical evidence such as fingerprints. Within minutes of their arrival, neon yellow tape marked DO NOT CROSS—A.C.P.D was strung between the trees and bushes that surrounded the house, and 4801 Twenty-seventh Road ceased being just another Georgian-style home nestled under the boughs of three huge oaks. It was now a murder scene.

As Schoembs and Coale worked, under the direction of Lieutenant Daniel Boring, the most senior officer present, they tried to ignore the sound of the phone ringing—ten, fifteen, twenty times; then it would stop, there would be a moment's silence, and it would start ringing again.

On the other side of the Atlantic Ocean, in Wales, Reggie Tucker was frantic. In the three months since he had left Arlington and returned to his native Wales to find a job, he had gotten used to calling his wife at odd hours because of the time difference. It had been expensive, but when she joined him in three and a half weeks, they would never have to call each other long distance again. And Susan was a person of very routine habits: she was always home when he called her in the late evening or early morning. He couldn't understand why she didn't answer now.

He had last spoken to her Friday evening; they had talked for almost an hour about the million little things she had to finish up at home and at her job as a publications editor for the U.S. Forestry Service before she moved to Wales.

She was next scheduled to call him at 6:15 A.M. on Monday, November 30. When he didn't hear from her, he called Monday night. No answer. He tried twice more that night, but no one answered.

She must be busy, he thought. She'll call in the morning.

When he received no call Tuesday morning, and could not reach her at work, he lost his composure. By Tuesday evening London time, he was calling every fifteen minutes, then every ten, then every five minutes. During several attempts, he let it ring twenty to thirty times. Desperately worried, at 1 A.M. he called Susan's cousin Brad Ingle, who lived in nearby Rockville, Maryland. Brad too felt that Susan was undoubtedly busy preparing for her departure but promised that he would go check on Susan immediately after finishing some work. His assurances did little to allay Reggie's anxiety.

At about 2:10 A.M. London time, 8:10 P.M. Eastern Standard Time, Reggie called his Susan again. This time his hopes were raised for a millisecond, because someone picked up the receiver.

It was a man's voice—but not Brad Ingle's. "Sorry," Reggie said, crestfallen. "Wrong number." He hung up.

Reggie redialed. The same voice answered.

At 8:11 the phone, which had been screaming ever since Coale and Schoembs entered the crime scene, began ringing yet again. As he had a moment ago, Lieutenant Boring instructed Schoembs to answer it.

"Hello, who the hell is this? Where's Susan?" cried the frantic, male, British-accented voice. "It's nighttime! What the hell are you doing in my house?"

"Sir, who are you, please?" Schoembs asked.

"I'm Reggie Tucker, Susan's husband! I'm calling from Wales. Now who the hell are you? Where's my wife!"

There was no doubt that this was by far the worst aspect of being a cop, something no one, regardless of experience or temperament, ever got used to.

"Mr. Tucker, sir, my name is Officer Rick Schoembs. I'm with the Arlington County Police Department. Sir, I'm very sorry, but I have some tragic news. Your wife, Susan, is dead."

Schoembs didn't give any details; in fact, he never even used the word *murdered* because standard operating procedure tells an officer that, at the initial stage of an investigation, everyone who has any relationship with the deceased

must be considered a suspect. Even—especially—the grieving husband.

After taking Reggie's phone number and politely repeating
that an investigating officer would call later that evening to
give more details about the death, Schoembs hung up and
went back to documenting the crime scene with one stack of
Polaroids after another.

While Schoembs was snapping the last of the pictures, homicide detective Bob Carrig, working the 2 P.M. to 10 P.M.
shift, squealed up to the scene. Carrig, a big man with graying
hair, affected the look of a Texas Ranger with his drooping
mustache, long sideburns, and cowboy boots. He hurried up
the lawn toward the redbrick house, just as Schoembs came
out to meet him with a fistful of still-wet instant pictures.
Carrig was a veteran detective. He had twenty years of police
work under his silver-buckled belt, but one brief look
through the photos turned his face the color of gray putty.
He went through the pictures again, shivering and squinting
under the cold December-night light of a street lamp. They
didn't get any better the second time. Steve Carter pulled up.
As Carter, a wiry detective with a long face and a carefully
coiffed pompadour, opened his car door, Carrig walked over
and thrust several photos at him as if he were revealing a
terrible poker hand. Carter looked at the pictures and almost
staggered back, as if he had been hit. "Aw, fuck," he said.
"Fuck!"

Ordinarily, the two men would have entered the home immediately, while they waited for Joe. But they were curtly
informed by Lieutenant Boring that nobody was going in
until his men had finished their initial photographing and
measuring. This was the rule: crime scene agents processed
and secured a scene, preserving it exactly as it was found,
then homicide detectives went in. Yet the detectives, who
hated to get their first look at any murder in a Polaroid picture, routinely broke the rule. Not this time. It was Lieutenant Boring's first murder scene after being promoted, and he
wasn't taking any chances. "I'm sorry," he said firmly, over
loud protests from Carrig and Carter. "No one goes in until
my men are finished." As he walked away, Carrig and Carter,

despite the gravity of the situation, exchanged quick grins. Though the news had predicted no more rain for the next few days, they knew a hurricane would be blowing up the driveway any minute.

"What the hell are you talking about!" Joe roared. "He's really not letting us into the scene?" He could barely contain himself. This was *his* murder. He should go in first! Too much chance of the crime scene technicians tainting or destroying evidence. Theoretically, they would only secure the scene, and leave all the evidence intact, but in fact the more people you had walking around, the more things were trampled and disturbed. In your usual smoking-gun-type murders it didn't matter: everybody knew who had done it, even some yahoo walking in off the street could tell. But this one was a whodunit, in which every minute speck of a clue might be critical. And a fresh scene just revealed clues more readily. He squeezed his eyes shut, imagining the places that were most important: the spots where the murderer had entered and left, the area around the body. Desperately, he hoped they wouldn't disturb anything.

"Joe," Carrig said suddenly. Joe turned to see Carrig holding out a handful of Polaroids. He grabbed them, carefully paging through each one. With every photo his eyes grew wider and his face tighter. "I can't believe it," he said at last. "I just can't—I can't—"

"I know," Carter said grimly. "Us too."

Carrig nodded.

"It looks just like—"

"Right," Carrig said shortly.

For a few minutes the impossible facts glistening in his hands quelled the fury at being shut out that had consumed him just seconds before. Then he heard the crunch of gravel, the grating grind of brakes, the opening of a car door. Hawkins was here—behind him was a car Joe recognized, Deputy Chief Arthur Christiansen's car. Boring strode—at an annoyingly slow pace—over to the deputy chief's car and got in. The door slammed and Joe saw their heads bent together in consultation.

24

A minute later Boring got out. "Okay," he said to Joe. "You can go in now."

They started in the basement. As Joe followed Schoembs down the creaky wooden steps, he thrust his hands deep into his pockets. The last thing he needed was to find his or, for that matter, any cop's fingerprints anywhere in the house.

Joe was aching to see the body, but right now he had to follow protocol. Schoembs would give him the initial tour. First the crime scene officer showed Horgas the right corner of the rec room, where someone had pawed through several cabinets and boxes of camera and darkroom equipment. Joe, however, immediately focused to the left, on a horizontal sliding window in the adjoining laundry area. One of the panes above the washer-dryer was completely broken out. A ragged hole had been punched through the lower-left corner of the glass that remained. A wooden rod, which had pre- viously functioned as a crude security device to prevent the window from being slid open, lay on the ground just outside. Several feet away from the base of the washer, on an orange throw rug, lay fragments of broken glass. Then there were two lengths of nylon rope. A chill washed over him. The rope. Right.

"I got to show you one more thing before we go upstairs," Schoembs said. He flipped off the laundry room light, crouched down next to the washing machine, and angled the flashlight beam across the white porcelain surface. Horgas leaned forward. There was a distinct demarcation line in the dust on the smooth surface. "Someone wiped it down with a towel or cloth," Schoembs said. Smart, Horgas thought. Whoever came through this window knew that the top of a washing machine was an ideal surface from which to lift fingerprints and shoeprints. Smart. Very, very smart.

They went up to the main level. No signs of a struggle, or even a burglary, just the pocketbook splayed and its contents scattered at the foot of the steps. No furniture was turned over, and all four cast-iron dining room chairs were squarely arranged around the table. A clear glass vase of dry flowers was centered pristinely on the shiny black marble table surface.

Just inches from this carefully placed vase was a half-eaten orange and, beside that, a long, serrated carving knife. Joe didn't know any personal details about Susan Tucker as yet, but after just a few minutes in her home he knew that she had been neat and orderly. If she had wanted an orange she would have cut it on a board in the kitchen and placed the sections on a plate. She was not someone who would have cut the orange on her immaculate table, much less have left a half-eaten section there.

"You son of a bitch," Joe breathed. "You killed her and then you waltzed downstairs and fixed a little snack!" Not only smart. Scary.

"Hey!" Joe cried, as he moved out of the dining room. "How come everybody's been using that air conditioner out there to get on the balcony! Isn't anyone thinking? If the front door was latched from the inside that's probably how the killer got out!

"Look at this floor!" he bellowed into Schoembs's face. "With your guys parading up and down there's no way you're gonna get any shoe impressions. And forget about any mud or other shit that may have fallen off this son of a bitch's clothes!"

Schoembs sighed and shook his salt-and-pepper head. He had become a cop fourteen years earlier because he wanted to "make a positive impact on somebody's life." At that moment, clearly, Detective Horgas was not that person. But he didn't interrupt, just let Joe blast on. He knew Joe was not the most diplomatic person on a crime scene, or anywhere else for that matter. Joe always found something to shout and complain about.

Detective Steve Carter had been at countless crime scenes with Joe over the years. He had known what was coming when he saw Horgas first hoist his massive frame lightly over the flimsy black railing (without, of course, stepping on the air conditioner). "When it's his ticket, he's going warp eight," Carter said later. "He wants this, this, and this—you can't keep his mouth shut."

Schoembs took him through the living room to the stairs. Joe paused over the contents of the purse as he began to climb; it was all too familiar. His eyes momentarily fixed on the smile emanating from the driver's license photo of a woman in her late thirties or early forties with short dark red hair and pink frame glasses. She kept staring at him, no matter where he moved his head. He turned his attention to the top of the stairs. Just like those before him, he did the best he could to hold his breath.

Susan Tucker didn't look anything like that smiling photo he had seen just moments earlier. *lying*

She was nude and ~~laying~~ facedown across the lower half of the bed; her face was almost completely blackened, her eyes swollen shut, and her head hung slightly over the bed's edge. A thick, dark red mucus oozed from her mouth and nose, soaking the coverlet and pooling on the gray carpet.

A brilliantly shiny, white nylon rope, similar to the one he had just seen in the basement, was tautly wrapped around her neck. The rope ran down the middle of her back where it was bound several times around each wrist. Her arms were folded akimbo behind her, the left lying across the small of her back, the right hand planted at her side. The hands were connected by a foot of rope and from the center dangled a length perhaps two feet long.

Joe bent down to closely examine the killer's handiwork. Shaking his head in disgust, he sucked in the putrid air through his tightly clenched teeth.

It was all ghoulishly ornate.

And it was Carolyn Hamm all over again.

Joe stood for a minute, swaying, as the full weight of this sank over him. It was impossible, of course. That guy they arrested was still in prison. It couldn't be.

But it was. And that's why Carrig and Carter were so shaken. It was all the same, the bindings, the hands behind her back, face to the side, the eerie submission to death. And Hamm had lived only four blocks away across South Walter Reed Drive. If it weren't for the trees, you could almost see Hamm's two-story home from Tucker's bedroom window. Was this a key—or only a weird coincidence? He stared down at the remains of Susan Tucker.

What lay in front of him was no longer a person. The body

was bloated, it was in such an advanced stage of decomposition that air bubbles had formed, separating her skin from her body. One such bubble covered much of the upper right side of the back. What had been Mrs. Tucker's skin was molting, peeling off at the slightest touch and displaying a yellowish black-and-blue tinge. Irregular, dark gray, reddish blisters covered the arms and legs. The taut rope had cut off the flow of blood to the hands, turning the fingernails midnight blue, the same color as the sleeping bag that Joe noticed draped over the buttocks and thighs.

Like the body, the room had been ransacked. Sweaters, blouses, and underwear lay half in and half out of the long, beige Chinese-style dresser. An empty metal file box leaned on a pillow at the head of the bed, its former contents, insurance papers and bank statements, littering the floor. An unopened box of Christmas balls, tragic memento of the holiday season, was perched next to the strongbox.

Other evidence of the killer's spree was scattered haphazardly in the adjacent bedroom. Sealed plastic Baggies containing commemorative and foreign coins were scattered around an oversized shoe box. This killer *was* smart, Joe thought. He knew better than to take the easily traceable, specially minted coins. Maybe he had taken something else from the room. Just as Joe was starting to look around, though, he was called outside to meet the victim's relative. That was how they would think of Sue Tucker now; she had lost her name and would be known from now on as the "victim," the "body," the "deceased." Cops had to step back like this. Otherwise they would never be able to cope with the horror that dogged their lives. Joe had accepted it long ago.

Ever since he had first put on the blues in August of 1968, he had wanted to work homicide. It was the most interesting part of police work—maximum freedom, maximum responsibility. Most important to Joe, it carried the ultimate challenge. "There is no more heinous crime than taking a human life," he said later, "and it is the *only* crime that carries the death penalty. I could be wrong, but I think almost every cop wants to work homicide. Being any other kind of detective—like sex, burglary, white collar—it doesn't compare." And giving the bad news to distraught relatives was one of the things that went with the territory.

Brad Ingle, a slight, soft-spoken man in his thirties, had been called to the scene to formally identity his cousin's body. Though the police were convinced Sue Tucker was the victim, standard operating procedure demanded a positive visual ID. Because she was a federal employee, further verification of her identity would be made at a later date by an FBI analysis of her fingerprints. Now, though, an ID was needed. Yet Ingle couldn't do it. He was so overwhelmed by his cousin's death that Joe couldn't get him even to look at any of the Polaroids. Ingle wanted to remember Sue as the vivacious person she had been and not the victim of some horrible defilement. After speaking to several neighbors, Joe was able to persuade one to verify that the puffy, blackened face was that of the lady who lived at 4801.

Though her presence seemed superfluous, the medical examiner, Dr. Frances Field, arrived at 10:15 P.M. She was there to make the official pronouncement of death and give the detectives some idea of when the homicide had taken place. Because the victim's skin had begun pulling away from the body, a condition known as "slippage," and due to the bloating from gas formation, Field, a veteran of over 3,000 autopsies, concluded that Tucker had been dead between three and five days. That placed the actual murder between Friday night and Sunday morning. Though she would eventually make her official findings at an autopsy two days later, Field ruled the death due to strangulation by ligature. Sue Tucker was choked to death by the nylon noose.

After about three hours at the crime scene Joe had seen enough. Every place he looked, the place said Carolyn Hamm. "I was being eaten away inside," he later said. "I wanted to get up to the station as fast as I could and pull out the Hamm file."

Homicide detectives often linger for hours at a crime scene after every shred of evidence has been gathered and all the technicians have gone home. "The scene tells you things," Detective Steve Carter said later. "The body talks to you."

While Horgas was attentive to any and all evidence, he was not one of those who liked to wait alone, beside the body in the dark, hoping for a mystical revelation about the killer. "Once I've been on the scene for a few hours, I know what I need for my case. I just tell the agents what I want done and leave," Horgas said. "All *I* have to do is catch the bad guys. I was never a crime scene agent like a lot of the guys on the squad so I don't really have an intense interest in how they collect evidence. The same goes for autopsies. I went to one training class where some guy went through the anatomy of a human body, how the muscles and the bones fit together and all this bullshit. As a detective I just need a general understanding of what happened and what I'm looking for. I don't have to know the names of bones or the name of the muscle that the bullet went through; that's what we have the experts for. All I have to know is that the person is dead. And this or that caused the death."

It was clear by now that there would be no smoking gun with Tucker. It would be solved by connecting something at the scene back to the Hamm murder. He hoped the killer had left something behind. Joe took Schoembs into the kitchen to speak to him privately. "Take as long as you want here," Joe said sternly, pronouncing each word as if it were a complete sentence. "This'll definitely be made through forensics. Print everything and anything he or they could have touched. And be careful with the body. When you turn her on to the gurney I don't want anything falling off and I want the ropes as is." Schoembs scribbled notes and nodded.

The sharpness of Joe's tone sprang now from pure anxiety. He, like everyone else who had walked through the crime scene, knew that whoever ended Sue Tucker's life was calculating and intelligent, someone who probably operated on his own and was intimately familiar with how cops catch bad guys. There was no obvious suspect, nor was it likely any informant would emerge with the murderer's name and address. They had nothing.

On the other hand, Joe had great confidence in Rick Schoembs. The agent had proven himself to Joe that past summer during the investigation of a suicide. It was a man who had shot himself in the head.

"It was a heavily wooded area and by the time some high-way worker found this guy he was falling apart. His body was still intact, but his head was just a skeleton," Joe recounted. "When the funeral people attempted to pick him up I was on the low side of the hill next to Rick. As they started to lift his legs his head came rolling off. Rick grabbed it like a first-class outfielder!"

As a veteran of literally hundreds of crime scenes, Schoembs also realized the gravity of the situation. He had seen worse crime scenes over the years—bodies mutilated beyond recognition, homes turned into shambles. Here the smell of evil was in the lack of disarray, the order of the scene. It was a precision killing: elaborate bindings, the absence of bruises or cuts about the body, the wiping down of the washing machine. An unknown assailant of razor-sharp stealth, who had to be gotten off the street—as soon as possible.

Instead of using the killer's exit, Joe crossed the living room to leave by the front door. As he passed the foot of the stairs, his eye again caught the smile of Susan Tucker looking up at him from the Virginia driver's license. Bending over, he eased it from her wallet with a handkerchief. Like Susan's cousin, Joe wanted to remember Susan Tucker as she had been.

As his vehicle pulled away from the curb, snaking its way through a sea of red, blue, and yellow lights blinking in the late-evening fog, Joe briefly gazed at the patrol officers making their way through the cul-de-sac to interview neighbors, who by now were all standing in their bathrobes on their front porches. The uniforms would be his foot soldiers for at least the next forty-eight hours. They would fan out through the vicinity and question anyone who might have seen or heard anything or anyone acting unusual. Horgas was not very hopeful that the door-to-doors would reveal any useful leads. This guy was too good to let anyone see him.

Joe roared down Columbia Pike, Arlington's primary thor-oughfare, trying to recall what he knew about the Hamm murder. Four years had gone by, but one fact stuck in his mind: the other detectives had felt at the time that Vasquez might have had a partner. Despite all the cajoling by the police and by his attorneys, though, Vasquez had not identified him.

As he drove down the avenue he had patrolled as a rookie, Joe was beginning to see the possibility that he could resolve Tucker's murder with relative ease. In the calm of his automobile, away from the pressure and turmoil of the crime scene, it all made sense. All I have to do is find out who Vasquez was tight with back then, he thought. There can't be more than a couple of guys. One of 'em has to be him.

Of course, the detectives assigned to the Hamm case had checked out Vasquez's known associates back in '84. Gone through them with a fine-tooth comb. But Joe knew he could probably do better. He prided himself on being one of the department's most skilled interrogators. Plus, four years had gone by—and there was another murder. Vasquez had had plenty of time to cool his heels, Joe told himself. He may not have wanted to talk then, but he'd be crazy not to give up his accomplice now. He drove down the once working-class street in downtown Arlington, now prettied up with yuppie sandwich shops but still dotted with tawdry bail bondsmen, that led to police headquarters. It was past midnight—but, of course, the lights were still on.

2

DECEMBER 1987

JOE WADED THROUGH THE EVER-PRESENT CROWD OF WEARY SOULS ON his way upstairs to the detective bureau. They were lined up on the worn wooden bench, waiting for some word about the release of a husband or friend, or the whereabouts of a towed automobile. At the single public phone a hapless mother holding an infant was vainly attempting to negotiate with a bail bondsman.

Though it was only two short flights up to his office, Horgas, like everyone else, never walked—a fact that was no doubt in the minds of administrators when they placed a collection of simple wooden plaques next to the elevator. The caption above the four proud faces on the plaques served as a daily, sober reminder of the peril of police work: OFFICERS KILLED IN THE LINE OF DUTY.

The robbery-homicide squad was housed upstairs in the Crimes Against Persons section, which also included the white-collar and juvenile–sex crimes squads. Set off from the rest of the section in a separate room measuring sixteen by forty feet, Joe and seven other detectives conducted their daily business of investigating the inhumanity their fellow citizens had visited upon one another.

Sitting in the right-hand corner at his cluttered gray metal desk, Joe was desperate to rip open the Hamm file. But first he had another task. Unfolding a small slip of paper, he began dialing the first overseas phone call he had ever made in his life. Though Schoembs had already spoken to Susan's husband, it fell to Joe to inform Reggie Tucker officially of his wife's death. He had done this before, but each time was like the first. As the phone rang, Joe stared at the driver's license he had just taped to the bookshelf in front of him.

"Yes?" There were 3,000 miles of ocean between them but Joe could see Reggie's tear-streaked face. No longer growling, he spoke to Susan Tucker's husband in gentle, compassionate tones. Beyond informing him that his wife was the "apparent victim of a homicide," Joe had another agenda. Tucker's loss was a tragedy, and he was in another country, but Joe could not yet discount him as a suspect.

Joe knew that more than 80 percent of U.S. murders are committed by persons related to or friendly with the victim, especially spouses and lovers, so he listened with great care. Tucker spoke haltingly, bewilderment and anguish soaking each word. Barring any unforseen evidence such as an insurance motive, it was this abject devastation that told Joe that Tucker had nothing to do with his wife's death.

Joe hung up to see a somber Detective Carrig, just returned from the crime scene, waiting to review the Hamm file with him. Retrieved from the "Closed Case" storage cabinet, the Hamm file sat at the head of the worn, cigarette-burned Formica table on one side of the robbery-homicide room. Joe ripped open the burgundy file folders as if they were his Christmas presents. Carrig did not share Joe's enthusiasm. Watching Joe spread out the file's contents was like witnessing a disinterment. The case had always been disturbing; knowing that Vasquez must have had a partner and not being able to identify him. It had been Carrig's case—and now another woman was dead.

Horgas first tore open the crime scene photography file.

The similarities to Tucker were blatant. "It really looks like the same fucking guy, doesn't it?"

All Carrig could do was nod.

"But Vasquez was guilty," Joe said thoughtfully. "When he confessed, what kinda feeling you get?"

"He gave us details about how he killed her, but we always thought he had a partner because he wasn't strong or smart enough to pull it off by himself."

"Then it's who he was tight with," Joe said, scanning through the other documents in the file. He frowned. It was obvious the investigators had followed up on Vasquez's associates back in '84: Larry Ranser, the neighbor who had helped discover Hamm's body; Max Zimmer, a friend of Vasquez; Charles Vandi, Vasquez's friend; Bill Kluge, Vasquez's alibi witness; and Alan Trenton, who had lived across the street from David Vasquez. There were about ten others, but these were the main ones. Joe ran through the notes again. "What about this guy Max Zimmer?" he blurted. "Vasquez lived near his house up until a few months before the murder and the house was right around the corner from Hamm."

"No way, Joe." On this Carrig was firm. "Not Max. Sure, they were friends. But Max is good people. I knew the guy personally even before Hamm went down. No way, not Max. Anyway, we checked him out, he had a solid alibi."

"Yeah, but he was much closer to Vasquez than any of these other three or four guys you had targeted. How could Zimmer not know something like this? Ain't it just as likely Vasquez was just covering up for his best friend? Besides, look at the size hole the killer went through. In Hamm it was smaller than Tucker, and when you consider how small Max is . . ."

"Forget it, Joey," Carrig insisted. "No way it's Max Zimmer."

The subject was dropped, but Horgas remained skeptical. Knowing Zimmer might have clouded Carrig's judgment. He would check out Zimmer with utmost care, and all of Vasquez's other cronies too. Vasquez had done Hamm with somebody else—Horgas was even more sure of this now, after seeing the photos, and he was going to stalk that second guy until he had him. Like the deer in hunting season, the biggest prize in the forest, the king stag . . . Joe would get him. But not now. Now it was close to 3 A.M., and time to go home, take a shower, and see if sleep was even a remote possibility.

It was not. He was still awake at 5 A.M., his mind going in a thousand directions. He caught himself in midthought, quietly got out of bed, and walked to his sleeping son's room. Leaning down, he gave him a kiss on the forehead. The events of that night were going to rule out any significant playtime in the foreseeable future. Then he returned to his bed.

At that same moment, across the Atlantic in a small village in Wales, Reggie Tucker was packing his bags. And back in Arlington, the crime scene agents were releasing Susan Tucker's body to the morgue attendants, who wrapped it in a clean white sheet before transferring it to the county hospital.

At six o'clock Horgas gave up on trying to sleep. The anxiety and excitement were too much. Horgas had been waiting for an assignment like this since he joined the robbery-homicide squad nine years earlier. The department had its homicides and had even made some important arrests over the years, including that of the assassin of American Nazi Party chairman George Lincoln Rockwell. Recently there had been a few drug-related murders. But Joe had enough competitive drive for three men, and drug killings were boring; who cared, on a certain level, if they killed each other? Susan Tucker's murder was different. This was a tough murder, a real murder, the kind that made his blood flow like he wanted it to.

He was first to arrive for the 8 A.M. briefing. This ritual occurred every day, when the squad's sergeant Frank Hawkins, a long-faced, white-haired man, came out of his back office to the center of the squad room to hand out assignments, hear status reports on the pending cases, and negotiate complaints or questions. On this December 2, though, routine was abandoned; a solemn silence replaced the usual banter about sports scores, informants, and vacations, and two of the department's most senior officers, Lieutenant Minnich and Deputy Chief Christiansen—never present at morning briefings—

filed in. They all gathered around the table, with Horgas at the head and the massive Hamm investigation file sitting before him like a gravestone.

Hawkins started the meeting at an easel with a huge sheaf of white paper. With his familiar red felt-tip pen in hand, he wrote in big bold letters:

Susan M. Tucker, Case No. 871201193, white female, 44, date of birth 7/10/43; 4801 27th Road South; cause of death—tentative strangulation/rope.

Below the case caption Hawkins sketched the two-story residence, marking the location of the body with an X. Alongside the house, he outlined all the relevant physical information gathered thus far.

They'd have to wait for the forensics, so Hawkins moved on to summarize everything Horgas and the other detectives had managed to find out about the victim in the few short hours since her body had been found. Who Susan Tucker had known, where she worked, her habits—any detail about her life might shed some light on the identity of her killer. Though the killer looked like an experienced criminal, no one at this point could discount the possibility that Tucker was killed by a friend or a person she had recently met.

She was by all accounts a quiet, unassuming woman. A technical writer for the United States Department of Forestry, she took the bus to work, arriving promptly at 8:15 and leaving at 4:45 in the afternoon. She brought her lunch with her and rarely carried over twenty dollars in her pocketbook. Colleagues said she was a reliable worker who during her seven years with the department kept to herself, made few friends, and never angered a soul.

Outside of work Susan was a homebody: a devoted wife with only a few friends. She was hardly the type to have an affair, let alone a one-night stand. Since her husband had gone back to Wales a few months earlier, Susan had ventured out only to go shopping with her neighbor, visit her cousin, and occasionally go jogging.

In retracing her final days, a neighbor reported that she

had last seen Tucker Thanksgiving morning, November 26. The last person Susan had spoken with was her husband on Friday, November 27, at 6:30 P.M. The detectives could find no one who had talked to her or seen her after that.

As Horgas had speculated, initial door-to-door canvassing had also yielded little. Several neighbors mentioned that sometime during the day on November 30 they had observed a tall white male in his midtwenties wearing a gray sweatshirt walking in the vicinity of Susan's home. "He didn't belong in the area and he wasn't heading anywhere," one of them reported. Another gave the same description but said the man was wearing a gray jacket. He had been seen at about 8 P.M. in the field behind the complex, staring in the direction of Susan's home before walking down into the woods. A third neighbor remembered a white male of similar description, in the same place, on the evening of Sunday the 29th. Finally, a woman who lived across the street from the Tuckers had told an officer she thought she heard fighting coming from the Tucker home around 11 P.M. on Monday. Before the interview was over, however, she changed her mind and said she thought the commotion was coming from the couple who lived two doors down.

They also evaluated all recent 911 phone calls, crime reports, and FORs, or field observation reports—recorded when individuals are stopped and questioned for activities that appear suspicious but not overtly criminal. Just after midnight, November 6, there had been a break-in on Twenty-eighth Street. The masked prowler had entered through an unlocked rear door but fled when he was seen by one of the occupants. Two days later, around the corner from the Tucker home, police received a report of a man in an army fatigue jacket hiding in the bushes. He fled before police arrived. No reports were received again until 1 P.M. on November 21, when there was a burglary on Thirty-first Road, three blocks away. Later that same day another woman, who lived around the corner from the Thirty-first Road address, called saying a man was trying to break into her home. By the time police arrived the prowler had gotten away.

On November 29 there was a flurry of activity: in addition

to a vehicle theft on Buchanan, a woman reported that at 4 A.M. she heard a scream in the vicinity of the Tucker residence; at 6 P.M. a prowler was seen around the corner from the Tucker residence, and then a similar complaint came in two hours later from a woman who lived several blocks away.

The meeting ended at noon with the delegation of assignments. The whole squad would work the first few days. There is an unwritten law of homicide investigation that if a case is going to fall together at all, it will usually happen within the first forty-eight hours of the discovery of the body.

Several men were sent to reinterview neighbors with an eye toward developing more details about the young man in the gray sweatshirt, the masked burglar, and the prowler in the bushes; others were assigned to review all the recent burglary and sex-related arrests throughout the county. Finally, one detective was charged with finding the manufacturer and retailer of the ropes.

After a quick discussion it was decided that Horgas's regular partner, Mike Hill, would be his partner on the case. Hill was a self-starter who understood Joe well and, unlike some others, was not put off by the blunt force of Joe's methods. Chuck Shelton, for instance, recounted Joe's phone call to him the night Tucker's body was found: "At three A.M. the phone rings at my house. 'You awake,' Horgas says. 'Yeah, I am now, Joe, I answered the goddamn phone, didn't I?' Without saying I'm sorry or giving any explanation Horgas fires back, 'What was the name of that guy that was Vasquez's friend, you know?' 'Wait a minute, Joe . . . I think it was something like Kluge.' 'What was his first name?' 'I don't know, Joe, I can't think of his first name.' 'OK,' he said, and that was the conversation. Never once did he say why he wanted the information, and it wasn't until the next morning that I found out about Tucker. Classic Joe."

As Horgas and Hawkins walked out of the PD they ran into Commonwealth Attorney Helen Fahey. Fahey was the kind of elected prosecutor who made her reputation on intelligence and thorough preparation; she would not get involved in the Tucker murder until a suspect had been identified.

Still, it was crucial for her to be kept informed of any serious crime. Joe gave her a thumbnail sketch of the homicide.

"Are you doing DNA?" Fahey asked.

"Not yet, Helen. We don't even known what we have right now." Horgas shrugged politely, but her question started his mind racing. He had read about DNA in a law enforcement magazine; it was touted as the first real breakthrough in suspect identification since fingerprinting had been perfected in the late 1800s. Each individual's DNA, or genetic code, was made up of nucleotides linked in complex, ladderlike chains; no two individuals were alike. And—supposedly—DNA could be retrieved from any human cell. Of course, it was brand new. It had been used in paternity cases, but in 1987 no one in the United States had yet used it in a homicide investigation. Joe made a mental note to find out more about it.

Though one day in the future DNA might provide the critical link to whoever killed Susan Tucker, right now Horgas needed the raw evidence. Like all homicide detectives, he knew that crime scene processors—though they clearly didn't hold the glory posts in any PD—were key to most homicides. The careful, deductive reasoning of men like Horgas was built on the latticework of detail extracted from the scenes by men like crime scene agents Schoembs and Coale.

"You have to be a super-observer," Schoembs had said. "You have to be very conscious about your surroundings and let your imagination run wild. You have to ask yourself, what could he have left behind by mistake or taken with him? Did he rip his shirt or could a hair have dropped off? You really have to put yourself in the bad guy's position to determine where he walked or how he broke into something or killed someone."

Schoembs and Coale had been assisted at the Tucker scene by Agent 50, the Ford 6000 series truck that had been converted into a self-contained crime lab. Aside from the routine equipment—video and still cameras, paper bags and envelopes to store evidence, standard fingerprint kits, and tools for taking tire and feet impressions, Agent 50 was also fitted with powerful halogen quartz lights for night work, its own generator, and a "laser gun" for processing latent fingerprints.

Schoembs and Coale labored over the Tucker scene for several days, processing every surface or object on which Tucker's killer might have left a trace of his presence; they combed the house for anything he had touched, dropped, sat on, bit, kissed or stood over in any conceivable bodily activity.

In fact, the crime was so heinous that after the first day of processing Schoembs and Coale changed the way they had traditionally worked a crime scene. Instead of working on their own, they decided to collect each item of evidence together. As Schoembs later said, "By the time we bring down a guy who does crimes like this it may be five or ten years down the road, and who knows what can happen to us?" By working in tandem, they guaranteed that if one of them was dead or unable to function, the surviving agent could testify that he had actually collected the specific item.

They videotaped everything and took hundreds of 35-millimeter photos, inside and out. These pictures would be reviewed by Horgas, constantly, as he worked, later they would tell the story to a judge and jury. Everything was documented, from the uncomfortable close-ups of the knots and bindings around Susan Tucker's neck and arms and the dark brown substance oozing out of her mouth and nose to the position of the orange on the dining room table and the lonely beans, apples, and film in her refrigerator.

Right after they took the photos they conducted a sweep to collect every item of consequence. Light bulbs in the bathroom and several other rooms were removed because it was thought that they had been unscrewed by the assailant (like wineglasses, light bulbs are excellent surfaces for recovering latent fingerprints). All the towels in the basement were taken, on the theory that the killer could have used one of them to wipe down the surface of the washing machine; the lengths of rope found in the basement bathroom were bagged for comparison to the bindings.

The men even took up shards of broken glass from the

laundry room floor with the rubber tweezers and swept soil from the basement steps.

They picked through the crucial but unfortunately soaked tangle of bedding as attentively as archaeologists at a major find. There was not much. "It was," as agent Schoembs later explained, "a very moist scene." All the clothing and bedding on and around the bed was a potential gold mine, for the assailant could have left behind fingerprints, blood, hairs, semen. Most of the potential evidence there, though, had been saturated by the puddle of body fluids released through decomposition. Blood and mucus had leaked out of every orifice of the body; pus had oozed from the huge blisters that had puffed up over the arms, back, and legs. And of course, blood and semen which stayed wet at room temperature too long would disintegrate and lose their identifying characteristics. Everything had to be quickly bagged and removed to either a refrigerator or the air-drying room in the basement of the PD.

Schoembs had first removed the blood-soaked blue sleeping bag draped across the victim's buttocks and followed this with the cover sheets, a brown corduroy blanket, and a simple white nightgown. As Tucker's body was moved onto the medical examiner's gurney, several dark hairs were taken off her right breast, photographed, and packaged in a small manila envelope. After the attendants placed the victim in the heavy black plastic body bag, Schoembs removed the turquoise printed bedspread, the mattress pad, and a pair of panties at the foot of the bed.

They moved on to the fine brushwork: fingerprinting. Sometimes crime scene processors get lucky when a fingerprint is actually visible to the naked eye, usually because the perpetrator either had blood or lipstick on his hands and touched a clean surface or, with clean hands, touched something dusty or oily.

The technology of "dusting" for fingerprints is fairly simple and has not changed for decades. There are two basic kinds, traditional black powder and, more recently developed, magnetic black powder. The traditional powder works best on smooth, nonporous surfaces, but because it is the consistency of finely ground pencil carbon, it is very messy to use. Most agents prefer the magnetic powder, a mixture of carbon and iron filings. A magnetic brush is used to fix the carbon/powder base around any available prints.

Dusting is straightforward, but locating the prints is not. Schoembs once worked on a fraud case where the investigating officer needed to identify the occupant of an apartment. The entire place had been cleaned out except for a couple of pieces of furniture. Dusting surface after surface revealed no prints. Just before giving up, Schoembs decided to dust one more surface. Knowing that the suspect was a woman and thinking of how, as Schoembs later said, "the female of the sex goes to the bathroom," he dusted the underside of the toilet seat lid. He recovered a clear set of prints that perfectly matched those of the suspect. The case Schoembs was most proud of, however, was the one he affectionately dubbed the "piggy bank case."

Entering the scene of a burglary, Schoembs was informed that many items and pieces of furniture had been moved around. "Surveying the daughter's bedroom," Schoembs later recounted, "I noticed a piggy bank sitting up on a shelf. If I was the bad guy I would probably have checked this out. The young lady, however, stated that the bank had not been moved." Shining his flashlight on the shelf at a 45-degree angle, Schoembs noted that though it was dusty under and immediately around the bank, there was a clear circular area several inches away that indicated that the bank had been recently moved. The bank was dusted and subsequently the recovered print was matched to the suspect.

Schoembs and Coale imagined everything the killer could have touched, then dusted it with magnetic powder. They dusted the light switch plates and the refrigerator door. Nothing. Similarly, no prints could be found on the banister leading upstairs or the marble dining room table. It was as if no one had ever even lived in the home. Yet it was consistent with other signs of the killer's intelligence. Obviously he knew all about the techniques used by police. They even removed the entire window and frame, hoping for prints or blood or microscopic fibers, and sent them to be analyzed by state lab technicians. Schoembs and Coale had painstakingly dusted every surface in Tucker's home that could possibly hold a print—the washer-dryer, the sink counter, dining room table, dresser top, telephone, jewelry box, strongbox, the telephone, basement window, the basement and main level banister, teacups, glasses, and, yes, the toilet seats in the two bathrooms.

No latent prints. Several prints were lifted from the back doorjamb but they were eventually matched to the victim's.

Yet the lack of prints did not completely surprise Schoembs and Coale because of what they had observed when they first entered the crime scene. "When I'd shown shone my flashlight over the surface of that washer-dryer, an area that someone *would have had* to have come down on as he went through that window, and an excellent surface for recovering prints, and I saw that it had been wiped down, it was obvious we were dealing with an intruder who knew a lot about police evidence collection techniques."

Despite intensive efforts throughout the first week to powder-process every conceivable surface in the home, only seven partial latent prints had been found. Unfortunately, they were so partial as to make it impossible to match them to any one particular person. Coale and Schoembs had been particularly chagrined at the absence of prints on the most ideal surface, the large shards of broken basement window-pane at the point of entry. These pieces were found lying in a neat pile on the ground outside the window. The killer had clearly worn gloves.

In a last-ditch search for prints, the crime scene team had painted the house with nyhydrin solution, a highly toxic solvent that meant wearing air packs and space suits and moving through the house as quickly as possible. Applied like paint, the procedure is similar to film development. If residual body oils are present, the print will appear in a purplish residue within twenty-four to forty-eight hours of application. When Schoembs and Coale returned the next day they discovered eleven partial prints cast in lavender hues. In the cold stillness of the empty house, there was a ghostlike quality to the light purple smudges found on the dining room wall. They would not know immediately whose prints they were, but they had a sinking feeling that they were unlikely to belong to Tucker's killer.

They had great hope, though, for the half-eaten orange. It appeared to hold a clear dental impression, which, like a fingerprint, could be used later to identify the killer. It was rushed to an odontologist. Though he labored over the fruit for hours, the doctor was unable to create a plaster cast. It had sat too long, and was too soft to give up an impression.

While Schoembs and Coale worked inside the house, Shelton, Carrig, Carter, and a phalanx of uniformed officers continued the door-to-doors. In addition to neighbors, everybody in her appointment book, and those who appeared on her phone bill and credit card receipts, they covered everyone who had entered the home in preparation for its being sold. They interviewed agents and buyers; housing inspectors, rug cleaners, painters, and carpenters. None of these seemed like good suspects.

Oddly, it was a neighbor, not a police officer, who found a potentially critical piece of evidence that week. Tim Brown, the man who had originally called to report Susan's disappearance, noticed a yellow-stained blue washcloth hanging from a tree as he was walking his dog. Reggie Tucker later would identify it as the washcloth Susan had used every night to wash her face.

Despite the disappointing fingerprint results, the agents had been able to give Horgas some positive news that week. Some of the hair fragments taken did not appear to belong to either the victim or her husband.

Susan and her husband both had reddish brown hair, but the ones found around her body were much darker. Two of these hairs were removed from the victim's belly when she was turned onto the gurney and three came from the pillow and sheets. Coale also retrieved two very tiny curly hairs from the basin and two near the spigots. While Coale could not reach a definitive conclusion with the naked eye, he felt these might be pubic hairs.

Upon being told by Coale about the hairs, Horgas had surmised the killer might have washed up or even showered after

assaulting Tucker. Working on this assumption, Horgas ordered
that the crime scene team remove the pipes and drains from
both the sink and bathtub. Wielding two-foot-long monkey
wrenches, Coale and detective Ray Spivey, another member
of the robbery-homicide squad, spent the better part of a day
dislodging the scum-lined, malodorous plumbing fixtures, a
task definitely not taught at the police academy.

Horgas attended the autopsy on Thursday, December 3.
Tucker's body was placed on the cold steel table the same
way they found her—facedown, head crooked slightly to the
left, arms folded behind. The harsh operating room lights
illuminated every detail of her defilement.

Dr. Frances Field presided in the morgue of Fairfax Hospital on—of all places—Gallows Road in the nearby town of
Falls Church, dictating tonelessly in front of Horgas,
Schoembs, and Coale into a microphone suspended from
the ceiling.

"This is the body of a forty-four-year-old white female,
sixty-seven and a half inches long, weight one hundred forty-
five pounds, brown eyes and red-brown dyed hair.... A
gold-colored ring is on the left hand. There is a grayish green
postmortem discoloration of the skin...."

She confirmed her on-scene evaluation of "strangulation
by ligature."

Aside from the damage to Tucker's wrists and neck inflicted by the bindings—the noose was bound so tightly it
cut a furrow in her throat—there was a remarkable absence
of any other trauma. There were no cuts or bruises, broken
bones, or bumps on the head—not a scratch anywhere on
her entire body.

Before Dr. Field turned the body over to make her Y inci-
sion, the first surgical step in an autopsy, where the ribs and
breast plate are pulled back, a PERK was performed by Field
and agent Schoembs. A Physical Evidence Recovery Kit (or
PERK) is a standard evidence-collection tool used in any serious physical assault case from rape to homicide. The kit itself
is a plain 5 x 8 brown manila envelope containing several
little plastic envelopes, labels, four sterile swaps, an ex-

tremely fine-tooth comb, a nail clipper, and a pair of rubber gloves. While Fields swabbed the interior of the victim's mouth, anus, and vagina, Schoembs extracted several strands of head and arm hair. He also combed her matted pubic hair and deposited any loose hairs in an envelope. Schoembs next clipped each of her fingernails. The clippings were especially important because they would reveal whether she had attempted to defend herself by scratching her assailant. The fingertips themselves showed no obvious injury, though, and neither did it appear that there was any blood or skin on or under her nails. Horgas would have to wait for the lab techs to do a microscopic examination of the interior of the nails. Still, given Field's findings and what Joe already knew about the assailant's killing methods, he was not sanguine that the white-coats would find anything.

There appeared to be nothing exotic about the bindings either, nothing but slipknots that could be tied by almost anyone. Joe noticed that the ropes, which had been dry when he was on the crime scene, were now soaked with blood and mucus.

"What happened to these ropes?" Joe asked, disturbed but controlled.

"Joe, in order for us to get her on to the gurney and out of the house, we had to roll her over on her back," Schoembs said as Dr. Field cut the ropes. "There was no other way. She was coming apart."

Horgas shook his head in disgust. They wouldn't pull anything off the ropes now.

On Friday, the day after the autopsy, the men gathered back in the squad room to go over the similarities between Hamm and Tucker. Hawkins used his ever-present red Magic Marker to make two lists:

Tucker	Hamm
WF 44	WF 32
Lived alone	Lived alone
Nude facedown on bed	Nude facedown on floor
Hands tied behind back	Hands tied behind back
Ligature around neck	Ligature around neck

Tucker	Hamm
Entry basement window	Entry basement window
Exit rear door	Exit garage door
Purse dumped in l.r.	Purse dumped upstairs hallway
No money in purse	No money in purse
Ransacking	Ransacking
Scene appeared wiped down	Scene appeared wiped down
Semen ?	Semen vagina

The women had lived near each other and both were professionally employed, both quiet and unassuming. And both, when killed, had had imminent plans to leave the country. There were no blood type results yet on anal and vaginal swabs taken from Tucker, but they had recovered semen from the rear-inside of Hamm's bathrobe, which had tested as a type O secretor and a PGM of 1.

Blood and other body fluids such as semen, vaginal secretions, and saliva can be typed by several different methods; each determination permits the technician to make a more refined analysis of the perpetrator's identity.

The ABO system, the most well-known one, breaks blood down into four categories: A, B, O, or AB. Once this determination is made, the lab technician uses the Lewis blood typing system to determine whether the particular person is a secretor or a nonsecretor of ABO Block Group Substances. Secretors are people who inherit from their parents the ability to secrete their amino blood group substances into their saliva and other body fluids. About 80 percent of the population are secretors; the remaining approximately 20 percent are referred to as nonsecretors.

Totally independent of the ABO system and always used in categorizing semen samples is the PGM blood typing system. The system is based on identifying the presence of the enzyme phosoglucomutase (PGM). Individuals possess one of three chromotypes—type 1, type 2-1, or type 2. Each chromotype is also subtyped: a type 1 can be a 1+ or 1- or a 1+1-; 2-1 can be +2-1, +2+1, 2-1-, 2-1+, and 2; and type 2 is divided into 2+, 2-, or 2+2-.

Most striking of all was the way each house was entered:

through tiny basement windows. The dimensions of the Hamm window were 14¼ by 11 inches and in Tucker 16⅜ by 13 inches.

"I still can't believe it!" Horgas shook his head at the scaled drawings of both windows Hawkins had taped to the wall.

"Four years ago we thought nobody could get through Hamm's window—that's why we staged that reenactment," Hawkins said. The task of "breaking into," Hamm's house through the basement window fell to Pete Tyler, the smallest man on the squad. "I hope you guys remember," Hawkins said, "he got in with *no* problem." If they were dealing with the same guy, then Tucker's window would be easy for him because it was several inches bigger than Hamm's window.

Hawkins moved on to a detective's least favorite subject: press policy. The surrounding community knew about the murder from the heavy police presence, but the PD's tight press policy had kept the murder out of the media. Now, though, they had to issue something. They agreed not to divulge the cause of death, the location and condition of the body, or any details about the dumping of the purse or the possibility of rape. They said only that a basement window had been broken to get in, and that the cause of death was unknown pending autopsy. And, Hawkins said sternly, under no circumstances should anyone learn that Tucker might be connected to Hamm.

A haggard, red-eyed Reggie Tucker arrived at robbery-homicide late Thursday afternoon. He was a slight man with a shock of red hair and a neatly trimmed beard, who, with each step toward Horgas, looked as if he would crumple to the ground. Tucker had not planned to come back to the States for a very long time. In several short weeks his wife was to have joined him in the lush, peaceful countryside of his native Wales. Instead he was here by Joe's desk, sitting in a hard-backed wooden chair, listening to the details of his wife's demise. Kindly, with a gentleness rarely seen in him by his coworkers, Joe explained to Reggie that they would have to take his prints and blood. Like everyone who had recently entered the house, his prints (and blood and hair samples) would be needed in order to isolate those of the potential suspect.

"We were just regular people," Tucker said as he wiped the black fingerprint ink off of his hands. "Susan and I moved into the home in nineteen eighty. We had a few friends in the neighborhood and mostly kept to ourselves. And I've been thinking about this since we spoke on the phone," Tucker continued in his rich but subdued Welsh brogue, "I can't think of one person who Susan regarded as her enemy. Not one. People liked Susan and she liked them. She loved her work. My wife was a writer. . . . She left for work at six-thirty A.M., taking I believe the number six bus that she picked up on South Walter Reed Drive. She took the four-forty-five bus in the afternoon, arriving home at about five-thirty. That was her routine for the last several years." This last bit of information was important to Horgas because it could be used in determining whether somebody had been stalking her.

Horgas also discovered that Susan Tucker was a very neat person. It would be unthinkable for her to cut an orange directly on their expensive marble table. And in the highly unlikely event she had done something like that, she'd never leave it there. Horgas's hunch had been correct.

Before ending the interview, Horgas showed Tucker samples of rope found on the basement bathroom floor. Tucker didn't spend a second examining them—he had never seen them before. If this was Hamm's killer, he had changed his MO. He was much more prepared; now he was bringing the rope.

That Friday night, Joe lingered over his desk before going home to take a shower. He knew he had to make one more unpleasant, though critical, decision.

Mike Hill stood beside him and they looked over the mile-long "to do" list. "We have everything we need from her, Joe," Mike said wearily. "I think we can release the body so her husband can bury her." Horgas nodded. Dialing Reggie at the hotel the police had asked him to check into, Joe fixed his gaze on Susan's driver's license photo, now a permanent fixture on his desk.

Horgas and Hill spent the next morning, Saturday, in the conference room sifting through the week's findings. They were well beyond the critical forty-eight-hour period now, and all they had were questions without answers. What was the motive? Had the suspect removed anything from the home that could later connect him to the scene? Going over the crime scene with Reggie Tucker, they hadn't pinpointed a thing; no photos were taken from the albums, the radio was on the right station, and a check of credit cards showed no unusual activity on the victim's checking or credit card account. Perhaps the suspect had left something behind at the crime scene—body fluids, hairs, or clothing fibers. The lab techs wouldn't know for about ten days. They kept coming back to what seemed like the main issue, though: Vasquez's partner. Hill had been assembling data. From an initial list of sixteen known David Vasquez associates, Mike had used background checks to narrow that number down to three leading suspects: Bernard Lawson, Charles Vandi, and Bill Kluge.

Lawson was a suspect in 1984, but he had appeared to have a rock solid alibi. Still, if any of Vasquez's associates fit the profile of a person who would commit such a crime, it was he. In his midthirties, he was a semifriend of Vasquez who had a long and checkered record, with multiple arrests as well as numerous FORs for loitering and suspicious behavior. Since 1981 he had been in and out of the correctional system for grand larceny, indecent exposure, and other offenses. A loner, he had also been hospitalized several times for schizophrenia and believed at times that he was Jesus Christ.

Charles Vandi, a car salesman, was number two on Horgas's list and had in fact been a prime suspect in 1984. Intelligent and employed on a full-time basis in a fairly demanding job, he seemed a highly unlikely friend for Vasquez. In explaining their friendship back in 1984, he'd told investigators that David was "a wonderful person who'd give you the shirt off his back." Vandi admitted that, except for

51

him, David had few friends. He sometimes loaned David money, but of much greater interest to Horgas was his admission that they also traded porno magazines. Furthermore, he had no solid alibi for the night of Hamm's murder. He thought he had taken a friend to the airport, but was unsure of it.

Then there was Bill Kluge, a marginal drifter like David. They had become friends in Manassas when David had moved there from Arlington, about six months before the Hamm murder. They had spent a lot of time together and been frequent drinking partners. Unlike Vasquez, though, Kluge had physical strength and at least average intelligence. He was also David's alibi witness, claiming David was with him in a bar the night of the murder. In fact, police had suspected that Kluge might have driven David from Manassas to Arlington to commit the murder, for Vasquez did not know how to drive and there was no bus that could have gotten him to Arlington in time to commit the murder and then back to work in Manassas early the next morning. Someone had driven him. And Kluge was as likely as anyone else.

Joe knew that the key to determining which of these men was the partner lay with Vasquez. He would go to Vasquez, ask him. There's no way in hell he's not going to tell me something, Joe assured himself. Nobody wants to sit in prison.

He dialed Rich McCue, one of Vasquez's defense attorneys.

"Rich, this is Joe Horgas. I think you heard we just had a murder over in Fairlington. Keep this between us. From what we got so far it seems there's some connection to the Hamm murder. Maybe David could help us out. If he gives me anything that leads us to this killer, we'll make it right for him. So I want you to go with me down to Buckingham." Since a deal was going to be offered, Vasquez's lawyer had to accompany him.

"Will Helen go along with this?" McCue asked, referring to the elected Commonwealth Attorney.

"I haven't spoken with her yet, Rich, but you can have my word on it." Joe would make the arrangements with Helen Fahey as soon as he hung up. He knew she would agree.

Joe's promise was enough for McCue. If Horgas told you something, McCue knew, you could rely on it—something that was not true of every police officer. "When do you want to go?"

"Nine-thirty Monday morning."

Buckingham Correctional Center, one of three maximum security prisons in Virginia, is located in the lush Blue Ridge Mountains two and a half hours southwest of Arlington. It houses some of Virginia's most dangerous felons.

After being cleared through an intricate complex of electronically controlled gates and doors, Horgas and McCue arrived at a small interview room. Vasquez shuffled into the room sporting a short, stringy beard and wearing his cap crooked slightly to the left. Sitting round-shouldered in his faded blue, ill-fitting prison garb and squinting under the fluorescent lights, David Vasquez struck Horgas as nothing but pathetic.

After introducing Horgas, McCue, who hadn't seen Vasquez since the sentencing almost four years earlier, broke the ice by launching into a discussion about the Washington Redskins. David, though, was apprehensive—the last time he had agreed to speak to a cop he'd ended up in jail.

Horgas had come prepared. In almost the same breath that he began speaking, Horgas pulled a thirty-five-cent cigar out of his vest pocket and offered it to David. Detective Shelton, one of the officers who arrested Vasquez, had told Horgas that Vasquez liked cigars. David's appreciation was clear; he passed the cigar under his nose and slipped it into his pocket so he could savor it at a later time.

"So how has it been in here for you, David?" Horgas asked. It was an open-ended question, yet Horgas was not prepared for the response. Vasquez crumpled in his chair and began to cry that his life had been pure hell. Far weaker than most of the inmates, he was constantly harassed and had, not surprisingly, been raped within days of his arrival at the prison. He had also had no visitors since the day he set foot in the prison. His only contacts with the world were his sporadic collect calls to the Harrison family, with whom he had lived for many years after his mother left Arlington, and to his friend Alan Trenton.

Playing off David's pitiful reaction, Horgas said: "Well, David, I might be able to help you, but you have to help me. There's another dead woman in Arlington and we think that whoever killed Hamm killed her."

McCue chimed in, telling Vasquez what the prosecutor had said. If Vasquez's cooperation led to an arrest, the CA would make that known to the parole board when David became eligible in two years.

"I can't help you," Vasquez said blankly.

Realizing he was dealing with a very fragile personality, Horgas spoke in soft, measured tones.

"We really need your help on this one, buddy. David. This is your chance to help yourself—and the community. We need to get this guy off the street because he's going to kill more women." But it was like talking to a wall.

Horgas took a deep breath and changed tactics. "Hey, you're a Catholic, right? So am I. Now we know that confession's good for the soul. Am I right or what?" Vasquez nodded his head in agreement.

"So—?"

"I'd like to help you, but I can't confess no sins to a priest if I didn't commit them in the first place," David whispered.

Next Horgas tried mentioning a few details from the Tucker murder, thinking he might arouse David's sympathy for the dead woman and her husband. This tactic didn't shake anything loose either.

"I can't help you guys," David said softly. "I'm here because of what I said to the police about a dream I had. . . . Sometimes I try to think about what happened, but I always come up with the same question. How could I have gotten there if I wasn't there?" Horgas recognized the response as almost identical to the one Shelton and Carrig said he'd given them back in 1984.

Horgas was the kind of detective who could get anyone to speak, and he tried every device he had ever learned to open David up. Yet Vasquez could not bring himself to relive the past. With each question he drifted further and further away, until he was no longer responding to questions at all. Instead he was wandering through a rambling, incoherent monologue about the dream and his arrest. And each time he came back to the same theme: "How would I get there?"

"We were in there for a little over an hour," Horgas later said, "but it was useless." Finally Horgas went out to inform the assistant warden that they were finished.

"You know," Horgas said to the warden, "I don't think Vasquez belongs here."

"Why's that?"

"He's innocent," Joe said flatly.

"Well, we got a lot like that in here," the warden quipped.

But Horgas was not joking. And, as they left the prison together, he said the same thing to McCue, without affect, as if it were nothing more than a fact of nature: "You know he had nothing to do with killing her. You know that."

McCue grimaced but said nothing.

"Ten minutes into the interview," Joe went on, "I realized he didn't have anything to do with it. The guy just doesn't fit. I don't care what the evidence was against him. He didn't do it."

McCue looked at him and said, "Why do you say that?"

"I look for emotion," Horgas explained. "If I arrest you on a robbery charge and you coldly respond, 'No, man, I didn't do it,' then I lock you up for robbery. But if you start scream-ing and crying and tell me with tears running down your face, 'It's not me! You got the wrong fucking man!' I'd say the odds are pretty good you're innocent—that is, unless I have your fingerprints."

"David didn't say anything different today than he did four years ago," McCue said as they got in the car.

"This guy doesn't even want to save himself. Come on, you saw him," Joe said emphatically. "He doesn't know shit! We offered him freedom—he didn't even bite. There were tears in his eyes!"

McCue shrugged.

"Listen. He's been in prison three years. Raped and who knows what else. There's no doubt he wants out to get back with his mother. All he'd have to do is tell us who was with him. A guilty man would give the guy up. Guys don't protect their friends once they're doing long time unless they're blood or really, really tight. And even then the human thing would be to say, 'Yeah, you're fucking right, there was something else,' and then he could just have given up a name, to send us off for a while, hoping we'd come up with it ourselves. David didn't even try to save his neck. It was pitiful."

McCue sighed. It was like dredging a river and bringing up clouds of mud and silt, obscuring everything, clarifying nothing.

For his part, Horgas knew that McCue wasn't the type of lawyer to plead his client guilty if he didn't think he was guilty. He must have had good reason. Although he and George Greten, the other appointed lawyer on the case, were young, and both general practitioners who had never handled a death penalty case, they had done a good and thorough job. They had plenty stacked against them. There were three taped interviews in which Vasquez confessed to the crime, and there were two independent eyewitnesses—a Muriel Ranser (the sister of Larry Ranser, a neighbor of Hamm's) and a Michael Ansari—who swore that they saw him in the vicinity near the time of the murder, even though he was supposedly living and working in Manassas about an hour away. It had been the most formidable case McCue had ever had, and now he found himself rearguing it with Horgas as they drove back to Arlington—yet he, the defense attorney, argued the prosecution, and Horgas, the veteran police officer, took the side of the defense.

"If the guy didn't know how to drive and there were no buses to get him the twenty-five miles from Manassas to Arlington, how'd he do it?" Horgas said.

"His buddy Bill Kluge might have taken him there," McCue said. McCue offered the theory that Kluge, Vasquez's alibi witness, might have been David's accomplice.

McCue reminded Horgas that he and his partner had tried everything. In the preliminary hearing they had tried to get the medical examiner to admit that the evidence was consistent with suicide, since there were no cuts and bruises on the body and no sign of a struggle. This didn't work: every other piece of forensic evidence proved that Carolyn Hamm had been murdered.

Next they focused on the proposition that David had nothing to do with the murder, that contrary to the eyewitness accounts of Ranser and Ansari, David had never set foot in Arlington in the period January 21–25, 1984.

That David did not know how to drive was unquestioned. Moreover, during the period of the homicide David had worked his usual day shift (7 A.M.–11 A.M.) at McDonald's, having come in to work on the morning of January 24 and 25 on time and appearing utterly normal throughout. There were no buses that could have taken him to Arlington and back in time for work.

McCue had also vigorously pursued alibis to put David in Manassas during the relevant time period. David had said he was bowling, but there was no one who could remember seeing him there. After Vasquez's arrest his mother, Imelda Shapiro, first told Carrig and Shelton that on the night in question she was at work and was unaware of her son's whereabouts. Shortly thereafter she changed her story, stating that she was home with him. Because she had wavered with the detectives and was unable to provide any other corroboration, the defense attorneys were unable to rely on her story.

McCue also searched for months to find evidence contradicting the sightings by Ms. Ranser and Mr. Ansari. Like the police, he came up with nothing. Ranser and Ansari were strangers to each other and their stories remained the same despite repeated interrogations.

Then there were the forensic results. It was encouraging that Vasquez's blood type did not match that found in the semen samples recovered from Hamm's body or her bathrobe, and that none of the shoe impressions outside the broken basement window matched David's shoe soles. Yet on the other hand, the expert McCue and his partner hired to analyze hair samples recovered from the murder scene was so certain that the hairs belonged to David Vasquez that they couldn't risk using his testimony, even though they had hired him. Though hair fiber analysis was not nearly as precise as fingerprint identification, it was still a fairly reliable technology.

If the hairs belonged to David, why didn't the semen? The lawyers were left with the theory that the bathrobe stain had nothing to do with the murder and in fact came from a previous lover.

Another problem was the fact that David was mentally impaired. He was unable to assist them effectively in his own defense and, they believed, could have been easily coerced into giving the confessions. And even if he had not been coerced into confessing, he clearly did not possess the mental or physical prowess to pull off such a crime by himself.

In addition to lining up witnesses to testify about David's minimal mental abilities, the defense attorneys had their client evaluated by two psychologists who jointly concluded:

> While extremely passive, Mr. Vasquez may seem reasonably engageable. This is in part due to his hesitation to overtly reject others for fear that they might be punitive to him. He is easily confused, owing to both a low intelligence and pervasive emotional condition, but seems reluctant to let others know he doesn't understand because of his pride. . . . It is also conceivable that he represses memories of emotionally laden events to an unconscious level.

The defense also consulted a psychiatrist who found that David was subject to suggestion and that his will was easily overborne by authority figures, such as the police. The doctor asked David, "How much is two plus two?"

"Four," David responded.

"Are you sure, David? You're sure it isn't three?" After several minutes of cajoling the doctor was able to persuade David that two plus two was three.

Despite David's low intellectual functioning, the doctors did not find that he suffered from any mental disease. This ruled out any possibility of an insanity defense.

After receiving the defense reports Commonwealth Attorney Henry Hudson (Fahey's predecessor) had David examined by a psychiatrist of his choice who, unlike the defense experts, found that, though David had "slightly low" intellectual function, he was competent to stand trial. He also concluded that David was capable of resisting suggestion by authority figures and otherwise exercising his own free will.

The showdown between the experts occurred on December 4, 1984, at the hearing to suppress David's three confessions. By far the strongest element of the defense strategy, the purpose of the motion to suppress was to exclude the three confessions on the grounds that they were coerced in violation of David's Fifth Amendment rights.

The very well researched defense brief filed with the court emphasized that David should have been read his Miranda rights as soon as he was confronted by the detectives because he was, contrary to Shelton and Carrig's statements, really a suspect. If he had been Mirandized during the first interrogation in Manassas, he would have been told of his right to remain silent, and perhaps the detectives never would have gotten him to talk. Relying on a well-established criminal principle known as the fruit of the poisonous tree doctrine, the defense argued that the original confessions "tainted" the remaining ones and thus all three should also be excluded.

The defense also challenged the circumstances under which David was interrogated—a small, windowless room where David was forced to sit at a narrow table between two constantly smoking, coercive detectives. They contended that the detectives lied to David (who was easily confused) about why they wanted to speak with him and fabricated a story about his fingerprints being found in Hamm's home. They alternately screamed and slammed their fists on the table. This was successful: after David began to cry and requests to speak to his mother were denied, he buckled and confessed.

Henry Hudson, of course, had a different perspective. He strenuously argued that Shelton and Carrig originally went to speak to Vasquez as a potential witness, since he was seen in the vicinity the night of the homicide. David voluntarily agreed to speak to them. Vasquez was not visibly retarded; he was able to read, hold down a job, and carry on a normal conversation. That the detectives became emotional or even fabricated certain facts did not in and of itself necessitate a finding that the confession was coerced.

At the end of that first interview, Hudson contended, there was ample probable cause to arrest Vasquez, but the detectives chose not to do so. And because David was not formally under arrest, he was free to go at the end of the interview; instead he freely chose to accompany them to Arlington.

While Hudson defended the first two confessions, he knew that the third tape was completely untainted. Unlike the first two interviews, the third statement was initiated by Vasquez. Without any prodding from Shelton, Vasquez independently launched into a description of his "terrible dream."

"It seemed to be a very rapid brief statement, a kind of stream of consciousness, on how the events occurred which seemed to me to be basically consistent with the crime scene," Hudson later said. "David was almost panting and the statement was uttered without hesitation and without intervention or suggestion."

The hearing continued for three days, an unprecedented time for such a proceeding in Arlington County.

The judge took the matter under advisement and did not issue his opinion until more than a month later on January 25, 1985, the one-year anniversary of Hamm's death.

To the delight of the defense, Judge Winston disallowed the first confession:

> In no sense was it mere questioning of a witness. Any fair reading of the tape or transcript will reveal this. Most significantly the interrogation occurred in the interrogation room. . . . All methods employed by the officers were those used to obtain a confession. None were those used to obtain information from a witness, which are usually soft and solicitous. Here we have a two-on-one situation at the police station, the use of the good guy/bad guy methods of interrogation and the careful use of factual misstatements of evidence.

The judge thus ruled that Vasquez should have been given his Miranda warnings and that the confession was illegally obtained. For similar reasons the judge ruled the second confession back at the Arlington police station illegal because it was tainted by the first.

To the horror of the defense, however, in the last paragraph of the three-page opinion the judge admitted the third "dream" confession. The judge's justification was that in between the second and third tape David had been given his Miranda warning, and still volunteered his "dream."

With just a slightly qualified win on the suppression motion, there was very little room for the defense to maneuver. In order to explain the third tape, unquestionably the worst of the three, the defense would be placed in the anomalous position of bringing in the first tape. "If we introduced the first confession," McCue later said, "then we were going to screw up our appeal rights on the suppression motion because we ourselves would have been putting the first tape into evidence. By agreeing with us and excluding the first two tapes, the judge created even more problems than he would have if he let all three come in."

By this time the defense had all but given up on finding any credible evidence that David Vasquez was not present in Arlington at the time of the murder. Then, just prior to the suppression hearing, someone stuck a note in David's mother's door giving the address in Florida of Bill Kluge, the alibi witness who had fled shortly after David's arrest (and whom the police believed might have been the second man). McCue immediately filed an out-of-state witness subpoena to have Kluge brought up to Arlington.

On the Friday morning before the trial was to commence, the defense received a call from Florida authorities saying that Bill Kluge was in their courthouse. Before Kluge got on the phone, McCue was planning on sending him an airplane ticket. His mind was quickly changed, however, when it became apparent that Kluge could not provide a solid alibi for David.

The final blow was Vasquez's response to the administration of sodium amytal or what is popularly known as truth serum. McCue arranged for the test in a last-ditch effort to establish David's innocence.

After asking Vasquez a series of questions relating to the murder of Carolyn Hamm, the physician giving the test informed McCue that there was no question Vasquez had actually been in Carolyn Hamm's home the night of her death. David gave the doctor essentially the same story he had given Carrig and Shelton almost a year earlier. Despite some inconsistencies in David's story, McCue's own expert was quite emphatic that this was not merely a dream but something Vasquez actually experienced. At that point, McCue told Horgas, he had no choice but to approach the Commonwealth Attorney's office for a plea. The idea of letting David take the stand and be cross-examined was insane. Henry Hudson, a tenacious prosecutor, would be able to get him to say anything he wanted—and that would lead to David's execution.

The prosecution offered to let David plead to second-degree murder and burglary with a sentence of thirty-five years. This would make David eligible for parole in seven years. Hudson was willing to make this relatively lenient offer because he knew the case was full of questions. After a short discussion Hudson also agreed to the defense request to let David make an Alford plea as opposed to a straight guilty plea. Under an Alford plea, the defendant doesn't formally plead guilty but does admit that if he went to trial there would be sufficient evidence to convict him of a more serious charge than the one to which he pled.

Hudson wanted a fast answer and he got it. David agreed that afternoon, and formally entered his plea of guilty on February 4, 1985.

Following his return to Arlington after speaking to Vasquez, Horgas went straight to the PD. He didn't say anything to anyone about Vasquez. All he said was that it hadn't been a very productive interview. Joe was known to be forthcoming with his opinions, especially on his cases, but the notion that his department had sent an innocent man to prison was simply too outer orbit to mention to anybody.

He had never faced such a dilemma in his long career. He had to weigh what was only a gut feeling, albeit a very strong one, against the faith he had placed in the detectives, prosecutors, judges, and even the defense attorneys he had known for twenty years. With all its cracks and fissures the system still worked, he told himself. If Vasquez was in prison it had to be for a very good reason. Maybe the real guy was a friend who set him up. Whoever the killer was, one thing was clear: he was out on the streets—and free to continue his rampage.

3

JOE CRACKED OPEN THE MASSIVE HAMM FILE AGAIN. HE'D HAD AN inkling there were problems before his trip to Buckingham penitentiary, but the Vasquez interview and his discussions with McCue convinced him that the problems were far more serious than he'd imagined. It was night now, and he was at his crowded desk. The hum of activity in the squad room had gone from a roar to a murmur. He could concentrate on the four feet of paper that groaned between the folders—the stuffed photographs, the teletypes, comb it all—and find that moment where the Hamm investigation went off track. He flipped slowly through the first pages. The opening days.

From what he read, it seemed that initially Carrig hadn't been sure Hamm was not a suicide. A suicide of sorts, at least—an autoerotic death. The other detectives had thought this was far-fetched. Yet Carrig, the most senior member of the squad, was not one to go out on limbs. With a commandant's barrel chest and tie clip in the shape of handcuffs, he was the picture of cautious authority. And accidental-autoerotic deaths were not as uncommon as most people thought. People—mostly men—got the ropes too tight or fell off chairs. And with Hamm there were aspects that suggested the possibility: the intricate bindings, the fact that there was no trauma to the body other than death. With a murder victim, you usually saw the cuts, the bruises, the signs of the struggle. Not here.

Carrig's partner Chuck Shelton thought this theory was too far out. He had no doubt that Carolyn Hamm was murdered. And just as Carrig appeared to be the most conservative man in the unit, Shelton seemed the most offbeat. He was the squad's sense of humor, a visibly relaxed man who liked to say that nothing was more important to him than his quacking desk phone shaped like a mallard duck.

"It's friggin' cold outside," he said later of the autoerotic death theory, "and here she is on her concrete basement floor. If you do something like this you find yourself a nice warm corner. Besides, look how her hair was all entangled in the noose. Tell me what woman would voluntarily tie anything around her hair like that." Also, the detectives did not find, as one tactfully said they usually did, "implements to fulfill the individual." Another item that was missing— and usually seen with autoerotic deaths—was padding between the ligature and the neck to avoid telltale rope burns.

This controversy, though, was resolved the next morning by the medical examiner. "Doc" Beyer dismissed Carrig's autoerotic theory outright because the victim's hands were tied so tightly around her wrists that there was no possible chance of her escaping. Beyer thought that Hamm had been hung by at least one other person. His opinion, though, was that the body had not been suspended off the ground because the noose was not very tight. Still, there were no bruises or cuts found anywhere on Hamm's body—just a slight abrasion on the left instep that indicated she had been dragged along the ground.

The medical examiner also found a petroleum jelly–type substance in the pubic hair and around the mouth. Lab tests over the next few days, Joe read in the file, had also established the presence of spermatozoa in her vagina as well on her labia and thighs. A test also revealed semen stains on the bathrobe recovered from the living room. Finally, Beyer estimated that Hamm was killed sometime after 10 P.M. on January 23, 1984.

Once the basic circumstances of the death had been established, it was time for any and all theories to be thrown on the table for consideration.

First off, Joe read that the handbag lying right inside the vestibule had suggested to the detectives that the killer might have broken into Hamm's home late in the afternoon and waited there for her to return. As soon as she came through the door, perhaps he grabbed her handbag, rummaged through it, and then got the idea to rape her. But then, Joe read, the assailant might have broken in intending to rape and kill—and gone through her bag only as he was leaving. Was this a career burglar who, this once, went far beyond his usual crime, or was it a murder for whom robbery was an incidental act?

Joe saw that the investigators had also tried to determine whether Carolyn Hamm could have had something to do with her own death. Did she get into a bad relationship? Pick up the wrong person at a bar? What were her habits with men?

In the first days of the investigation the department intensively canvassed the neighborhood to find out as much as possible about the victim. Although it was not unusual in a yuppie bedroom community like Arlington, they were still surprised that even Hamm's closest neighbors knew next to nothing about her. All they said was that the lady lived alone, kept to herself, and was an attorney who worked long hours at a prestigious firm in D.C. This much was leaked to the press, and the headline in the January 27, 1984, edition of the *Arlington Journal* read, HANGING VICTIM STRANGER TO NEIGHBORS. Carrig and Shelton didn't do much better in combing the neighborhood for potential witnesses. Not one person they interviewed noticed anything out of the ordinary on the 25th of January or the day before. Even the head of the neighborhood watch program had nothing to say.

Thus Carrig and Shelton put much of their initial effort into developing a personality profile of Hamm. Casting a wide net, they had called every name in her Rolodex and appointment book as well as all those whose numbers appeared on her phone bills and with whom she corresponded.

The profile which emerged was that of a stable, well-educated, single woman who never smoked or drank alcohol. An attorney specializing in historic preservation, she was passionate about old buildings, traveled widely, and liked listening to the Beach Boys and Vivaldi. She was definitely *not* the type who frequented pickup bars, and in fact was something of a loner who had very few romantic relationships. During their search of the home, Joe saw that the forensic team did discover an angry letter from an ex-boyfriend dated several weeks before the killing. The boyfriend was quickly ruled out by Shelton, however, when he was proven to be in another state at the time of her death.

Her friends Bess and Dave were the last people to see her alive. On Sunday evening they watched the Superbowl at Carolyn's home and ate take-out fried chicken. Carolyn was in a great mood because she was going on vacation to Peru that coming Friday with one of her closest girlfriends. Chillingly, Bess told the police of sitting around with Carolyn two weeks before the homicide and talking about their greatest fears. "I said I was afraid of drowning," Bess recalled. "Carolyn said her greatest fear was that someone might break into her house and get her." Joe shivered, imagining the terror she must have felt when she faced her murderer, and then willed himself to turn the page.

Next he saw a copy of a report prepared by Rich Alt, a detective in the burglary unit. On the morning of January 27, 1984, Alt had received a routine request to go back and see a break-in victim he had spoken to a week before. The victim, Wilma Thoreau, had first called the police a week earlier because she had returned to her house to find that someone had broken in through a basement window. Strangely, nothing was missing except forty dollars and two gold chains. Instead, the intruder had left items behind.

Neatly positioned in the center of her bed was a paper bag containing three porno magazines, a carrot, and several lengths of venetian blind cord. On the floor at the foot of the bed, Miss Thoreau had found a bucket containing several bags of marijuana, drug paraphernalia, razor blades, and a small vial of white powder, which was later discovered to be the topical anesthetic procaine. These items had been retrieved by Alt and duly noted in his report.

Thoreau then called Alt back a second time because her next-door neighbor admitted to her that his house had been broken into the same night. He said he had not told the police because the intruder had taken some things he did not want police to know he had in his possession.

Following his meeting with the woman, Alt stopped by the neighbor's home. The nervous young man immediately admitted that some magazines and the procaine were stolen from his home. Though a prescription drug, procaine was used on the street as a sexual stimulant. Alt issued a standard warning about illegal substances and left.

Driving back to the station, Alt thought, this is really one for the books. A guy breaks into one house, steals some stuff, and breaks into the house next door to do who knows what.

Shortly after he sat back down at his desk, Alt's sergeant briefed him on the Hamm homicide. The full weight of what he had just discovered on Dinwiddie Street—and what he had retrieved from Thoreau's home a week before—came crashing down on him. The Dinwiddie Street address was no more than two blocks from Carolyn Hamm's home. In minutes Alt was at Shelton's desk and within the hour Shelton was in Wilma Thoreau's home.

A few short minutes reviewing the Thoreau scene and Shelton was pretty sure the intruder was the same person who had murdered Hamm. Thoreau, a winsome twenty-eight-year-old brunette, was probably his first attempt. He only failed because he got tired of waiting for her to come home. He tried again with Hamm and was successful. There seemed little doubt now that he'd try a third time.

"When we put two and two together," Shelton later explained, "I went back down there to speak with Thoreau. She asked me, 'What should I do?' I said, 'I would pack my shit and get out of Dodge until we get this thing under control.' I never said that to any citizen in my entire career, but it was so obvious that it was the same guy."

The complexity of the Hamm case had just increased exponentially in less than eight hours. The Thoreau incident clearly seemed to mean that, as one detective later said, "we had a homicidal maniac on the streets." Experience told them that if they didn't find this deranged individual soon, they would be *forced* to tell other single women in Arlington what Shelton had told Wilma Thoreau.

Despite the obvious danger to all women in the area, the department did not want to alarm the public. A tight lid was put on the case. Throughout the first week of the investigation the department's media officer Tom Bell continued to describe what had occurred as a "suspicious death." Attempting to allay community concern, Bell also informed the media, on January 27, that "we have no reason to believe there is a mass killer stalking the neighborhood."

This party line was not easy for all the officers to follow. "We had some horrendous arguments," said a detective who insisted on remaining anonymous. "I told Hawkins that it was in the public interest to release more information so people could protect themselves." Hawkins was adamant. He didn't want any information leaked on Hamm or Thoreau. It was not until January 31, with the release of the autopsy report, an official document, that the department publicly conceded that Hamm was a murder victim, the first of 1984. Hawkins, however, continued to enforce the "no further comment" policy on the particulars of the case.

Sitting at his desk on Saturday, December 5, 1987, Joe remembered the pressure to get the Hamm case solved. It had not been some back alley stabbing, or the murder of someone who lived a high-risk life, like a prostitute or drug dealer; it had been the murder of a prominent attorney, young, a woman from a distinguished firm. And even though he had not worked on the case directly he recalled the urgency in the squad room; he recalled how the top brass—the administrators who usually stayed in their offices, at their desks, behind their closed doors—were hovering in the bullpen all day, pacing, anxious, acting as if they wished they could go back to being foot soldiers and tackle the case themselves. And when the department was keeping it hush-hush with the press, Joe remembered, it was like being in a pressure cooker. Every minute, ticking. Find the guy before he does somebody else. Joe turned back to the file and read on.

Following normal procedure in narrowing down suspects, after ruling out any possible boyfriends—and in the absence of a husband—the investigators turned their attention to the last persons to have seen the victim alive and then those who discovered the body. Hamm's close friends Bess and Dave were quickly eliminated. Carrig and Shelton then turned their attention to Larry Ranser, the young neighbor who had helped discover the body. Darla Henry, Hamm's friend who had asked Ranser to accompany her into the home, had already been fingerprinted and checked out. Considering the nature of the crime, she was never seriously thought of as a suspect. Ranser, though, was a possibility. Carrig and Shelton asked him to come to police headquarters on January 28, 1984.

An athletic young man who lived with his mother, Ranser was visibly shaken during his interview with the detectives. Speaking disjointedly, averting his eyes, Ranser told the detectives that he had been leaving his driveway when the lady asked him to go with her into Hamm's home.

Ranser said that though he hadn't personally known Hamm, he was able to guide Hamm's friend around the house because most of the homes on the street were built by the same developer. He also insisted that except for calling the police on Hamm's phone, he kept his hands in his pockets the entire time he was in the house.

"So the only place your fingerprints should be in that house is on the telephone, right?" Shelton interjected.

"Maybe on the front door too." Ranser qualified. "I can't remember."

Following the interview, Ranser agreed to be fingerprinted and gave sample of his blood and hair. He also offered to submit his boots and sneakers for comparison to several prints that had been found outside Hamm's basement window.

Later that day Shelton wrote in his progress notes, "Ranser

appears to be a fairly unstable individual. I anticipate additional interviews."

Joe saw that on Monday morning, five days after the discovery of the body, Shelton and Carrig didn't have much of anything that made sense. The only thing really important had been the information gleaned from Thoreau, and that had mainly told them the guy was likely to do it again. Moreover, weirdos were starting to come out of the woodwork.

In one of many similar reports Joe came across, an officer stopped a white man in his late twenties on Sunday night, four days after the body was found. He was standing in front of Hamm's home. "Subject stated," the report read, "that he was trying to get some vibration as to why victim was killed. Subject checked out and was sent on his way."

Then finally Joe came to the first break in the case. At 8 A.M. Monday morning, February 1, Shelton's duck phone had quacked. It was Muriel Ranser, Larry Ranser's sister. She said she wanted the detectives to know that when she went to visit her mother on the previous Monday—presumed to be the evening of the murder—she saw a man walking up the street in her direction. She had pulled her car up in front of Carolyn Hamm's house at about 8:15 P.M. because her mother lived on the street. The man continued walking toward her and stopped about six feet away. She had recognized him as David Vasquez, a neighborhood person she had known for about fifteen years. He wore glasses, a jacket, and had his hands in his pockets.

Ms. Ranser, in her early thirties and a salesclerk, went on to say that Vasquez had been a janitor at her high school and that there had been rumors that David had stolen various garments from the girls' locker room.

That evening on the street, she said, Vasquez stared at her in a way that gave her a "creepy feeling." Then she turned and walked down the street to her mother's home.

Ranser underscored that she herself had always been uncomfortable in David's presence. Whenever she had worked in her front yard in the past, she had always gone inside immediately upon seeing him approach. Ranser was unsure whether David had personally known Hamm; she did, however, have a memory of seeing David walk by while Hamm was sunbathing in her front yard.

Shelton hung up. "Bobby, we might have something really hot here!" he shot at Carrig. It was more than just the call from Ranser. Another witness had mentioned Vasquez. That morning Shelton had read a memo from patrol officer Roger Estes:

Information from Michael Ansari received 1/28/84 at 17:20 hours: Since I have worked in this area I got to know Mr. Ansari as a personal friend. I value his opinion highly. He is an alert individual. Mr. Ansari discussed an individual who is mentally very slow. The individual came to Mr. Ansari's mind after the homicide. Mr. Ansari stated the subject is weird; this is due to his attitude towards women. He peers at them for long periods of time. The subject's name is Dave, about 30–35. Last name unknown. Lives with [neighborhood family named]. Dave possibly works at Wakefield High School as a maintenance man. He is described as a white male of latin descent, about 5'10", medium build, very stooped shouldered posture, thin beard [and] very nearsighted. On the day of the homicide investigation, Dave came to the corner of 23rd and S. Culpepper Streets, looked awhile [at the police activity], then left. It was strange to Mr. Ansari who stated the whole neighborhood was interested in what happened, except Dave. Dave has been known to have temper tantrums but has not been known to have ever hurt anyone.

Ansari's observations were given particular weight because he was a retired military officer, Joe recalled. And the two independent sightings of Vasquez in the neighborhood— though neither appeared to involve anything illegal—marked Vasquez as the first person who seemed promising to check out.

Joe moved on to the next page. Shelton and Carrig immediately paid a visit to Arnold and Debra Harrison, with whom David had resided before moving to Manassas. Their two-story gray frame house was just around the corner from the Hamm scene.

Mr. and Mrs. Harrison told Carrig and Shelton that they had become a surrogate family to David Vasquez seven years earlier, after his mother moved out of the neighborhood. Vasquez lived with them until finally moving to Manassas the previous June to rejoin his mother. They said he got a job as a janitor at McDonald's. Since then he would come back once in a while to collect his mail, but both husband and wife agreed that they hadn't seen David since November of 1983.

Joe saw that when Carrig informed them that someone had seen David on the block just last week, they appeared to be genuinely surprised.

Joe could also see that they were willing to supply any information they could to the detectives. In his late thirties, David was a quiet man, turned in on himself, with only a couple of friends and zero contact with women. He had a hard time holding a job.

He also did not drive; but he did take evening walks around the neighborhood. "Not for exercise," Arnold Harrison told Carrig and Shelton, "but to look around."

Joe then came to the search of David's room, unhesitatingly allowed by the Harrisons. "There were piles and piles of books and magazines with women's pictures, only a couple that I would classify as harder porn than, let's say, *Playboy*," Shelton later said. In one periodical Shelton noticed a picture of a woman bound and gagged with a rope around her neck. More disturbingly, they also discovered an envelope containing a number of amateur photos. There were women in bathing suits and cut-offs washing a car, apparently unaware that they were being photographed through a screen door. Then there were shots of teenage girls playing lacrosse and soccer at nearby Wakefield High. The photos were taken from a distance—probably, Shelton surmised, through a locker room window.

The photos were technically legal but were clearly "peeper pictures" to Carrig and Shelton. The girls were not aware they were being photographed and all were partially undressed. Along with the pictures they found a handwritten three-page list with the names and birthdays of several hundred famous actresses and female TV personalities.

Joe noticed that before they even identified Vasquez, Carrig and Shelton had been directed by their superiors to pay a visit to the FBI's Behavioral Science Unit in Quantico, Virginia. The unit specialized in crimes such as rapes and homicides in which the local authorities had not been able to identify even a possible suspect. These special FBI agents were unlike traditional law enforcement officers in that their primary investigative tool was criminal profiling—a forensic science technique they had pioneered.

Analyzing the available evidence of the crime (including the age, sex, and race of the victim, the method of killing, the condition and location of the body, whether or not the victim was sexually assaulted, et cetera) and matching this evidence with the psychological and behavioral criminal profiles developed over the years, the agents could make some fairly remarkable and accurate predictions about the identity of a killer. These included the number of people involved in the crime, the approximate age, education, sex, race, and even the general area in which the assailant might have resided.

Since they had made the appointment with the FBI unit before they identified Vasquez, Carrig and Shelton hoped to use the meeting to determine whether Vasquez fit the profile. They also wanted some pointers on how to confront and interview their suspect.

Shelton and Carrig had sat around an oval conference table with senior agents Roy Hazelwood and John Douglas, discussing the evidence and showing them the ropes, photographs, and autopsy report. "The individual who was involved in this was a white male in his thirties," Hazelwood commented. Looking over the photos, he continued: "I see a lot of immaturity here, but at the same time I see someone who's a little more mature." He explained that the immature side to the killing was the dumping of the purse and the theft of a few dollars without taking the credit cards. Other aspects of the scene, though, particularly the ornate bindings and lack of wounds or bruises, suggested a mature personality. These two different "personalities" could mean Hamm was killed by two people, with David being the immature one; or the perpetrator could be just one person with a complex multiple personality having mature and immature sides.

Horgas noted that the day Carrig and Shelton were in Quantico, two of the four detectives assigned to assist them—the sum total of the "Hamm Task Force"—were back in Arlington gathering background information on Vasquez. Burglary detective Cindy Brenneman and Ray Harp from the sex crimes unit went door to door with David's photo. Several neighbors positively identified him, but most did not know who he was. A record check revealed that he had never been convicted of or for that matter charged with any sex crimes; his only conviction was for stealing coins from a Laundromat at nineteen.

Hoping that they might be able to discover something about the killer—perhaps his profession—from the bindings the detectives also interviewed a Coast Guard officer. He informed them that the pieces of cord from Hamm's hands were tied with a square knot, and the bindings around her neck were composed of three half hitches. These were all extremely common knots, which did not require any special skill, training, or occupation to fasten.

Now Carrig and Shelton were ready to confront Vasquez. At the very least he was a potential witness, someone who had been observed in the neighborhood the night of the homicide and might have seen something. On the other hand, it also looked as if he could be a suspect. What they had been able to discover about his personality seemed to match the FBI profile. Still, during their hour drive to the McDonald's in Manassas where David worked, Carrig and Shelton were nagged by the inconsistencies—David did not drive, for example, and lived at least an hour south of Arlington. How had he gotten to the scene of the crime after work and back again in time for work the next morning? Perhaps he had caught a ride with someone and gone back to Arlington to visit a friend. If so, and if the friend verified his story, that would be the end of this line of inquiry.

Joe came now to the transcriptions of the interviews with

Vasquez. These ran well over a hundred pages, and the tiny print seemed to swim in front of Joe's eyes. He had read enough. He would come back to this later, he thought, and closed the file.

The hours Joe had already spent reviewing the file had told him that the investigation had some obvious problems. But he had no idea yet of how muddled it got when Vasquez was interviewed. On that day in 1984, when Carrig and Shelton strode into the fast-food restaurant, they immediately recognized the rather short, thin man with the dark, stubby beard and wispy mustache who was mopping up a spilled soda. Wearing a brown McDonald's standard-issue baseball cap crooked to the side, he never looked up at the approaching officers until they were two feet away from him. If their background investigation had not informed them that he was about their age, they would have assumed he was at least fifteen years younger. His demeanor was that of a teenager.

Though Vasquez seemed initially nervous, he also appeared impressed that these two cops had come all the way down from Arlington to get his help in investigating "an incident" that had occurred in his old neighborhood. They asked David if he would accompany them to the local Prince William County Police Department for a interview. Carrig had assured David that he was not in any trouble but that he and Shelton did not feel comfortable speaking in front of all of David's coworkers.

Sitting in the small interview room, the detectives commenced the discussion in a very casual, soft-spoken manner. They asked Vasquez a variety of background questions, mostly confirming what they already knew about him. He was a fringe person, a loner who at thirty-seven still lived with his mother. His was hardly a story of success, but in an effort to gain his confidence Carrig and Shelton were understanding and supportive. Vasquez told them of moving from job to job. Of one employer who fired him, Vasquez explained, "I told them I was doing my best to clean the rooms."

"They just didn't like your product, huh?" Shelton responded.

"Right," agreed Vasquez. "My product."

Once the groundwork for trust was laid, the real questioning began. Carrig took the traditional tough, no-nonsense-cop approach and Shelton the soft, understanding one.

"All right, this is Monday," Carrig began in a grave tone. "Two weeks ago Monday. You know where you were?"

Vasquez didn't hesitate. "Two weeks ago Monday, I was here working."

"What time you get off?"

"I got off at eleven A.M. Then I went home, then I decided to go bowling. But I had to walk."

"Do you know what time you got home?"

"Around five, 'cause I bowled about four games."

"What did you do the rest of the night?"

"Stayed at home, like usual," David said matter-of-factly.

"Who was there?" Shelton asked.

"Ah, my . . . mother," David said, peering at Shelton through his thick, smoke-colored glasses. Uncertainty colored his voice for the first time.

"All night?" Shelton asked.

Vasquez moved in his chair and looked to the ceiling.

"Ah, ah, was she there or not? Or was she working? She got so many days that she'll work in the daytime or work at night—"

"David, David!" Carrig said raising his voice above Vasquez's.

"What?" Vasquez said meekly.

"You were in Arlington that day," Carrig said as if he were stating an indisputable fact of nature.

"How could I be in Arlington? I was here two weeks ago."

"David," Carrig said more insistently, "you were in Arlington that day, that's *why* we are here talking to you."

"We know you *were* in Arlington," Shelton echoed.

"Now think about where you were last Monday," Carrig said.

"Oh, two weeks ago last Monday, all right," Vasquez said as if he were on the verge of uttering something important.

In the same breath, however, he said, "No, I, ah, didn't even enter Arlington for two weeks at all, sir. At all."

Vasquez shifted uncomfortably and rubbed the furrow of his brow with his knuckles.

After almost two weeks of grueling, uneventful investigation, David's denial seemed the first glimmer of light. Why would he lie? Two separate people had independently placed him in Arlington—solid proof. Ranser and Ansari could have no reason to make up their stories. David, on the other hand, if he was involved, had every reason to deny it.

"Let me tell you where you were," Shelton said in a kind, supportive voice. "On Wednesday about one-fifteen in the afternoon you were in Arlington. In the neighborhood. On Monday two different people saw you there."

"I haven't been over there since November. That's the only time I have been over there, sir," David pleaded.

"Now wait a minute, you can get me right on this, OK? We just want to know why you were there. We're not disputing the fact that you *were* there, because the people know you. We want to know why you were there. If you are telling us that you weren't there that makes us a little weary. Do you understand what I am saying?"

But David held to his story; he was in Manassas.

"There was a burglary in your old neighborhood," Shelton declared, turning the interview down a new avenue. "Is there any reason why your fingerprints should be inside that house?"

"My fingerprints?" Vasquez replied, puzzled.

Carrig and Shelton lied to Vasquez about his fingerprints, which was both standard and legal in interrogation. Though it might seem to violate the American sense of fair play, deception is not only an integral part of police interrogation, it has been sanctioned by the United States Supreme Court. The only restriction imposed by the court is that the fabrication cannot be used to subvert the voluntariness of the person's right to remain silent or their right to an attorney. As Shelton later commented, "It's like putting the cheese in the trap. If the rat is hungry he'll come and eat. A lot of these guys don't know if you have their fingerprints or not. The goal is to let the person you're interviewing explain why it's impossible that his fingerprints are in the house because he was, for example, in Atlantic City at the gambling table. If that's the case, then he's caught me [in a lie]."

But David would not budge. "Don't ask me [how my fingerprints got there because]; I wasn't there."

Shelton and Carrig continued to press. "Help yourself, damn it!" Carrig shouted. "Tell us why you were in the neighborhood and we will call it a day."

"Neither he nor I are monsters, OK? We are not going to jump up and tear your head off," Shelton quickly followed up. "We are both reasonable men here to listen to your side of the story. . . . We are the ones that can help you. . . . When you play the game, you play as best you can, but it's over. You've got to tell us now or you're going to hurt yourself. . . . We are the ones that can help you. We do it all the time."

"My mother's the only one who can help me. I know she can," Vasquez said shakily, the stress of the interview becoming progressively more apparent. "She's working right now, I don't want to disturb her," he said, almost speaking to himself.

Moments later came the first fissure in the dam: "Maybe I might have gone there for a visit."

"OK, now we're starting to come around a little bit," Shelton said with an air of relief. "[But] who were you visiting, why were you there?"

To these and other questions Vasquez was unable to give a clear answer. He even backpedaled on his admission that he might have visited Arlington.

"How did you get there?" Shelton said exasperatedly.

"How did I get there?" David repeated. "I want to know. Because if my mom was working and she can't drive [me] and I don't drive—"

"Listen, if you borrowed somebody's car I could give a shit. I mean, we're certainly not worried about giving you a ticket for driving without a driver's license."

"No way! I won't drive without my driver's license and I don't drive."

Every question yielded a qualified answer. "I might have,"
or "I don't remember, but . . ." And each answer took the
investigators two steps forward and one back. Slowly,
though, Vasquez did admit that he had been in Arlington
and had gone to Hamm's home. Still, after he admitted going
into the house, ostensibly for the purpose of helping her move
some furniture, Vasquez said, "It was my imagination that was
there, [but] how my body would get there if I didn't . . ." He
couldn't seem to settle on an answer.

Though over the next hour David Vasquez admitted he
had intercourse with Carolyn Hamm and then killed her, his
statement could hardly have been called a "confession." Vac-
illating and equivocating at every turn, his account of the
incident was incoherent and inconsistent.

Carrig: David, did you have sex with her?
Vasquez: No.
Carrig: David, we'll be able to find that out very easily.
Vasquez: If I did I . . .
Shelton: Where did you have sex with her? On the second
floor. Or was it in the basement that you had sex
with her?
Vasquez: Uh, no.
Shelton: So, it wasn't on the second floor. OK. So we're
down to the first floor. The living room, is that
where you had sex with her?
Vasquez: Yeah.
Shelton: Where?
Vasquez: Right in the middle of the living room . . .
Shelton: Was she naked when you had sex with her?
Vasquez: Maybe.

Following this exchange, David explained to Shelton that
Hamm had *asked* him to tie her up because she was into
bondage, something David himself didn't like. Even more remarkable, David told the detectives that Hamm asked him to
kill her. "I told her no, I didn't want to do it and she said,
'Do it!' "

> Shelton: Tell us how you did it.
> Vasquez: I grabbed the knife and just stabbed her, that's all.
> Carrig: Oh David. No David! Now if you would have told us the way it happened we could believe you a little bit better.
> Vasquez: I only say that it did happen and I did it, my fingerprints were on it.
> Carrig: You hung her.
> Vasquez: What?
> Carrig: You hung her!
> Vasquez: Okay. So I hung her.

After being shown a crime scene photo of the victim lying on the basement floor, Vasquez also conceded he had sex with the body after Hamm died.

Two grueling hours later, just when Carrig and Shelton believed they had an airtight confession, Vasquez took off his glasses, rubbed his eyes, and in a manner that seemed to indicate he was talking to himself said, "I know I did it, but I don't know how my fingerprints got there. I wasn't there. I know I wasn't there. I know I wasn't . . . I know I didn't do it. How would I get there if I didn't drive and I didn't hitchhike?"

The interview had reached the point where Shelton and Carrig felt that they had to move it to Arlington. If David was going to give up the goods, Shelton and Carrig wanted him to do it on their turf where they had access to the entire case file. Though he had clearly given up some critical information, Vasquez was equivocating. Because his story was so murky—and because the case was too important and too high profile—they didn't feel they could seek an arrest warrant without some input from their superiors. And yet, with what Vasquez was saying, an arrest warrant was now critically needed.

Sitting in the small interview room in Manassas, Carrig and Shelton were in the twilight world of constitutional rights. Vasquez's confession had taken them largely by surprise. On the drive down to Manassas they had felt he possibly had some involvement, at least as a witness. But they had not formally targeted him as a suspect and thus they had not informed him of his Miranda rights—the right to remain silent and the right to an attorney. Designating someone as a suspect has very specific legal implications. It means that there is probable cause to believe the person committed a crime and thus grounds for an arrest.

David could have refused to accompany Carrig and Shelton back to Arlington. He could have said, "I don't want to talk to you any further"—but he didn't. His only requests were, first, that they call his mother and tell her to meet him in Arlington; and second, that somebody stop at his workplace to pick up his sweater.

David slipped into the backseat of the maroon Ford. Here was a man who the two detectives thought might be a vicious, sadistic killer, yet he was neither handcuffed nor shackled. On the ride back to Arlington they all smoked 35-cent cigars and talked about a car show Vasquez had recently attended in D.C.

Upon their arrival David was escorted directly to the interrogation room in the major crimes division. A second interview commenced. This time, however, Vasquez was given a Miranda warning. They were playing for keeps now. Anything David said could and would be used against him.

Sitting in the windowless interrogation room in the rear corner of the squad room, Vasquez shifted uncomfortably in the hard-backed wooden chair. As he had in Manassas, he wavered between admitting he was in Hamm's home and protesting that "I don't even know how I got to that place." Carrig and Shelton were bewildered. They were used to guys who looked them right in the eye and said, "Go fuck yourselves." David couldn't seem to settle on an answer to anything they said to him. He only appeared sure of one thing: that he hadn't been in Arlington in six months. Yet, in a rambling and inconsistent account, he continued to repeat the detail of how he had bound Carolyn Hamm, had sex with her, and hung her. Listening to him, Carrig and Shelton couldn't shake the feeling that he was a little dull to pull off such a spectacular crime by himself. And they had proof to support their position—two sets of fresh footprints were outside the point of entry. There had to be a second guy.

Vasquez had been talking for about fifty minutes, with a seven-minute break to wolf down a hot dog and soda. Carrig left the room to discuss the next step with his superiors. He took the tape recorder with him. Shelton stayed behind. He had no interest in prodding Vasquez to continue, for any new questioning might give him a chance to change his story yet again. As he had in the drive up from Manassas, Shelton simply began shooting the breeze with Vasquez. He discussed their favorite bars, and deep-sea fishing. There was no tape recorder on. "It was just guys talking," Shelton would later say.

Without warning, Vasquez stopped speaking in midsentence.

Dropping his head, casting his eyes vacantly at the dark green, pockmarked metal table, he said in a low rumbling tone, "I have horrible dreams." Vasquez was not addressing Shelton, just talking at the air. Shelton sat up ramrod straight. This was not the same David Vasquez he had been talking to all day!

Shock immobilized Shelton for a few moments. Vasquez was completely transformed. He seemed clear, certain. The vacancy was gone.

Holy shit, Shelton said to himself, I don't have anything to write on—let alone a tape recorder. Moving silently so as not to disturb David's trance-like monologue, Shelton cracked open the door and tried to catch the attention of someone, anyone in the squad room. He motioned to Detective Cindy Brenneman, one of the Hamm task force members, who was standing at the opposite end of the room and mouthed, "Get me a tape recorder." She didn't understand. He tried again. She still didn't get it. Finally, in a tone he was sure would startle David, Shelton blurted, "Get me a fucking tape recorder!"

Everyone in the major crimes division heard this, yet David continued speaking undisturbed. By the time Shelton got the tape recorder plugged in, David was five minutes into his "dream."

"Girl was in my dream, it's a horrible dream, it's a horrible dream, too horrible, I got myself in hell by breaking the glass," he said breathing heavily, moaning. "The dryer was hooked up, cut my hand in glass. I need help, then I went upstairs, she kept coming out, she startled me. I startled her. We both kinda screamed a little bit, she told me what was I doing. I said I came over to see you. My dream's too horrible to go back in it again."

"What happened in your dream after you startled her?" Shelton asked, dumbfounded. This was incredible! He had just finished a hypnosis course, yet he hadn't done anything, used anything—and David was talking as if hypnotized. His meandering, meek persona had vanished; now he seemed cold and intimidating.

"She wanted to make love. She said yes and no and then she said OK and we went upstairs to her bedroom. Kissed a little and then took each other's clothes off. Bit her, I guess hard, then she told me would I tie her hands. . . . She said there's a knife in the kitchen, cut string off the blinds, just tie me. Then I asked her while I was tying her hands if it's too tight. She said no. . . . Walk downstairs . . . took her pictures, she's nice. . . . She said tie me some more. . . . I brought . . . some big rope and . . . she told me the other way. I says what way is that? She says, by hanging. I says no, don't have to hang, no, no, no, no. She said yes and called me a chicken. So I did it. I tied it to the car and threw it over the beam and then I put the rope around her. I was gonna pull and then I says I can't do it. She call me a chicken again, a couple of times. I says I can't. She call me man or mouse. And I says neither but I'm not . . . I was like I said in that dream, dream was so dreamable, that dream. And she says do it. So I did it. I tried to hold on to rope, she was off the ground already. Try to hold rope as tight as I could but . . . I couldn't. The rope burned my hands, God it hurt. I let her down. I couldn't tell if she was dead or alive. I went back upstairs, got the camera, took some pictures of her. Put her on her belly. God. See her face 'cause I didn't know if she was dead or alive. I was in my underclothes. . . . That dream, dream, dream, dream. That dream trying to get dream to go away but I couldn't."

After thirty minutes, Vasquez was emotionally spent. "I don't want my dream anymore. That dream, too much," he said in a voice reduced to a heaving whisper.

"Okay, David," Shelton said soothingly, "put your head down and relax. Okay. Just relax, David. I won't make you think about your dream anymore, okay?" Shelton still didn't comprehend the full import of what he had just heard.

Vasquez's "horrible dream" was critical. Vasquez had initiated an independent corroboration of what he had said in the two previous interviews. Moreover, by presenting a fundamentally different persona, Vasquez seemed to confirm what Shelton and Carrig had been told by the FBI's behavioral science unit about a possible dual personality profile.

Some departmental brass initially had some reservations about the reliability of the dream confession because in late 1983 Shelton had taken a class in investigative hypnosis. Investigative hypnosis is used to help witnesses refresh their memories but not to get suspects to confess, and there was some concern that Shelton might have used his skill to influence Vasquez's "trance." Though Shelton was aware of this concern, considering the nature of the confession he was able to persuade the bosses no hypnosis was used on Vasquez.

Ultimately the decision to arrest Vasquez was made at the top levels of the department. Deputy Chief Packett, Lieutenant Minnich, Sergeant Hawkins, and Commonwealth Attorney Henry Hudson all met with Carrig and Shelton. They hashed it out for over an hour. The bottom line was that, despite all the problems with the interview, they couldn't afford to put Vasquez back on the street after what he'd said and after two different people had placed him at the scene.

Carrig, though, was dragging his feet, deeply bothered by the nature of Vasquez's confession. "I didn't have a whole lot of choice," he said later, "because the higher-ups would have done it anyway. And then in any job you got to worry about your career. . . . When you got the Commonwealth Attorney, who I thoroughly respect—I mean, he's a cop's prosecutor—and you got Hawkins, who was not only the sergeant but also a homicide detective at one time; you got Minnich, who had years of experience as a detective . . . so you could say to yourself, well, maybe I'm wrong."

The department's silence on the death of Carolyn Hamm was broken a few hours later.

For immediate release:
February 6, 1984, 6:30 p.m.

Arlington police have charged David Vasquez with the murder of Carolyn Jean Hamm. Hamm was found dead in the basement of her home at 4291 S. 23rd Street, Arlington on Wednesday morning, January 25, 1984. She died from asphyxiation by hanging. . . .

The arrest of David Vasquez follows an intensive around-the-clock investigation by a team of twelve detectives. Many hours of interviews with friends, relatives, co-workers and neighbors of Ms. Hamm coupled with an in-depth analysis of all available evidence has led to the arrest of Vasquez on the charge of first degree murder.

David Vasquez is a 37 year old male. He resides in Manassas, Virginia, and is employed as a porter for a fast food restaurant. Vasquez is being held in the Arlington County Detention Center.

On the surface, it looked good. Back in 1984 the arrest looked so good to Horgas that he dropped his concern about the masked rapist. Rapid police action had solved a brutal crime, and the community could now rest easy once again. But those involved knew there was still the second man. None of the detectives really felt comfortable about closing the case and accepting the idea that Vasquez, alone, was guilty.

There were so many factors. Vasquez was physically weak (coworkers had confirmed that he had great difficulty unloading even thirty-pound boxes from the supply trucks), and it didn't seem possible that he could have overpowered Hamm or hoisted her on the noose by himself. Carolyn Hamm had outweighed him by at least thirty pounds. Unable to drive a car, he worked in Manassas the day of the crime and reported to work on time at 7 A.M. the next morning.

There were no buses that could have made this possible, so someone had to drive him. Who was it? And where did he spend the night? And who had been his "brains"? Vasquez's intelligence was diagnosed as being in the Dull-Normal to Borderline range, and—unless the possibility of a split personality concealed a deeper intelligence—he seemed incapable of conceiving this crime and carrying it out. And whoever had planned the crime had probably left the semen on Carolyn Hamm's bathrobe too, because the blood type did not match David's. Swabs from the victim's vagina and inner thighs revealed a different blood type than that of David Vasquez.

The investigators were particularly perplexed by this last fact because the hair strands taken from the bathrobe, bed, and a blanket in the living room were found to have the same visual and microscopic characteristics as the pubic hair of David Vasquez. It was possible that David raped Hamm but did not ejaculate. However, it was also possible that he had not sexually assaulted Hamm, and that the hair did not belong to him but to the mysterious other man. Hair analysis is not nearly as precise as other forensic identification techniques such as blood typing and fingerprinting. David's hair only had the same *characteristics* as the hairs removed from Hamm's body, but this finding did not mean that the recovered hairs definitely belonged to Vasquez.

Nevertheless, he had to have been involved. Even if he did not actually rape Hamm, they were sure he was at least on the scene. Everything in his confession pointed to it.

Detectives not even directly involved with the investigation felt strongly about the second-man theory. Because there was a consensus among the investigators that the same person who killed Hamm had also broken into Wilma Thoreau's home, soon after his arrest Vasquez was taken down to the burglary squad room to be interviewed by Rich Alt. Prodded by Shelton and Alt, Vasquez returned to his dreamy state, but he gave up nothing on the Thoreau break-in. He just continued discussing details of the Hamm killing. Alt was genuinely amazed when all David would say about Thoreau was "I don't know. . . . I don't remember."

"We were convinced then," Alt later recalled, "as I am convinced today, that the person that committed the Thoreau burglary committed the Hamm murder. And yet David never said anything. He would talk about the homicide, yet not talk about the burglary. It was bizarre . . . because the burglary was a much lesser crime."

Alt, a rookie detective at the time with only one year on the squad, had doubts about whether Vasquez had killed Hamm. Following his interview with Vasquez, Alt approached one of his superior officers.

"Don't you hear that everything [that Vasquez confessed to] he'd been told [during the interrogation]?" he exclaimed. "He's regurgitating what they've told him!" *see below*

"I was making a statement that was against what they thought," Alt later remarked. "They did not take it kindly. [From his] facial expression I knew that he was very perturbed, and to my recollection I got up and left."

Alt did not believe, however, that David was not involved in the crime. "When Shelton [asked Vasquez to think] back to the crime . . . all of a sudden, boom, his whole personality changed. He sat straight in the chair instead of slouching. His voice grew deeper. It was weird. The fact that I didn't agree with the way the interview went did not mean that I thought David Vasquez was not guilty of *something* involved in this crime."

Like the other investigators, Alt felt sure of one thing: Vasquez had been on the murder scene. He knew too much not to have been. Still, there almost had to have been another man.

But they did not have the second man. And they did have David Vasquez.

Vasquez was formally arraigned on capital murder charges in the early-morning hours of February 7. His mother, Imelda Shapiro, a petite woman in her late fifties, wept inconsolably as the charges were read. He was charged with capital murder because he killed his victim during the course of a rape and robbery. He was also charged independently with rape, robbery, and burglary. The capital charges meant Vasquez could be executed in Virginia's electric chair if he was convicted.

After the court appearance, Shelton and Carrig brought David back to the major crimes division, where Shelton attempted to get David to repeat his horrible dream in Carrig's presence.

"What we want is for you to just kind of get yourself into a state where you can really think about your dreams," Shelton said. Within a few minutes Vasquez lowered his voice, sank into his chair, and repeated his dream. They had it—all over again. All the details. They looked at each other and nodded. No question: Vasquez had been there.

In a county where homicide was a rare occurrence, the Vasquez prosecution was given the highest priority. Henry Hudson took the case himself.

Hudson, a diminutive man with boyish looks and watery blue eyes, was law enforcement through and through. Unlike most prosecutors, he began his career as a deputy sheriff and then went to law school at night. After reviewing all the evidence, Hudson had no doubt as to Vasquez's involvement and his culpability. He remained intrigued by the possibility that Vasquez had a split personality, but that still did not dissuade him from his conviction that Vasquez had "all the trappings of a homicidal maniac." Remarkably, despite his uncompromising perspective and his determination to prosecute Vasquez all the way to the electric chair, the Commonwealth Attorney still believed that Vasquez played a secondary role in the actual commission of the murder and rape.

Though Vasquez maintained he had committed the crime by himself, "We utilized every technique and strategy to try to discover who the second person may have been," Hudson later said. In addition to reinterviewing everyone who had known Vasquez, newly developed laser fingerprinting technology was used to analyze almost every surface in the Hamm home. All these efforts proved unsuccessful.

For a while, Carrig and Shelton focused on one of David's best friends, Bill Kluge. Kluge, Vasquez had told the investigators, was the last person he saw prior to the homicide. A strong, well-built man in his early thirties, Kluge had lived in the same complex as David in Manassas and the two often went out together. It was Kluge who had brought Vasquez's mother to the police department the night of the arrest and who appeared in court the next day for David's arraignment. Since they were such close friends, Shelton and Carrig thought that they would have easy access to Kluge whenever they needed him. When they tried finding him a week after David's arrest, though, they discovered that Kluge had vanished.

The possibility of a second man—such as Kluge—was only one of the many questions that still bothered Henry Hudson up until the weekend before the trial. Even though he had won the right to use Vasquez's third confession, he was bothered by the inconsistent forensic results. "It was not the strongest or weakest case," he later commented. "It was the type of case we could win or lose."

Despite the heinous nature of the crime, Hudson agreed to let Vasquez plead to a reduced charge of second-degree murder because, as he told the press at the time, "we lost so much of our evidence [at the suppression hearing] we felt . . . the potentiality for acquittal was very great."

Not surprisingly, the defense expressed quite a different perspective. "If we went to trial and he had been convicted he could have received the death penalty," Rich McCue commented to the *Arlington Journal*.

After David entered his plea on February 4, 1985, Hawkins walked into his office and wrote CLOSED next to Hamm's name on the massive homicide tally sheet that hung on the wall.

Yet the plea bargain didn't sit well with all of the detectives, and the second man lingered in their minds.

"They were sending us back to our units," one of the members of the Hamm task force later said. "I said to Sergeant Hawkins, 'What about the other guy?' He told me that they were closing it on this guy. We didn't feel the investigation was complete. But we were told that was it and we were out of it. I basically tried to forget about it . . . but I thought there was still somebody out there."

Carrig and Shelton didn't forget it. "I felt that maybe after the court case was over, the pressure was off, he might loosen up a little bit," Shelton later recounted. "Before David was transferred to state prison, I would visit him an average of three times a week for probably a month after the case was over. I used to bring him cigars and the sports page. I knew he liked to fish so I brought him my fishing magazines. I told him I had a little boat. We even talked about me taking him out on the Potomac when he got out of jail. But the real reason I went to see him was to get him to give up that second man. I let him know that I thought nobody really knew the whole story. Nothing worked. After about a month of beating my head against the wall, I stopped visiting him on a regular basis. The last time was September of nineteen eighty-five."

Shelton and Carrig desperately wanted that other man, but the case was closed. The work of the department had to go on. Three years cranked by; 1985, 1986, 1987. Throughout the constant stream of cases, the robberies, the murders—each one prosaic and predictable, no more stranglings—the two detectives still felt a tense, nagging undercurrent. The second man was still out there. They felt themselves waiting, waiting, always waiting and trying not to ask themselves: When was he going to strike again?

4

DECEMBER 8, 1987, THE SEVENTH DAY AFTER THE DISCOVERY OF Susan Tucker's body, Horgas dragged himself in early after another sleepless night. He couldn't shake the visit with Vasquez from his mind. Innocent! He was sure of it. David Vasquez had had nothing to do with Hamm's murder four years earlier. But now he had another murder, and there was paper piled a foot and a half high on his desk. Messages, progress reports, memos, witness interviews. He hadn't had a chance to look at any of it.

Now he started paging through it. This he would throw away, this he would file. There was nothing. Nothing that shed any light on—

He stopped.

Focus. The paper trembled ever so slightly in his hand.

REQUEST REGIONAL BROADCAST: OCTOBER 6, 1987
REF: FOR POLICE INFORMATION ONLY—NOT FOR PRESS

THIS DEPARTMENT IS INVESTIGATING TWO HOMI-CIDES. THE FIRST OCCURRED ON 9–18–87 AROUND

MIDNIGHT. A WF-35 WAS FOUND IN HER APARTMENT ON 9–19–87 AT 0940 HRS. SHE HAD BEEN BOUND WITH HER HANDS TIED BEHIND HER BACK. SHE HAD ALSO BEEN RAPED. THE APARTMENT WAS ENTERED THROUGH AN OPEN REAR WINDOW WITH THE SCREEN CLOSED. THE SUSPECT RAISED THE SCREEN AND ENTERED THE APARTMENT. THERE WAS NO SIGN OF ANY STRUGGLE IN THE ASSAULT OR THE MURDER.

ON 10-3-87 AT 0140 HRS THE VICTIM, WF-32, WAS FOUND IN HER BEDROOM THE HOUSE WAS ENTERED FROM A SECOND STORY WINDOW THAT WAS OPENED BUT THE SCREEN WAS CLOSED. THE SCREEN IN THIS CASE WAS CUT OUT AND LAID ON THE SEC-OND STORY PORCH.

IN BOTH CASES THE VICTIMS WERE STRANGLED TO DEATH. ANY DEPARTMENT WITH SIMILAR CASE PLEASE CONTACT RICHMOND BUREAU OF POLICE OR DETS. GLENN D. WILLIAMS, DET SGT N.A. HARDING. THANKS FOR YOUR HELP IN ADVANCE.

/S/ GLENN D. WILLIAMS, HOMICIDE

Fingers still trembling, Joe stabbed out the Richmond phone number from the teletype. Within ten seconds he had Detective Glenn Williams on the line. Tension clawed at the back of his throat while Williams spelled out the details in a soft Southern drawl. One woman bound with a red patent leather belt and extension cord, the other with a kneesock and shoestring. Both raped, both found with Vaseline around the vagina and anus. Then, to Horgas's surprise, Williams mentioned a third rape-murder. They weren't sure if the third murder was related to the first two, though the semen samples and the similarities in the crime scenes had definitely proven that the first two killings had been committed by the same man.

The third murder had occurred just over the county border in neighboring Chesterfield and was being handled by another police department. The victim was a fifteen-year-old Korean girl who had been raped and strangled in her bedroom. She had been hog-tied with a white rope, which had been wound around her neck and wrapped three times around her wrists. If it was the same guy, Williams said, he had radically changed his modus operandi. He had targeted a much younger girl of a different race, and he had brought along his own bindings to kill her instead of relying on those he could find at the scene.

Williams also told Horgas that his department had sent the semen samples to a lab in New York to be DNA "fingerprinted." While the local forensic folks were able to categorically say, after performing the most detailed blood identification procedures available, that the semen in both Richmond cases carried the identical blood type, they wanted to get a much more refined analysis.

Horgas still didn't know any more about DNA fingerprinting, the procedure Helen Fahey had mentioned six days earlier. It was obviously something that he had to find out more about since forensics were going to play a key role in identifying the killer.

The FBI's Behavioral Science Unit had also been brought in, Williams said. After a careful review, they surmised that the killer was a white male in his twenties to thirties who resided in the Richmond area.

Horgas gave Williams a thumbnail sketch of the Tucker murder. Since forensic tests were not yet back from the lab, all Horgas could provide were the details of the crime scene. As he listed these, the similarities seemed obvious to him. To his amazement, though, Detective Williams shrugged them off.

He doubted that Tucker's murder was related to those in Richmond. Everything they had in Richmond told them it was a local boy. Anyone who killed two women in one specific Richmond neighborhood would never travel 100 miles to Arlington to kill another one. Williams spoke with impatient certainty, as if these facts should have been obvious to Horgas.

Joe didn't buy this point of view, but he could sense that

for Williams, the subject was closed. No relation between the Richmond and Arlington murders. So Joe switched tactics. "Anything else going on down there?" he asked.

"No, not really." Williams wanted to get off the phone.

"Really? Not even in those areas where the girls lived?" Joe pushed.

"We do have this black guy running around doing some shit," Williams said offhandedly.

"Whaddya mean?" Joe tried to keep the excited quaver out of his voice.

"Nothing to do with these killings. It was this black dude who'd raped a white woman a mile or so away from where one of these girls was killed. Actually it was a burg-rape. She woke up and he was on top of her. He wore a mask and threatened her with a knife."

"That's it?" Joe asked.

"Come on, man, you really want to know more? The FBI says our guy is a white boy."

"Humor me," Horgas insisted.

"OK. The guy spent a lot of time with her. First he made her shower, then he made her drink a half bottle of Southern Comfort. He also had some kind of a bag tied around his waist. That's where he got the rope. As he was tying her hands behind her back the people from upstairs came home and he split."

"We had another murder up here back in nineteen eighty-four," Horgas said, the words coming out in a rush. "We think it's . . ." He skidded to a halt. If Williams didn't think the current murders in Richmond had anything to do with Tucker's killing in Arlington, he was hardly likely to believe the story about Vasquez being the wrong man in the Hamm case. "Let's just say there's a relationship between the eighty-four murder and the one we got now. And just before this lady in eighty-four was killed, we had a masked black guy running around with a knife, doing a bunch of rapes."

"So?" Williams inquired with a touch of sarcasm.

"I'm just saying it's kind of a coincidence. That's all."

"Well," Williams said decisively, "we're looking for a white guy—not a black guy. But if you want to come down, we're having our weekly task force meeting on the homicides tomorrow morning. The guys from Chesterfield as well as a couple of prosecutors will show up. You can ask all the questions you want."

That was nice of him, Joe thought, replacing the receiver, since he basically thinks I'm full of shit. Joe drummed his fingers on the phone, feeling the furrowed crease that seemed to have found a permanent place on his forehead during the past week dissolve into a big, triumphant smile. The guy who did the two Richmond women was the same one who killed Tucker—he was sure of it. Dead sure. And Hamm too. But what he really zeroed in on was the rape. It had always been there, in the back of his mind—even though nobody else ever thought it was significant—the masked black rapist who had worked the area between the summer of 1983 and the early winter of 1984. Then, right around the time Hamm's body was found, there was a really vicious sex case not more than six or seven blocks away from her house. A married woman in her thirties, sexually assaulted and sliced up.

A few minutes later Horgas was in Sergeant Hawkins's office, asking for permission to go to Richmond. Hawkins immediately approved the out-of-jurisdiction trip; after all, he was the one who had placed the teletype on Joe's desk. But Joe was careful not to mention the rapes. Hawkins would say he was crazy; after all, Hawkins and everyone else had quickly dismissed his ideas about the black rapist back in 1984, when Hamm was killed. No, there was no way he could mention it. Joe hadn't even told Hawkins he thought Vasquez was innocent.

Hawkins did impose one condition on the trip: Shelton, not Hill, would accompany Joe to Richmond. Hawkins said it was because he wanted someone in Richmond who was familiar with Hamm. Horgas knew full well there was another, more subtle reason for sending Chuck Shelton: damage control. The Tucker murder's apparent relationship to the Hamm murder posed a tense and—potentially—an extremely embarrassing situation for robbery-homicide. Shelton, Carrig, and the others might have made a very big mistake. Eventually, this murder would be solved, and life would go on. Hawkins had to protect the department.

Yet none of this was talked about as Joe and Chuck drove down to Richmond. Instead they commented on the beauty of the countryside, and the palpable difference in atmosphere between Arlington and Richmond.

The Mason-Dixon Line, on the border between Pennsylvania and Maryland, is the official demarcation between the North and South. But the South, the real South, doesn't start until one reaches the former capital of the Confederacy, Richmond, some 200 miles away. Those who whiz down I-95 on their way to Disney World and the warmer climes of Miami Beach see only the cigarette-shaped smoke stacks of Philip Morris. Even with their windows tightly rolled down, drivers will detect the musky, pungent aroma to which Richmonders are oblivious. Here tobacco is still king.

Horgas and Shelton knew that Richmonders regarded Arlington as not really being part of the Old Dominion. Those who lived in the communities bordering the nation's capital—such as Arlington and Alexandria—did not speak with that soft drawl heard on the streets of Richmond; in fact, it was common knowledge that most who inhabited the D.C. suburbs were not even natives; many were transplanted northerners.

Arlington, though, took pride in its unique identity, and it also prided itself on having a modern, progressive police department. One of a handful of nationally accredited police departments in the country, Arlington's was the most educated police force in the state of Virginia. Horgas and Shelton shared an unspoken nervousness about dealing with Richmond; though it was the state capital, and a city accustomed to a high violent crime rate, to them it was a backwater town with a provincial police force.

But these thoughts were overshadowed, a few hours later, by the simple horror of the crime scene photos. There had been three victims in the Richmond area: Debbie Davis, Dr. Susan Hellams, and Diane Cho. Horgas and Shelton slowly circled the rectangular conference table, examining each set of pictures in turn. On each dead face there was the same contorted, agonized expression they had been on Susan Tucker and Carolyn Hamm. Color blowups of the impossibly small points of entry, the tautly elaborate bindings, and the characteristic slipknot nooses told Joe all he needed to know. He watched as Ray Williams and Glenn Williams—the Richmond detectives in charge of Davis and Hellams, known around the department as the Williams boys, although they were not related—huddled over the Arlington photos documenting the slaying of Susan Tucker. Their wide eyes and slow nods suggested to Joe that they saw the same connections he did.

Shelton and Horgas were given the basic facts of the cases: Davis and Hellams in Richmond, Cho in nearby Chesterfield County. The first murder dated back three months, and they still didn't have anything. The detectives appeared exhausted and overwhelmed. They had hit one brick wall after another. And, unlike the Arlington killings, the Richmond murders had been slavishly covered in the media. The community was now in a state of full-blown hysteria.

Then Horgas quickly presented the facts of the Tucker murder to the Richmond and Chesterfield squads. He finished up by saying that they had preliminarily tied the murder of Susan Tucker to a 1984 killing.

"We got a guy doing time in Buckingham for that murder," Joe said. The detectives looked up in surprise from the photos and interview summaries. There was a moment's stunned silence.

"Well," asked Ray Williams, "can we get down there to speak with him?"

"It wouldn't be worth it. I was just there on Monday. He's got nothing to say. It's unclear what he knows about anything, even the eighty-four murder," Joe responded wearily. He really didn't want to say any more. He himself did not yet really understand how Vasquez fit into the picture—if he fit at all—and he was acutely conscious of Shelton sitting next to him, not saying a word. Anyway, it wouldn't help these Richmond guys to hear details about the Hamm case, not yet. But they were looking at a single perp in all these killings, he thought; that much was clear.

"When you look at Debbie Davis lying there on her bed and look at Tucker lying across her bed," Joe said, "there's no question they were done by the same guy. Right? And that goes for Hellams and the Cho girl. I mean, what are the odds? All these murders just happened, during the same period of time? You got either two different killers doing the same thing or it's the same guy. I'd put my money on it being the same guy!"

But to his amazement, Ray Williams snorted condescendingly. "The murders occurred over a hundred miles apart! How can there be a connection?" He went on to explain, in a pedantic teacher-to-student voice, that Hamm and Tucker appeared linked not just because of similar modus operandi but also because they occurred only four blocks apart. It would be impossible for Joe to apply the same reasoning to the Arlington–Richmond connection because the cities were so far apart.

Joe tightly sucked in his next breath. For an instant speaking was difficult. Then he turned his stone hard face away from Ray and addressed the assembled group. "Who's been working homicide here the longest?"

"I been here twenty-five years," volunteered M. D. Scott, a tall, square-jawed man with silver hair.

"Did you ever see anything like this before?" Joe inquired, gesturing to the photos spread across the table.

"Well, I've seen them with their hands tied and shot in the head or their throat was slashed. . . ."

"But you ever see *anything* like this?" Joe repeated.

"Well, no," Scott said.

"And so don't you think it's much more than a coincidence?"

"It's a coincidence," Ray cut in. "We've been on this for months—it's a local guy. These types travel, but not more than a few miles. They don't spread out over a hundred-and-twenty-mile area!"

There was a general murmur of agreement around the room.

"Anyway," Williams said pointedly, "what kind of forensics you boys have to back up what you're saying?"

Horgas stiffened in frustration. Though a week had gone by since Tucker's body was discovered, he was forced to admit that he had no lab results.

"Really!" A smile played around Ray Williams's mouth. "What kind of operation you have going on up there? We get our results in less than two days."

Horgas could say nothing to this.

Ray shrugged. "Don't you think it's kind of difficult to talk about these cases being connected if you don't have your forensics? I guess Glenn told you an outfit up in New York is doing DNA fingerprinting on our samples."

Ray went on to inform Horgas proudly that this was the first time a Virginia police agency was using DNA analysis in a murder investigation. About a month earlier on November 5, a semen sample from Davis's bedding and one from Hellams's slip had been hand carried to Lifecodes in New York, one of three privately operated DNA labs in the United States. The results weren't back yet.

Now Glenn Williams joined the action, a tinge of sarcasm in his voice. "Hey, Horgas, tell us, exactly how many homicides have y'all had up there this year?"

Joe shrugged. "Four or five."

"Well, we had seventy-six," Ray put it haughtily.

Joe got the message. These "boys" had tackled more homicides just in this year—1987—than the Arlington PD had handled since the midseventies. "So you have a dangerous town," he said defensively. "What does that have to do with what we're talking about?"

"What it means," Ray spelled it out, "is that we know what the hell we're talking about because we see a lot more murders than you-all do."

Joe didn't buy the logic that violent cities turn out better homicide detectives. Horgas said to himself, Screw them. They're wrong. Just like Hawkins had been wrong about the black rapist, and Carrig and Shelton and McCue wrong about Vasquez. If he could get the truth. The truth. It seemed to be completely buried in possibilities, equivocations, contradictions. Would he even know it when he saw it?

But he wanted the truth now, wanted it badly. It was a

stronger want than he'd ever had for any target, and he was a man who had crept many miles in the darkest woods, not so much as crackling a dry leaf on the forest floor, tirelessly stalking the swiftest, the most intelligent, silent deer. This want was a hundred times stronger. He would get it. Bag it. And right now—he set his mouth in a thin, obstinate line— that meant swallow the rage.

So he listened with full outward respect as the other detectives spelled out the details of each crime. This took some effort, especially when it came to Ray Williams, for he and Ray would prove to be a mismatched and flammable duo. Each had a singular reputation in his squad. The young and aggressive Williams was seen by many as a hot-dog, while Horgas—plodding and analytical—was perceived by even his close friends as opinionated and extremely competitive.

Nevertheless, he gave them all his attention. He glanced away only to study the detailed crime scene photos. First the men stressed how unusual it was that these crimes had occurred in Richmond's quiet, affluent South Side.

Downtown Richmond still had the refined, rolling-lawns-and-cobblestones feel of the Old South. The majestic state capitol designed by Thomas Jefferson, the historic St. John's Church where Patrick Henry delivered his famous speech, the grand Jefferson Hotel (used some fifty years earlier as a movie set for *Gone with the Wind*) all carried the visitor back to another, gentler time. This atmosphere crossed the James River to Richmond's South Side, where three originally independent towns—Westover Hills, Forest Hills, and Woodland Heights—had been annexed to the city of Richmond in the first half of the twentieth century. South Side is mostly composed of two- and three-story frame homes built around the turn of the century as well as several clusters of brick garden apartments constructed in the 1940s.

Drew Gillespie, the Richmond city councilman who once represented this district, had described it as "a well-established community of middle- to upper-income-level folks of all ages. It's a quiet place where kids buy houses on the streets on which they grew up. And because it's such an ideal area we have people fighting to buy a house here."

On the quiet Indian summer morning of September 19, 1987, Joe learned, a Forest Hills resident called central police dispatch not to report an emergency but rather a strange circumstance. Upon arriving home the night before at about 10 P.M. he had noticed a white Renault Alliance hatchback parked at an oblique angle in front of his home, its engine running. Going out that morning to get his paper he noticed the car was still running. The owner was nowhere in sight.

After running the plates through the computer, the responding officer, rookie John Harding, discovered the owner lived no more than a hundred yards away in a large garden apartment complex. After getting no response to his repeated knocks, he asked the landlady to let him into the one-bedroom first-floor apartment.

Ray Williams was at Eighth and Main in downtown Richmond when he got the call to respond to a homicide in South Side. A native son and a ten-year veteran of the bureau, his first reaction was that it was strange to have a homicide in that part of town. Richmond's overall murder rate had skyrocketed in the past few years, of course. A lethal combination of urban poverty, crack, and easily available handguns had given the former capital of the Confederacy what was now the highest homicide rate in the South. The same detectives who used to carry small, wood-handled, snubnose .38 revolvers now wore powerful 9mm semiautomatics.

"Forty-five-twenty Devonshire," Williams mused. "I haven't been called over there in as long as I can remember. That's a nice neighborhood. Must be some kind of domestic."

Because the forensic team was still working in the back of the first-floor apartment, Williams toured the living room when he got there. Nothing seemed disturbed. No furniture or lamps were knocked over, the VCR and TV sat squarely in a cabinet, and the floor was immaculate. Very strange. Because a domestic homicide was usually the culmination of a prolonged battle, the house should be in complete disarray.

In the bedroom the body of a slightly heavyset woman named Debbie Davis was lying facedown diagonally across the bed. She had wavy, medium-length auburn hair and appeared to be in her midthirties. She was clad only in a pair of blue jean cut-offs, enough for Williams to assume she had not been sexually assaulted. She still wore her gold earrings and bracelet. Davis's only visible wounds were a slight abrasion on her nose and one on the lower lip. These, however, were clearly not the mortal ones.

He had viewed countless mutilated and ravaged bodies during his tenure. Like all homicide detectives, he had tried very hard to divorce himself from imagining the pain the deceased had to have experienced in the moments prior to his last breath. But here Williams was unable to do that. The utter agony this victim had endured at the hands of her slayer screamed out at him as he examined the apparatus of her death.

A blue wool kneesock was wrapped around her neck and knotted behind. A metal pipe, later discovered to be a vacuum cleaner extension, was shoved underneath the sock to form a crude tourniquet. The tourniquet was twisted so taut that the medical examiner would later be unable to manually remove it. When she cut it at the autopsy the next day, there was an audible popping sound.

The victim's right wrist, planted by her hip, was tied with a length of black shoestring. The free end ran over her shoulder and was looped around the left wrist, which was cocked behind the small of her back. The shoestring was fiendishly rigged; any movement of one hand would put increased pressure on the other.

Aside from the torture done to her body, the bedroom, like the living room, was largely undisturbed. Half a glass of Coke wrapped with a paper towel sat neatly on the wooden nightstand at the head of her bed; next to the glass was a copy of the legal thriller *Presumed Innocent*.

Moving into the kitchen, a forensic investigator pointed to the point of entry, an open window above the kitchen sink. The width of the opening was only twelve inches, and situated immediately outside underneath the window was a rocking chair. It was later discovered that this chair had been stolen early Saturday morning from the home of an elderly pensioner who lived on nearby Forest Hill Avenue.

Studying the twelve inches of open window, Williams

thought it would be nearly impossible for anyone to hoist himself through such a narrow slot. He tried to lift the screen higher. No effort would budge it. What made the entry even more amazing was that to get onto the kitchen floor the intruder would have had to boost himself over a dish drainer rack positioned directly under the window. Not one of the dozen glasses was broken, let alone disturbed.

After three hours they had very little concrete information about the assailant except how he got in and that he killed her in the early morning hours of September 19. As for the victim, a quick on-the-scene background check told them she was not a prostitute, a person with a criminal history, or even a flamboyant type who ran with the wrong crowd. Debbie Davis just didn't fit the profile of the victim Ray and his partner Glenn Williams had typically seen sprawled out in a parking lot on a Friday night. She was just a plain, quiet, simple lady. It had not been a domestic argument, not been a drug hit. Why the hell would somebody kill her?

"It was the first homicide either of us had ever seen where the victim was bound and tied," Ray Williams later said of him and his partner. "The way the killing went down was more repulsive to us than the typical shotgun to the head or slit throat. We knew we were dealing with a really cruel son of a bitch. This guy was different because he was so intimately involved in her death. He didn't shoot her from six feet across the room. He felt her die."

The autopsy the next morning, though, revealed an even higher level of brutality.

Dr. Andrea Blumburg's conclusion on the method of strangulation was the first surprise. An examination of the underside of the eyelid revealed a condition known as petechia. "Petechial hemorrhages," Dr. Blumburg later explained, "are ruptures of capillaries that look like fine pinpoint hemorrhages. They are caused by extreme pressure on the vascular supply preventing the venous return to the neck." This meant that the killer had intermittently tightened, then loosened the tourniquet over a period of forty-five minutes to an hour—torture, pure and simple.

Next, in contrast to Ray Williams's initial assumption,

Davis had been sexually assaulted. Though she was wearing a pair of cut-offs when her body was discovered, Davis had in fact been vaginally and anally raped. The high-intensity operating room lights also revealed tears at the entrance to the vagina—an indication of brutal force, or use of an object, during the rape.

Finally, and tragically, Dr. Blumburg found absolutely no evidence of any defensive wounds. Either Davis was too fearful to fight back or thought her cooperation would make things better. And there was a third possibility: he so quickly overpowered her that she did not have a chance to fight back.

The ensuing in-depth background check on Debbie Dudley Davis revealed nothing further about why she had been murdered. She was an accounts receivable clerk at a newspaper called *Style Weekly* and worked a second job at Waldenbooks in nearby Cloverleaf Mall. "She was the nicest, sweetest homebody," her cousin told the local paper.

Divorced several years earlier, she had no man in her life at the time of her death and had not even dated recently. Her neighbors informed the investigators that she was open and friendly and never had any wild parties. Drug use appeared out of the question. Her ex-husband and an ex-boyfriend were interviewed, checked out, and quickly eliminated as suspects. Similarly, exhaustive interviews at both of her jobs failed to turn up anyone who held a grudge against her. And the door-to-doors produced nothing either—except for one neighbor who said she noticed two suspicious white males nearby around the time of the murder.

As far as why Debbie Davis had been a victim, nothing seemed to fit. Years of homicide investigation had taught both Ray and Glenn that a victim often places herself in harm's way. While random homicides do exist, they are rare, and most murder victims know their killers—usually very well. But in this case, they sifted through all the relationships in her life and found nothing.

Neither did the forensic lab reports provide any leads. Despite the use of nyhydrin solution, no usable prints could be identified on the point of entry, bedroom walls, or anywhere else. Similar results were obtained after dusting and laser printing the Renault. There were, however, four rather large semen samples on her bed linens and comforter. Preliminary testing had indicated that they were pure samples, meaning that they were probably not the result of postcoital spillage. One explanation offered by the lab technicians was that the assailant had masturbated on his victim. In addition to the deceased's hair, examination of the bedding and nightgown disclosed numerous white, black, and tan animal hairs; a very dark curly hair; and a Caucasian facial hair not belonging to the victim.

On September 29, 1987, the publisher of *Style Weekly* offered $10,000 for information leading to the arrest and conviction of Debbie Davis's killer. There were no immediate takers.

After two weeks of nonstop work, the Williams boys told Joe, they knew no more about the identity of the killer and the motive for the murder than they had known the day the body was discovered. Every twenty-hour day brought only more frustration.

Horgas noticed that Ray became visibly disturbed as he began his next sentence. It was as if Ray was reliving the moment two months earlier.

"On Saturday, October fourth, my phone rang at two-fifteen in the morning. It was central dispatch," Ray said, shaking his head. "They wanted me to respond to a homicide over on West Thirty-first Street. A husband had just come home to find his wife dead. I got this real terrible feeling, because I knew the address was on the South Side."

West Thirty-first Street was located in the Woodland Heights section of the South Side, a little over a half mile east of Debbie Davis's home. The 500 block was ideally situated, just three blocks from the park and a stone's throw from the James River. Turning left off Semmes Avenue, South Side's main thoroughfare, Williams saw the collage of red, blue, and yellow lights illuminating a two-story frame home on the west side of the street.

"What d'ya got here, officer?"

The nervous young man in uniform told Ray the woman had been found by her husband in the bedroom closet.

Driving up several minutes later, Glenn Williams noticed his partner standing forlornly in the yellow circle of porch light. In baffled, defeated silence they walked inside.

From the doorway of the second-floor bedroom with blue curtains and dark-stained hardwood floors, they could see the top half of her body. She was lying sideways, faceup on the floor of the closet. Her body was crunched into a space no more than two feet wide and five feet long, her head lodged between a white valise and the wall.

Aside from the black knit skirt and white silk slip that were clumsily bunched up around her waist, she was nude. A very fair-skinned woman with a Rubenesque figure, she had light reddish brown hair that cascaded in soft curls to her shoulders.

Her flushed face had the contorted look of an excruciating death: the lips had a bluish tinge and her mouth was painfully agape; vacant chestnut eyes looked up as if desperate for someone to help her. Fresh blood had coagulated about her nose and upper lip.

A red leather belt designed with a longitudinal slit in the middle was tied around her neck with the free end of the belt pulled through the slit and knotted. Attached to this end was another, black belt.

Her left leg was bent up at a right angle and was leaning against the wall. A magenta quilted belt was knotted around her left ankle, then loosely tied around the right. She wore red socks and red leather sneakers. Her right hand was firmly secured against her right hip, and an electrical extension cord was wrapped around it four times, the same number of times around the left wrist, which had been folded at a right angle across the small of the back. A navy blue knit woman's tie was wrapped over the extension cord.

Though no bruises or defensive wounds were obvious, there was a symmetrically shaped five-inch black smudge on the midsection of her right calf; upon closer examination it seemed to be the partial configuration of a shoeprint. The killer had held her down with his foot while he strangled her.

As in the Davis scene, except for the irregular bloodstains

on the bedding, there was no sign of the violence that had occurred only hours before. Everything was eerily in its place.

The forensic technicians did not have to look far for the point of entry. Adjacent to the closet was a large bedroom window with its screen neatly cut out. On the back balcony sat an air-conditioning unit no more than a foot from the window frame. On the unit was an opened jar of Vaseline with light red pubic hairs in it.

Gazing through the shorn screen, the detectives were immediately struck with how difficult it would be to climb the fifteen feet up onto the balcony without a ladder. This perp was agile, strong, and determined. Standing on the tarpapered balcony, they also saw how easy it would be for the killer to peep through the victim's window from the unlit, overgrown, grassy alley bordering the backyard fence. On the ground below them they saw a three-foot length of white rope curled in a large clay planter.

A slight man with horn-rim glasses was slumped in a living room chair, his face buried in his hands. Marcellus Slag, the victim's husband, told the detectives that his wife, Susan Hellams, was a thirty-two-year-old neurosurgery resident from the Medical College of Virginia. Susan had called him earlier in the day to say she was going out to eat with friends. Upon his arrival home at about 1:30 A.M. he assumed she was not there because he had to open the front door deadbolt lock. After showering he got into bed without turning on the bedroom lights. Feeling immediately uncomfortable because the bed was unmade, he got up and turned on the overhead lights to remake the bed. It was then that he saw the red blotches on the comforter.

Frantic, he ran to the closet on the other side of his bed to throw some clothes on so he could check the house, and found her.

The medical examiner who had arrived during Slag's interview determined from the body temperature, 98 degrees, that Hellams had died between midnight and 1 A.M. This finding suggested that Slag had just missed the killer. The detectives surmised from the haphazard way the body had been thrust into the closet that the killer may have actually been in the home and bolted when Slag's car pulled into the driveway.

The Davis murder told the Williams boys that the killer was dangerous; Hellams told them how dangerous. With Hellams a bad case became a nightmare.

"He was like no other criminal I had even seen," Ray Williams later reflected. "He was like a ghost. He slipped in . . . did his thing and floated away. It was like dealing with a shadow. Nobody saw anything, nobody heard anything. . . . I had to in a sense respect him because he was so damn good. He scared me because of the threat he represented to the public."

That night he jotted down the obvious in his progress notes.

"This offense along with Debbie Davis seems to be related as far as ligature strangulation and numerous points in the investigations." The "numerous points" included that both were killed on a Friday night; entry into the homes was through a rear window, and there was a complete absence of prints. The victims were stockily built white professionals in their early thirties who lived alone. Though Hellams was married, she, like Davis, lived by herself most of the time. Her husband, a law student at the University of Maryland, came home only on weekends.

The autopsy conducted the next day provided even starker evidence of the similarity between the two cases.

In first examining the body Dr. Marcella Fierro, the medical examiner, noticed "a faint musky odor reminiscent of seminal fluid" emanating from the body, especially around the mouth, gluteal fold (the area where the buttocks meet the thighs), and buttocks.

Before she went any further, Fierro swabbed a clear solution all over Hellams's body. Shutting off the lights, she then ran a laser over the body. The recently developed procedure was used to identify the presence of any foreign substances or injuries on the body that were not apparent to the human eye. The procedure was similar to film development processing. The technique was so sensitive it could detect fingerprints left on the skin.

Fierro discovered no fingerprints, but when she ran the laser over the thighs, buttocks, breasts, and perineal skin, large areas illuminated, showing the presence of semen.

The doctor also noted "a curvilinear black mark on the lower right leg as well as one on the right side of the head, which resulted in a patterned compression" where the killer had held her down. Closer examination later revealed the black substance to be roofing tar. Scrapings later were matched to the tar found on Hellams's balcony.

The ligature style was almost identical to the one found with Davis. The FBI would later find that the ligature knots as well as those about the wrists and legs were identical to Davis. The noose was very taut and attached to its free end was an extra length of material, the most likely purpose of which was a control device to tighten and loosen the noose. There was, however, one difference. The petechial hemorrhages were far more extensive; to Dr. Fierro this meant that Hellams was subjected to a much longer period of strangulation and torture than Davis. For Ray and Glenn Williams the doctor's finding indicated that if it was the same killer, he was getting much bolder, remaining in the home longer.

Like Davis, Hellams suffered a type of abrasion to the nose and lip that indicated she was pushed face first into an object rather than struck with a fist or object. Noticeably absent as in the Davis homicide was any evidence that Dr. Hellams had tried to defend herself physically.

Hellams had four separate injuries to the anal area, each more serious than the single one suffered by Davis. Preliminary lab results confirmed the presence of semen in the vagina and anus. Several large spots of pure seminal fluid also stained her slip and skirt. Animal hairs were found in the bedding and panties, yet Hellams did not own an animal. The hairs found in the jar of Vaseline were matched to the victim's pubic hair. A combing of the victim's pubic hair, moreover, uncovered no unidentifiable hairs.

The clearest proof that Debbie Davis and Susan Hellams were killed by the same person was the serological typing of the semen.

Samples extracted from anal and vaginal swabs, the sheets,

and the comforters revealed that the assailant was a type O secretor and had a PGM of 1. Because only 13 percent of the population possessed these factors, they could much more easily eliminate potential suspects and ultimately convict the killer. The only problem was that before they could test the killer, they had to catch him.

After listening to all this Joe was more certain than ever that the man who had killed Davis and Hellams in Richmond was the same man who killed Tucker—and Hamm. But he didn't say this. Instead he said: "Now tell me about the rape."

A look went around the table that said: Is he ever stupid.

"Please," Joe amended. God, this was hard for him. And Shelton just sat there, not saying a word. "Just for my information."

Glenn Williams shrugged at Clay Hamilton, the detective who had been in charge of that investigation, as if to say, Who gives a shit, tell him.

Hamilton sighed in acquiescence. First, though, he repeated their earlier assertion that the rape was simply not connected to the murders.

"OK," Horgas said. Was that what they wanted to hear? "Just give me the details, please."

The victim was a thirty-two-year-old white woman named Ellen Talbot, Hamilton told him. She was single and lived in a first-floor apartment on Westover Hills Boulevard in South Side. At about 3 A.M. on November 1 Talbot was awakened by a black male in his late twenties, about six feet tall, wearing a ski mask, brown cotton work gloves, and dark pants and armed with an eight-inch carving knife. The intruder also carried a knapsack from which he removed a rope to bind the woman's hands. While taunting and threatening her with his knife, he made her drink a half bottle of Southern Comfort he'd also brought with him.

What followed was a three-hour nightmare of sexual torture that included repeated rapes, forced oral sex, and brutal penetration with a vibrating dildo—another of the rapist's tools. The torturer attempted anal rape but was unsuccessful.

Finally, toward 6 A.M. the muscularly built man (who'd remained silent throughout the assault) removed yet another piece of rope from his knapsack and began trying Talbot's ankles together. At this point Ellen's sobs alerted her upstairs neighbors, who had just arrived home. When they came down to investigate, the rapist fled through the kitchen window—his point of entry—taking with him nothing except several of the victim's accounting textbooks. As he raced across the backyard into the adjoining woods, he dropped the books.

While the attack appeared to bear some resemblance to the South Side murders, the task force believed there were too many substantial differences. First, Ellen Talbot didn't die. If the past three months had taught Ray and Glenn anything, it was that this strangler wouldn't let any of his victims survive. And based on their meetings with the FBI, the task force knew that the killer was a white man over thirty, not a black man in his late twenties. The task force was devoting an enormous amount of time and energy to targeting white males.

Hamilton and the others also pointed out to Horgas the other inconsistences: Ellen Talbot was five foot four and weighed only 98 pounds, petite compared to the other victims. The rape occurred on a Sunday morning, not a Friday or Saturday night. The rapist did not masturbate on the victim or place a noose around her neck. Analysis of the ropes used to bind the rape victim's wrists and ankles, furthermore, did not reveal that they were cut by the same knife used to cut the rope in the murders.

Horgas had to admit, they had been very thorough. It sounded good. But he didn't believe it. His gut told him that the man who'd raped Ellen Talbot was the infamous South Side strangler—and also the man he was stalking in Arlington. "OK," he said. "Let's get back to the murders."

Their next problem, the detectives told him, had been dealing with the public and the press. Glenn Williams slid a thick file of news clips across the table to Horgas.

The morning after Hellams was found, the headline of the

Richmond Times-Dispatch screamed: 2ND WOMAN STRANGLED ON SOUTH SIDE.

It was imperative not to scare the public and not to give out any details that might compromise the investigation; they had to be very careful. Frightened and concerned citizens would read the paper, but so would the killer.

Following a frenzied press conference, the next day's front-page story lit the community-wide spark of fear.

SECOND SOUTH SIDE WOMAN STRANGLED:

LINK IS FEARED

An MCV doctor was found slain in South Richmond yesterday and police investigating the links between her death and a recent homicide said a serial killer could be at work. ". . . In each case there was a forced entry with the murderer cutting the screens and entering through an open window. Each victim was strangled. Both victims were white between the ages of 30 and 35."

The police chief was quoted as saying, "We would certainly encourage those who have to travel at night and have to travel alone to avoid it if possible; if not, do it in pairs." Though he steadfastly refused to provide additional information on further similarities between the two deaths, anonymous departmental sources did so. The source even said he "had a gut feeling that it's the same guy in both cases. We've got some yo-yo on the loose, and he needs to be caught." One thing that no police source told the press, however, was that sinking sense the detectives shared that, as one later put it, "this guy was going to have to kill a few more people before we were going to catch him."

The last several paragraphs of the article told readers about the victim in the second strangling, Richmond's sixty-third homicide that year. The paper learned from a colleague that Dr. Hellams "was a doctor through and through. . . . She was very concerned with the poor, the indigent, the downtrodden. She cared deeply for her patients." A friend described her as "kind of a Renaissance woman. She balanced her life with classical music, literature and dance . . . [and] medicine." Another said: "It seems so senseless that someone who devoted her life to saving others should have it so tragically taken away."

Since this was the first serial murder in Richmond's history, there was no blueprint for the investigation. "[It was] learn as you go," Lieutenant Robert Childress later admitted. "My immediate response was to borrow people from everywhere I could find." A task force led by the Williams boys was formed, which included four additional homicide detectives, a sex crimes investigator, a massive complement of plainclothes detectives, and a contingent of officers from the Selected Neighborhood Apprehension Program (SNAP), which had been formed two years earlier to combat the drug-related violence in the predominantly black housing projects. This was the first time the unit would be deployed for a non-drug-related effort.

The first priority of the fifty-member joint task force was to saturate the surrounding neighborhoods with officers. It was a massive show of force, which, it was hoped, would provide a little comfort to a terrified community. In addition to interviewing everyone who had lived within a mile of the murder victims, the task force had the seemingly impossible job of maintaining twenty-four-hour surveillance of all areas within a five-mile radius of the two homicide sites.

They believed the killer traveled by foot. Debbie Davis's abandoned vehicle seemed to be proof that the killer came to her home by some means other than a car. The detectives surmised that following the murder Davis's killer attempted to steal her car but deserted the vehicle because he was unfamiliar with a stick shift. Furthermore, the door-to-doors revealed that no one had noticed any unfamiliar automobiles in the vicinities of either murder. The rocking chair found under her kitchen window suggested that the killer had carried it from the nearby porch from which he had stolen it.

Neighborhood watch groups blossomed overnight. Violent death had been all but unknown in South Side before. Prior to Hellams's death, "we had what you call a very small organization," said neighborhood watch president Betty Miller.

"When I moved here a few years earlier, it was very challenging to get people interested in their community. It took two gruesome murders to see that neighborhood watch is really a valuable thing. We had about seventy-five percent of the neighborhood organized in a very short amount of time."

Numerous meetings were held, the largest one being a week after the murders, at the Woodland Heights Baptist church, which was located diagonally across from Dr. Hellams's home. In addition to the over four hundred people who packed the room, every important Richmond city official and high-ranking police officer was present. Fear and anxiety was etched on all their faces.

"There is not a higher priority in city government than bringing this person or persons who have committed these homicides to trial," said City Manager Bob C. Bobb. "We're asking people not to panic and not to arm themselves."

"Just because the killer has struck on Friday nights doesn't mean he or they won't change their pattern. Consider yourself vulnerable at any time," a sober Captain Stuart Cook added. "I wish I could tell you that you need not worry if you are not in your thirties or of a certain build, but the killer could prey on all people, not just women in their thirties."

Though he steadfastly refused to give any specifics about either case, Cook gave concrete guidance aimed at removing or at least limiting the killer's opportunities to stalk and attack. People listened attentively as he and a community information officer suggested particular methods of safeguarding their homes: using dead bolt as opposed to spring locks, securing their windows with screw locks. Though it might detract from the beauty of their homes, residents were told to severely cut back all shrubbery around the windows and doors so as to deprive the killer of a potential hiding place.

"Be nosy," Cook said. "Nosy neighbors are good neighbors. Know your neighbors, watch out for them. Don't leave windows open. Don't leave a ladder lying around; chain it to a tree. And most importantly, women should not be out walking alone.

"When you know you're heading home," he said to the

single women, "call your next door neighbor and say, 'I'll be home in thirty minutes; please keep an eye on me while I walk into my house, and then I'll call you. If you don't hear from me within thirty minutes then call me and call the police.' "

The cautionary words should have helped to allay the residents' fear, but the more people heard, the more they panicked. It was frightening to know that the killer could be anyone, a neighbor, coworker, even a friend. Everyone became a suspect, someone to fear. And the bureau refused to divulge details of the murders. Cook's reply to each inquiry was the same: "The results of the investigation will be shared with the Commonwealth Attorney's office and a decision will be made as to whether it will be made public." Frustration was added to fear. As one resident said, "I don't have any more sense of what to look for than when I came in [to this meeting]."

Joe paged through the newspaper clippings. It was obvious that people were in a frenzy of apprehension.

> At least two South Richmond hardware stores were sold out of window locks yesterday in the wake of the two slayings. . . . "They're about to run me crazy," said Hugh Gunter, owner of Gunter's Inc., a hardware store in the Stratford Hills Shopping Center. . . . Since Saturday, Gunter said his supply of more than 50 window security devices had been sold and he estimated he would not sell that amount in a month. "This has been a pretty severe shock to this part of town. It really has the people in this area terribly, terribly concerned," he said.

"I got phone calls from several women asking, 'Should I move out of this area?' " Cook later commented. "If they could be a potential victim—a single professional woman living on the South Side—I told them, 'I can't give you any official advice but if you were my sister I would suggest that you go live with our mother for a while.' "

The first week of intensive investigation by the largest task force in Richmond history, the detectives told Joe, had revealed nothing. Desperate to obtain some direction, they turned to the FBI's Behavioral Science Unit, the same group who had advised Shelton and Carrig. A meeting was held on October 9 in the Commonwealth Attorney's conference room.

The Richmond police had listened attentively to FBI Special Agent Judson Ray, a man who spelled precision from his clipped manner of speech to his starched knifelike collars. "He is likely a white male about twenty-five to twenty-eight, but remember you can't completely rule out that he is black," Special Agent Ray told them.

The race of the killer was especially critical to focusing the direction of the investigators. Judson Ray's opinion was based on the historical fact that serial murder has been almost exclusively an Anglo-perpetrated crime. Law enforcement had only identified one black serial killer in recent times: Wayne Williams, the Atlanta Child Murderer. National crime statistics, moreover, indicated that female rape and homicide victims were much more frequently raped or murdered by someone of their own race than another one.

The absence of any sign of a struggle, most notably the lack of any defensive wounds, pointed to the assailant's possession of immense upper body strength. The absence of prints or any other clues, on the other hand, told the FBI that the killer was intelligent and probably had a prior criminal record for burglary or sexual assault.

The timing of the murders on a Friday night suggested the killer had a full-time job, the FBI agent told them. Both on and off the job, however, he probably kept to himself, especially after a killing. It was extremely unlikely that he would talk to anybody about the crimes. He had problems maintaining relationships with women but probably had a few female relationships. There was no doubt in the agent's mind that the killer experienced difficulty having normal sex.

The killer was not a schizophrenic, but he did have two distinct sides to his personality, one careful and methodical, one out of control. Judson Ray further surmised that the killer wandered the neighborhoods at night looking for his victims. Once she was selected, he most likely monitored her activities for a brief time, then struck when his opportunity for success seemed greatest. Ray was not as clear, however, on what triggered the killer's murderous intentions. In all likelihood he was set off by some significant life event involving a woman: breaking up with a girlfriend, an argument with his mother, even being slighted by a female coworker.

The profile presented at the FBI meeting immediately piqued the detectives' interest in Dwayne Arnold, a black male in his early thirties who had just been paroled from prison. Though he wasn't white, Arnold seemed to fit the profile; he lived by himself in a South Side apartment located not far from the two victims. Most significantly, he had been incarcerated for breaking into the home of a South Side woman and sexually assaulting her. The detectives were also drawn to him because he had a reputation for having verbally harassed women in and around the downtown business district.

After a week of round-the-clock surveillance, Arnold was stopped going into a drug house. He denied any involvement in the murders and willingly submitted his blood for comparison. Arnold's blood type did not match that found in the semen at the scene.

Most of the names developed by the task force during the first few weeks did not arouse as much interest as Arnold, yet every one was thoroughly checked, regardless of how remotely related to the murders he appeared to be. In addition to the routine names lifted from Rolodexes, letters, and appointment books, the investigators added dozens to their list: every person to whom each victim had written a check or made a credit card charge in the last year, all the doctors and patients with whom Hellams had had recent contact, and all of Debbie Davis's accounts receivable customers at *Style Weekly.*

An avalanche of names also came pouring in by phone and letter from the frightened public. "Every hour we'd get calls that somebody was seen walking in the area that had never been seen there before," Ray later said. "Or we'd get calls about vehicles that were unfamiliar to a particular person."

Among these were some good leads. One woman called about the strange man she met at O'Toole's, a famous South

Side watering hole. This aroused Ray and Glenn's interest, because they had learned that both Davis and Hellams had frequented this neighborhood bar—and anything that seemed to establish a link between the two women was very important. They had checked out many possible links: within days of her death Ms. Davis had had a medical procedure performed at the Medical College of Virginia (MCV), where Dr. Hellams had worked; also, both women shopped at Cloverleaf Mall. These coincidences led them nowhere. But the man at the bar—that was interesting.

The woman had told Ray Williams that she wanted to meet him in Forest Hill Park at 11 P.M. because she didn't want anyone to know that she was speaking to the police. Sitting on a wooden bench under the soft light of a street lamp, the petite twenty-five-year-old told the detective that she met the man, a powerfully built thirty-year-old about five foot eleven, while having a drink at O'Toole's long mahogany bar. He initially appeared shy and quiet, averting his eyes and mumbling as he spoke. She learned he lived adjacent to Forest Hill Park and worked at a local café. He was fascinated by astrology. After they decided to go sit in a back booth however, he abruptly changed.

"He couldn't keep his hands off me. I tried pushing him away, but he kept roaming his hands over my breasts, neck. Everywhere. He told me about everything from his father who had beaten him with a belt buckle, how close he was with his mother and the difficulty he had making friends." More disturbing to the young woman was the man's obsession with the recent deaths of two neighborhood women. He incessantly talked about the cases.

After doing a background check and conducting round-the-clock surveillance for several days, a task force member paid Leland Hutton a visit.

The unassuming white male who answered the door told the detective that he had no particular reason for being interested in the murders other than they had occurred in his neighborhood. He willingly agreed to accompany the officer downtown for a blood test.

Hutton fit every aspect of the profile perfectly except he was a type A secretor. Wrong blood type.

In the heretofore tranquil neighborhoods of Westover Hills, Forest Hills, and Woodland Heights, many took Captain Cook's advice "to be a nosy neighbor" quite literally. Every neighbor was a suspect and every neighbor was a spy. Individuals felt compelled to report the neighbor who for years they had thought was a little strange; and girlfriends reported dates who appeared to be just a little too anxious for that good-night kiss.

As Lieutenant Childress explained it to Joe, the investigation uncovered "a lot of weird ducks."

"Four different ladies told us about a certain medical professional who fancied himself a stud. Each told us about his playroom," Childress later recalled. "He tied them to his bed, hit them with whips, and used a dildo." A brief investigation revealed he was weird but not the killer.

Several women called about a South Side accountant who was also partial to bondage.

And a number of residents reported that a gentleman in their area had for years been peeping in neighborhood windows. Upon confronting him with his neighbor's' allegations, the police were astounded when he readily admitted to being a veteran Peeping Tom.

Fear altered the community's appearance too. In the waning days of October the area was lit up like a Christmas tree. Porch lights and living room lamps burned brightly through the night into the dawn. People abandoned their solitary evening constitutionals down by the James River, opting instead for neighborhood group walks with high-intensity flashlights. The already unreal atmosphere was made that much more peculiar by the regular intrusion of roving television minivans, patrolling the streets and looking for the ideal story for the 11 P.M. news.

Residents felt a responsibility to be on patrol as well. Upon arriving home one night around 11:30 P.M., Karl Mattingly saw two unkempt men sitting in a beat-up Chevy parked just up the street from his house. When they were still there at 12:30 A.M., he decided to act. Going out the back door, he slowly worked his way up behind the brown car. In seconds he had his .45 caliber semiautomatic stuck at the side of driver's forehead.

"Get the fuck out of the car! Now!" he screamed.

One of the men reached into his jacket, and Mattingly cocked the weapon.

"Hey! Cool down, man. We're cops," said the driver. "Here, all I'm gonna do is take out my ID. Just be cool."

"These guys were undercover," Ray Williams explained. "If calmer heads had not prevailed, we would have a shoot-out, because this guy really believed these fellas were the Strangler."

"And that's how things went until Cho was murdered?" Joe asked.

"Right," said Williams. "Late November."

Ernie Hazzard, the stocky, ruddy-faced Chesterfield County detective in charge of the Cho investigation, with his gangly, chain-smoking partner Bill Showalter, took the floor and explained that the Cho family lived in Chesterfield Village, a massive garden apartment complex. The residential community was located just west of the Chippenham Parkway, the dividing line between South Richmond and Chesterfield County. Jong and Kum Cho, their children, fifteen-year-old Diane and and twelve-year-old Robert, lived in a three-bedroom, first-floor, corner apartment.

A freshman at nearby Manchester High School, Diane was a serious student who had her goals set on being a doctor. In fact, that Saturday night, the last thing her parents heard her doing was typing a paper at about 11:30 P.M.

Mr. and Mrs. Cho left the next morning at about 6 A.M. to open their convenience store in Richmond. Because Diane had stayed up late doing homework, they did not want to wake her to say good-bye. At around noon Mrs. Cho called the house, only to discover that Diane was still sleeping. She asked Robert to wake his sister, but the boy refused. Because Diane had gotten very angry with him for waking her in the past, he wanted his mom to be the one to do it.

Diane had still not come out of her room by the time her parents returned at 3 P.M. Opening Diane's door, Mrs. Cho

121

noticed her daughter still buried beneath the woven orange cover, only her shoulders exposed. Diane was a deep sleeper, but Kum Cho had never known her daughter to sleep so late.

Kum's piercing scream brought her husband and son running. Her hands were working desperately to untie the intricate knots around her daughter's neck and arms. Seeing that his daughter was dead, Jong Cho wrenched his sobbing wife's hands off the ropes and led her into the living room.

Senior Chesterfield County detectives Showalter and Hazzard were shocked by the complete lack of any sign of struggle. In stilted English, Mr. Cho informed the investigators that nothing was broken or out of place. It was exactly how he remembered it when he went in to say good night the previous evening. Unfinished math and grammar homework assignments were neatly arranged on her wooden desk; the walls were adorned with colorful ribbons and a collage of photos of her young friends.

The plump, coconut-skinned girl with short, permed black hair was lying diagonally across her bed, her head facing the wall. She was nude. A shiny white rope was looped in a slipknot around her neck, the free end draped across her shoulder blades. Her wrists were bound by a darker, heavier weight rope measuring approximately four feet.

Turning her over, the investigators observed that the rope had cut a deep furrow in her throat. And even if she had tried to scream, the wide stripe of silver duct tape stretched across her mouth would have prevented it. Though there were no obvious wounds anywhere on her stomach or chest, her entire pubic area was drenched in blood.

More perplexing than the cause of the bleeding, however, was a horizontal figure eight drawn in nail polish on the side of her left thigh just above the knee. She had just polished her nails the night before, but the polish on her thigh was a different shade. Neither parent had ever known their daughter to paint symbols on her body.

Diane's killer obviously gained access through the open bedroom window, not a difficult feat considering the bottom ledge of the window was only four feet off the ground. Hazzard initially surmised that the killer had removed the screen, which was found propped up against the house directly under the window. He later learned from Mr. Cho, however, that Diane often removed the screen herself so she could lean out the window to chat with her friend who lived upstairs. A careful forensic inspection revealed no footprints outside the window or any identifiable fingerprints on glass or frame that could not be matched to known individuals.

Hazzard and Showalter had never seen such a boldly executed homicide. The victim's bedroom shared adjoining walls with her parents' and brother's, and yet no one had heard anything. The detectives theorized that the killer had probably broken in when Diane was sound asleep and immediately slapped the tape across her mouth. Yet it was also possible that he watched her from outside and, when she left to take a shower at about 11 P.M., he entered the room and hid in her closet. When she came back into the room he could have taken instant control.

"It was a gutsy move that showed how sure of himself he was," Showalter commented. "One thing was obvious—this guy had to be watching her for some time to know when the ideal time to strike was."

In the ensuing days, the Chesterfield investigators thoroughly canvassed the apartment complex and conducted extensive interviews with Diane's friends and teachers at Manchester High. "We were hunting to see if she was into drugs, stealing, porno—anything that would give us some type of lead as to why this occurred," said Showalter. All the hours of investigation, though, merely confirmed what Diane's grieving parents had told the police that first day. She was a simple, thoughtful fifteen-year-old girl. An honors student, she was active in school chorus, loved to draw, and was liked by everyone whom the detectives questioned.

The girl who had a bright smile for everyone died from "asphyxiation due to ligature strangulation." She was so fiercely raped that the medical examiner found multiple tears in her hymen and a one-inch-diameter lacerated hole in the septum of her vagina—the midline structure running through the vaginal canal. These injuries were, however, only partly responsible for the copious amounts of blood, because she was menstruating at the time of her attack. Dr. Fierro also determined that the young girl was anally raped.

Aside from the wounds inflicted by the ligatures, the only other surface injuries were large petechial hemorrhages about her eyes, face, and shoulders; the medical examiner also noted there was a faint patterned impression of unknown origin on her right shoulder. The laser examination of the body revealed a greasy substance similar to Vaseline on the perineum and the back of her legs and arms. Seminal fluid was also found on her legs and buttocks.

Dr. Fierro found a complete absence of defensive injuries. In fact, the medical examiner observed that Diane's nails had obviously just been polished that evening. "They were perfect," she later said.

Fierro removed numerous black hairs, which were ultimately confirmed to be from the victim herself. Several red hairs were identified, but it was later determined that they belonged to one of the forensic technicians who removed the body from the home.

Despite the crime scene and forensic similarities between Cho and the Richmond victims, Horgas was surprised to hear that Hazzard initially did not believe that Cho's death was the work of the South Side strangler. Hazzard pointed to the differences: Diane was only fifteen years old; she was Asian, not white, and the murder occurred with her family sleeping in adjoining bedrooms. Moreover, Hazzard emphasized, the other victims did not have their mouths bound with duct tape, nor did their killer draw a figure eight on their thighs.

Hazzard admitted, however, he changed his mind after speaking to Ray Williams. There was no doubt in the Richmond detective's mind that the South Side strangler had struck again.

Ray Williams argued that the race and age difference were significantly outweighed by some striking parallels. The killing occurred on a weekend night; the killer entered through a first-floor screened window, a window that was obscured by a bush; the girl's hands were intricately bound behind her and she had a slipknot around her neck; the petechia proved there was an extended period of strangulation; she was not only vaginally and anally raped but copious amounts of pure semen were found on her body and on the sheets, indicating that the killer had masturbated on her. Williams also stressed that the age differences could be easily explained: though only fifteen years old, at five foot three and 140 pounds, Cho's frame was in fact very much like those of Davis and Hellams.

Even after consulting with Richmond, though, Chesterfield authorities refused to definitively link Cho to the South Side strangler because they feared alarming the public. In Richmond, however, many residents breathed a strange sigh of relief because they thought the killer had left South Side for the suburbs. Richmond police interpreted the third killing far differently.

Diane Cho's murder convinced the Williams boys and other members of the task force that the killer had gotten not only much bolder but much hungrier for a kill. Moving into a new jurisdiction could have meant he changed his killing fields or it could have been his way of playing with the police. There was no better way to prove his intelligence to the massive task force he had undoubtedly been reading about than to kill in Chesterfield and then come back to kill somewhere else. Maybe South Side. Maybe someplace new.

Three days after Diane Cho was killed, Ray and Glenn Williams told Horgas they got an anonymous call that convinced them they'd hit pay dirt.

"An individual who worked at the Medical College of Virginia told us that an orderly had recently been discussing details about the murders," Ray Williams explained to Joe. "He was a powerfully built white man in his late twenties who lived alone." Background checks told the detectives that the individual had a record for sexual assault. If anyone fit the FBI profile, it was this guy.

After three days of round-the-clock surveillance, which produced no probable cause to arrest the man, Glenn approached him directly. Under the pretext of wanting his assistance in the investigation of the South Side strangler, Glenn asked him to go down to police headquarters and the man willingly agreed.

The interview took place in the homicide squad's interrogation room. Ray Williams watched from behind a two-way mirror.

"If I were to commit a crime like this I would just walk around the neighborhood at night looking through lighted windows," the man began. He continued for three hours to discuss how he would watch the victims for a few nights and then break into their homes. He provided particulars on both the Davis and Hellams crime scene, knowing details not reported in the newspapers—like the length of the shoestring used to choke Davis and the fact that a vacuum cleaner pipe had been used as a tourniquet.

During the session he voluntarily gave a blood sample, which was rushed to the lab for analysis. Glenn slammed his fist into the table when Ray returned with the disappointing results.

"It turned out that his caseworker spent a lot of time walking the halls of the police station," Ray said, his voice still tinged with the bitterness of almost catching the big one. "And she had picked it up from a policewoman. . . . I guess the guy just wanted to confess. He wanted to be famous."

Despite their public stance that the murders were not related, Chesterfield authorities agreed to form a joint jurisdictional task force with Richmond. They could not ignore the November 25 serological results. The semen found at the Cho scene had the same blood factors as that found in Davis and Hellams.

As of November 27, Showalter and Hazzard reported directly to the Richmond police bureau instead of coming into their own offices. The two extra investigators, however, were hardly sufficient to meet the increased workload presented by the third murder. With the death of Diane Cho the task force had to reinvestigate all those leads previously pursued plus all the leads independently developed in the Cho inquiry.

Cho's case renewed interest in one of the links established soon after Hellams was killed—Cloverleaf Mall. Credit card receipts and checks had established that Susan Hellams not only shopped at the mall but bought books at Waldenbooks, where Debbie Davis worked. Diane Cho regularly visited the mall with her friends and was at the mall the day she was killed. Some task force members postulated that the killer selected his victims at the Cloverleaf Mall and followed them home. The stakeout teams now had to expand their turf to the mall.

As the Williams boys summed up their presentation, it was obvious to Joe that the investigation was swallowing them up. By the first week of December, Ray and Glenn Williams were frustrated and exhausted. In two and a half months they had eliminated over 750 suspects from all walks of life— from delivery boys to dentists. And they had probably given a cursory review to more than five times that number. "Hours and hours of work," Ray said, "that didn't amount to a hill of shit."

The meeting between the Richmond and Arlington contingents broke up at about three in the afternoon. The detectives promised each other that they would be in touch if there were any new developments, but it was obvious that they did not relish the prospect of future conversations with each other.

Horgas and Shelton stopped about halfway back to Arlington to get their messages. Deanne Dabs, a technician for the Northern Virginia State Crime Lab in Fairfax County, had called to report that preliminary tests on the vaginal and anal smears revealed the presence of sperm. It was too soon, however, to type the samples. Then there was another message, one that totally flabbergasted Joe: a reporter from the *Richmond Post Dispatch* had just called the department seeking information on Joe's visit.

The meeting in Richmond was to have been top secret. No one in Arlington outside those invited, including other officers, knew about Joe's visit. Someone in Richmond had talked. Well—he would have to work with them, but he didn't have to trust them.

Despite the apparent similarities it was premature, to say the least, to link publicly the murders in the two cities. Serial murder hysteria was wreaking havoc on Richmond's citizens and police officers; now Horgas feared it was about to engulf Arlington.

But there would be another, terrible side effect from the press coverage.

The killer would know a detective in Arlington was on his trail.

5

BY THE TIME JOE WALKED BACK INTO THE ROBBERY-HOMICIDE SQUAD room, he was more certain than ever that the infamous South Side Strangler was responsible for the death of Susan Tucker. The meeting had been slightly contentious, but—for Horgas— also enlightening.

Especially the rape of Ellen Talbot.

Of course, Ray Williams and the other Richmond detectives had discounted it. But he could feel the truth with a growing certainty, that her rapist and the strangler were one and the same. And that he was the same masked black man who'd raped all those women in Arlington during the summer of 1983. And *not* David Vasquez's partner. No way.

But could he, should he abandon it? Vasquez confessed to killing Carolyn Hamm, don't forget. He confessed.

No, Joe decided. This is how it happened. One is never a hundred percent sure, but when your instinct says yes, you have to act on it. You have to. Just keep an open mind.

Plus, on the practical side, if he could prove he was right about this, there would be no denying that the ACPD had arrested the wrong man for killing Carolyn Hamm. And now more than ever he needed his administration's support. He knew his special complement of officers was about to go off the assignment and return to regular duty. He was in the second week of the investigation already; the department had a lot of other responsibilities. But he was still going to need help. A task force! Hawkins would have to go for it. Stressing how hard he was looking for Vasquez's partner was going to help. No, he wouldn't abandon the Vasquez partner theory, because of another thing: if he could disprove the involvement of Vasquez, he could prove his own theory. The one no one bought into. The masked rapist who operated alone.

Though he desperately needed help, it was not his style to delegate the hands-on investigation. He solved his own cases. Now, with the most important murder of his career, he would do it the same way.

But there was a huge amount of glorified gofer work to be done. Every single file related to the masked rapist had to be pulled out and studied. Not only those files but every single burglary that had occurred between the summer of 1983 and winter of 1984. Because the masked rapist was obviously someone who knew how to break into houses. And who knew? Maybe he'd find a break-in or two that could somehow be linked to the rapist.

He needed to learn as much as possible about the rapist's MO—how he got in, how he attacked them, what he said. The rape victims, he knew, were the only living eyewitnesses he had. They had seen the man who killed Hamm and Tucker—and Hellams and Davis and Cho. Nobody else believed it, but he knew it was the truth.

Horgas, along with his partner Mike Hill, was given a task force of two new detectives: Dick Spalding of burglary and Ed Chapman of sex crimes. He needed men from these two squads. As a homicide detective, he would not have known how to locate or best interpret rape and burglary files, nor would it have been diplomatic for him to demand that the detectives drop everything and start pulling closed cases. Each squad had its own turf and was naturally protective of the work that it did.

The four men met on Friday, December 11. It was the first

time either Chapman or Spalding had been assigned to a homicide.

Standing at the front of the room, Joe methodically laid out his analysis for the two newcomers and Mike Hill, who of course had heard it before. He ticked off twelve similarities between Hamm and Tucker, from the point of entry to the dumping of the purse to the style of the killing. Chapman and Spalding slowly nodded their heads in apparent agreement as Joe went through his points showing that one man killed both Tucker and Hamm.

"So you guys do see the connection here, right?" Joe asked enthusiastically.

"Sure, Joe," Chapman responded guardedly. "I see the possibility of what you're saying. But we'll never know till we actually get this guy."

Horgas fought down disappointment. Didn't anybody see that this was the truth?

"Okay," he went on, returning for a moment to the party line. "He might be one of Vasquez's associates. One of the guys Carrig and Shelton looked at back in eighty-four." Chapman and Spalding sat up straight. This was obviously what they'd been expecting to hear.

"I went to see Vasquez on Monday," Joe said quickly and dismissively. "He wasn't any help at all. So we're just going to have to go out and bring in all his friends for questioning. Hill put together the list." Hill nodded. Chapman and Spalding looked at him gravely.

Obviously they still believe this, Joe thought desperately, but he barreled right on without missing a beat. "But aside from the guys who we know hung with Vasquez back in eighty-four, I got an angle on someone else. Ed, remember that masked black guy we had running around here back in the summer of nineteen eighty-three?" Joe was trying to keep the enthusiasm out of his voice.

"Yeah," Chapman said, confused. His look said, Why you bringing him up?

"I don't know if you remember this guy, Dick." Horgas turned to Spalding. "But he was raising hell in Arlington and Alexandria. He attacked several women on the street and a bunch in their homes." Though several of the rapes had included residential burglaries, Spalding had not been made aware of them because they were assigned to other members of the unit.

"From everything I've learned in the last few days, this guy didn't stop in eighty-four," Joe continued. "Since September there have been three murders in Richmond that are almost identical to Tucker and Hamm. Entry through a rear window, female victims raped, hog-tied. Cause of death each time strangulation by ligature—the whole nine yards. What got me on to this black dude is that between the second and third homicide a masked black guy breaks into a first-floor apartment through a rear window, binds and rapes a woman. This woman lives not a mile from the first two hits. So what I'm thinking is that all of this was done by the same guy— the masked black rapist who was operating around here starting back in eighty-three."

"One person did all this?" Chapman asked skeptically. "Where you gonna find evidence to support this? I mean hard evidence."

Spalding did not say a word, but his stony silence said it all. Well, Joe thought, screw them. They were a "task force" only in the narrowest sense of the word. In fact they would have to do whatever he asked them to do, and that meant Spalding would go through all the burglary files and Chapman the rape files. And then he would show them who was right.

Spalding and Chapman were under no illusion as to the "task force." "We were there more as gofers," Spalding later said.

Spalding proved an ideal choice for the job, even if he didn't go along with Horgas's theory. South Arlington had been his beat for a number of years, and he knew it inside out. "Fairlington has always been conducive to burglaries," the thirty-year veteran said, "because there's a lot of shrubbery [where a thief can conceal himself.]" Spalding didn't find any unsolved burglaries in Fairlington that seemed related to the Tucker murder, but he did notice that after the murder, burglaries in the area plummeted. "Anybody who may have been doing burglaries in Fairlington certainly didn't want to be associated with a murder," Spalding explained. The ten 1984 cases he pulled from storage and reviewed in connection with the Hamm murder didn't suggest anything either.

It took Chapman four days to gather all the masked rapist files. As Horgas sifted through the dog-eared manila folders and arranged them in chronological order, he was astonished by the sheer number and variety of attacks. Commencing the last week of June, 1983, and continuing through January of 1984, nine Arlington women and one Alexandria woman reported being raped and sodomized by a young, well-built, masked black man armed with a knife, who usually stole cash from their pocketbooks. During the same period there were three abductions and five attempted abductions of women by a man fitting the same description.

According to the files, the investigators were stymied. Some detectives thought all the attacks were the work of a lone serial rapist, others believed, based on the number of attacks, that there were two masked rapists operating. Despite six months of investigation no arrests were made.

Even worse, for Horgas, was the shape the case files were in. Out of order, missing critical documents, they reflected all the problems and confusion that had plagued the investigation. Unbelievably enough, the PERK kits, which contained the vital hair and semen samples, could be located in only three of the nine rapes. Chapman discovered the evidence from one rape sitting in the same spot in the property room where it had been originally and temporarily placed immediately after the attack more than four years earlier. Horgas was most outraged of all to discover that critical evidence such as victims' clothing had actually been destroyed or was marked TO BE DESTROYED. Of the evidence that remained, one case had never even been sent to the lab for analysis. This told Horgas the investigators had given up. Departmental rules strictly required preserving all evidence until there was a final resolution to a crime, but because there was limited storage space, investigators often disposed of evidence when they had little or no hope of ever apprehending the perpetrator. I could never do that, Horgas thought. He organized the jumbled files and brought what remained of the original evidence to the lab.

He had already taken the Tucker evidence to the state lab on December 11, the day he first met with Chapman, Spalding, and Hill. The Northern Virginia Bureau of Forensic Science in Fairfax County did all the fingerprint comparisons; firearms examinations; and drug, chemical, and toxicological analyses.

It was unusual for Joe to have any direct contact with the lab techs; typically he had stayed only long enough to turn the evidence over to a receptionist and sign the proper forms. Routine tasks did not appeal to Joe. He was not what anyone would call an exacting guy; his evaluations, for instance, had often harped on his sloppy desk. As for his paperwork, well, he liked to say that he was not a paper man; he liked catching the bad guys rather than writing the whole thing up. He never wrote long, glory-packed reports. They were plain and simple, sometimes—according to his superiors—painfully so. And whatever it was the white-coated techies at the state lab did, hunched over their beakers and propane burners, had never interested him. That was their job. And it didn't matter as much as what he did, did it? Until now.

Now, suddenly, nothing was more important than what the lab did.

Because this was going to be a forensics case. He had been certain of it ever since he first laid eyes on Tucker's molting body. The killer was an intelligent criminal, especially skilled at infiltration. His kills were too well planned. He'd never let them catch him casing a home or fleeing. Yup, he thought, the Richmond officials might as well save their reward money. No one was ever going to be able to claim it.

Horgas had never had a case like this before, one he couldn't nail all by himself. It was clearly shaping up to be the biggest case in his career. Still, he had to grit his teeth and bet everything on the diminutive woman at the state lab, the one with the closely cropped, dark auburn hair and rosy cheeks who looked like a school nurse.

Deanne Dabbs supervised the serology section. The unit

was charged with typing, comparing, and identifying blood and other body fluids as well as analyzing and comparing hairs and natural fibers. She was now as important as—no, more important than anyone on the task force.

Horgas's request to meet with her was surprising inasmuch as he had not said more than ten words to her in the ten years she had worked at the lab. And when she saw Horgas sitting in the waiting room she was astonished all over again—by the sheer volume of what he had brought. There were three dozen bags and boxes of Tucker scene evidence.

"It's this murder we just got," he said, gesturing to the pile around him, "but before I let you have this stuff we gotta talk. I want you to have the whole picture about what we got here because it's a lot bigger than just Tucker's murder."

Aware that his prior, casual attitude toward the lab might interfere with them giving him the 110 percent cooperation he wanted, Horgas wanted Deanne to sense what he saw as the immense import of the case. He needed to let her know that she was an integral part of the team. Above all, he did *not* want her to see this as just a run-of-the-mill murder case.

Sitting at a lab table amidst bottles and test tubes brimming with varied colored solutions, Deanne listened intently as an animated Joe spun his theory about Tucker, Hamm, and the South Side strangler. Dabbs was immediately impressed by his passion for the case. She was well aware that he had never before expressed any interest in the lab, having always seemed to view it as a giant machine that produced neatly typed reports to help convict people at trial.

Dabbs was also amazed at the volume of evidence. She could not recall ever receiving so many objects for analysis before; the average case required her to examine not more than half a dozen articles. On that day Horgas had brought with him, among other things, a maroon skirt and blazer, a red nightgown, white bra and panties, a brown throw rug, bedding, washcloth, more than twenty small plasticine bags, each containing a fiber or hair, and the ropes used to bind and strangle the victim. Dabbs was already in possession of the blood and other body fluid samples delivered to her office by the medical examiner following the autopsy.

"So do you see how big this case really is, Deanne? I mean, if I'm right, and I think I am, this guy is just going to keep on killing," Horgas said forcefully. "He's gotta be stopped."

"I see what you mean, Joe, really I do," she said supportively. "I'll get to your evidence as soon as we finish up this rape that just came in."

"No, you can't do that, Deanne. This case can't wait. I know you've got a long waiting list, but this one is really important. This may have stopped for four years but he's really going at it now. You know what? The last victim was a fifteen-year-old. He killed her while the rest of her family was sleeping in the same apartment. You gotta start now. Today if you can."

Deanne was not put off by his aggressive style. Actually, she was quite captivated by Joe's obvious sense of purpose. Joe's intensity convinced her that the killer was an immense threat to everyone and had to be taken off the streets immediately.

She had already seen the killer's work. It was she who, several years earlier, had examined the crime scene samples taken from the home of Carolyn Hamm. After David Vasquez was arrested, she'd been asked to compare his blood type with the typing results obtained from a swatch of Hamm's bathrobe. She remembered the phone call from the concerned assistant Commonwealth Attorney who had just read the report of her findings. Her conclusion after comparing the vaginal slides with Vasquez's blood sample was that David was not a "contributor"—his blood type was completely different from the blood type of the semen sample extracted from the slide.

Because the attorney was perplexed as to the source of the stain, Dabbs explained that since the victim's body had not been found in the dining room where the bathrobe was, it was possible that the semen stains could have been from a prior incidence of consensual intercourse—that is, intercourse with a lover.

The other explanation, of course, was that the bathrobe stains came from the perpetrator—and the perpetrator was someone other than David Vasquez. If Joe's theory were borne out, she realized, she would soon be reexamining the results she had obtained in the Hamm case back in 1984.

In inimitable style, Horgas of course wanted everything done yesterday: immediate typing of every stain and hair fiber on the clothes, sheets, pillows, blankets, and washcloth he had just presented to her, a complete analysis of the autopsy samples, and comparisons of all these results to those obtained in Hamm and the Richmond murders. Though she agreed to give the Tucker case first priority, the natural processes of blood and hair analysis prevented her from moving very quickly. Horgas could not rush the analysis techniques, though he would have liked to.

Soon after Horgas left the lab, Dabbs informed her two assistant serologists that for the near future they would take over the day-to-day running of the lab while she would devote full time to the Tucker murder. Over the next several days, Dabbs found herself talking to Horgas numerous times during the day, sometimes three to five calls per hour.

"I had lots of questions about different pieces of evidence," she said later. "Anytime I called he was always available, and if he wasn't available he would call me right back. He was trying to help me and of course I was trying to help him."

Within a week of her meeting with Horgas, Dabbs discerned a strange osmosis taking place. Like most scientists, she prided herself on objectivity. Her role was simply to analyze specimens and write up results. Whether her efforts resulted in an arrest was entirely incidental to her task. With each passing day, however, she found herself becoming more deeply involved with the progress of the Tucker investigation. Her daily conversations with Horgas routinely went beyond a particular lab-related inquiry, and she found herself asking him how his leads were developing, whether he had received any responses to his teletypes, and so on.

Working day and night on the samples she obtained the first results—on the samples delivered after the Tucker autopsy by the medical examiner's office—shortly after Horgas's visit. It was, as she later commented, "pretty much record time." The results were off the record, however. Because of paperwork, the official findings could not be processed and delivered for at least three more weeks. And now there were even more samples: that same week Horgas had delivered fifteen more items, including drains from all the sinks in the home.

The first news was critical but, to Horgas, not very surprising. Tests on vaginal and rectal swabs received from the medical examiners's office were positive for semen. The next results arrived December 15. Dabbs reported that a semen stain was found on the Tucker's nightgown and two negroid hairs were discovered on the blue washcloth that had been discovered by Tucker's neighbor two days after her body was found. The next day Deanne called again, informing Horgas that the one long white hair and two black hairs removed from Tucker's pillow were animal hairs; the white one from a cat and the black from a dog. The numerous short red hairs lifted from the blanket were mustache hairs. Results delivered the following day were even more fruitful: the tiny black hair found on the underside of the top sheet was identified as a fragment from a negroid hair. In addition, three complete negroid hairs were found on the sleeping bag. Dabbs also confirmed that the small stain on the white blanket was semen and that the huge wet area on the blue sleeping bag that investigators had found draped over the victim was a pure semen sample.

This was a strong piece of luck. In Dabbs's experience it was extremely rare to extract a pure semen sample from a sexual assault crime scene. Whether it was a vaginal swab or stain from panties or a bedsheet, the semen was typically found mixed with vaginal secretions. A semen stain such as that found on the sleeping bag typically indicated that ejaculation had occurred prior to coitus or the donor had masturbated. Remembering the discovery of such stains at the Richmond crime scenes, Horgas immediately wanted to know if the Tucker samples matched those of the other victims. He was dismayed to discover that it would take Dabbs at least another week to perform all of the typing tests.

Yet Dabbs had some excellent news for Horgas too. With the help of a powerful microscope, Dabbs had identified five of the hairs as belonging to a black person. This was the first positive confirmation that Horgas was indeed on the right track.

Hair analysis is not nearly as precise a forensic science as fingerprinting, but technicians are able to make many gross determinations such as whether the hair is animal or human, what race the individual belongs to, and to what part of the body the hair belonged. The certainty of the identifications, though, strongly hinges on sample size. Optimum results are obtained from full hairs consisting of both the root and tip. Anything less is considered a fragment. "If the root is missing," Dabbs commented, "depending upon how long the hair fragment is and from what part of the body the hair originated, we may or may not be able to do very much with it."

The easiest identification to make was race. Because African-American hair tends to be curly, it exhibits buckling, an attempt by the hair to fall back onto itself, which causes a minute crinkle. Microscopically this hair shows clumping of the pigment runnels. In Caucasian hair the pigment runnels are more evenly distributed throughout the length of the hair.

Head hair and pubic hair are the easiest to analyze, because they have the most characteristics associated with them and able to be analyzed with a microscope. Arm hairs and leg hairs tend to be much finer, much shorter, and more often exposed to weathering as well as abrasion from clothing.

The major problem in hair analysis and comparison is that hairs are so easily transferrable. One picks up errant hairs sitting on a sofa or a bus seat, or even shaking hands with a friend. During close-contact crimes, such as rape or murder, hairs are effortlessly transmitted, but strange hairs found at a crime scene could also have come from virtually anyone the victim had contact with in the last week or even month.

While it was too soon to identify the sources of the Tucker hairs, Horgas was able to safely conclude that the mustache hairs belonged to Reggie Tucker, Susan's husband. With no proof other than his theory, Horgas concluded that the negroid hairs came from Tucker's killer. Since Susan Tucker did not own an animal, the presence of those hairs had raised the possibility that they also came from the killer or Susan could have picked them up from a friend. The fact that similar animal hairs were found at all three Richmond scenes seemed to support the theory that the killer shed the animal hairs; Dabbs even raised the possibility with respect to the dog hairs that the killer could have brought the animal along with him as a method of controlling his victim. Horgas had never heard of an assailant doing anything like that, but in this case anything was possible.

Horgas's wildly enthusiastic response to the results of hair examination prompted Dabbs to do a little investigating of her own. She called her friend and colleague Mary Jane Burton, who worked at the main state crime lab in Richmond.

"Mary Jane, I'm working on a case up here that I understand might be related to several you're doing down there. I don't know the victims' names, but the killer is known as the South Side Strangler," Dabbs began. "I don't have any typing done, but I was just wanting to informally find out what your hair analysis results looked like."

After giving Mary Jane her preliminary results, Dabbs was amazed to hear how closely some of her findings tracked those obtained in Richmond—numerous light and dark animal hairs, reddish blond human facial hair, and dark limb hairs and hair fragments. Dabbs was crestfallen, though, to discover that the dark hairs had not been positively identified as being of negroid origin. Burton informed her counterpart that she had specifically found several dark limb hairs not belonging to the victims but they were of insufficient quality to draw any definitive conclusions as to race.

Dabbs threw herself back into analyzing the samples. On December 22, she completed her analysis of the Tucker murder semen stains. She called Joe to tell him that the perpetrator would have the following blood characteristics: O secretor, PGM 1 (PGM subtype 1+), and Pep A 1. This was identical to the blood type Richmond had obtained from semen on Debbie Davis's sheet and Susan Hellams's thigh.

It also matched the semen samples that had been typed in 1984 from the Hamm murder. At that time the lab had analyzed the semen stains as O secretor and PGM 1. The more detailed steps of classifying the PGM chromotypes into subgroups such as 1+, and the classification of the PEP enzyme (in this case, A 1) were not developed until after 1984. David Vasquez had been classified as an O secretor as well, but he had a PGM of 2–1, not 1.

Joe reacted ecstatically to the news, but Dabbs cautioned him that while these findings could certainly be used to eliminate potential suspects, they would not allow him definitively to identify the perpetrator, since these blood characteristics were found in fully 13 percent of the population. Similarly, the blood match did not prove beyond a shadow of a doubt that the same person had committed every murder. It may have been statistically unlikely—but it was still possible—that the killings were the work of different perpetrators who happened to share the same blood type.

Joe, however, was more certain than ever that his theory was correct. While Deanne had been analyzing evidence, he had been interviewing the nine rape victims.

The first was twenty-eight-year-old Roberta Schwartz, assaulted in early June 1983. As he listened to Ms. Schwartz's phone ring Joe stared at the smiling driver's license photo of Susan Tucker taped to the bookshelf. He knew that the lady at the opposite end of the line, and the others he would be interviewing, were the lucky ones. Luck was relative, however. These women had clearly been to hell.

Ms. Schwartz was not enthusiastic about meeting to discuss the rape, but she agreed when Horgas told her that the rapist was "at work again—but this time he's not just raping women. He's killing them."

On the morning of December 15, a petite brunette with dark blue eyes hidden behind gray-tinted glasses sat in the small interview room at the back of the squad room. Inhaling deeply on a cigarette Roberta Schwartz described her ordeal, which began in the parking lot of a supermarket at about 1 A.M.

"As I approached my car, a young black guy rushed up to me and stuck a long-bladed knife up to my face. He was a skinny man in his early twenties, about five-eight. He had a white T-shirt pulled over his head that had eyeholes cut out and he had something covering his hands. He forced me into the car and made me drive around. After driving for about fifteen minutes he made me pull over. All the time I was driving he kept threatening to cut me." Schwartz stubbed out her cigarette and lit another one.

"And then what happened?" Joe said. His voice was full of compassion, because now she was going to tell the worst part.

"He was really hyped up. First he opened the glove box and searched around, asking me where my change was. I think he found some. Anyway, then he forced me to climb over him and get out the passenger side. With the knife at my back he had me walk into this wooded area near where we parked."

"We were standing in the woods there and he says something like, 'Suck my dick and do it good.' I hesitated but did it after he thrust the knife at me and threatened to cut me. I did it for I don't know how long."

"Do you know if he—uh—ejaculated?" Horgas asked.

"No. No he didn't. After he pulled out of my mouth he told me to take my clothes off, put them down on the ground, and then to lay on top of them. Can you believe that? It's like this son of bitch didn't want me laying on the ground. I first told him I wasn't gonna do it.

" 'Look, bitch,' he said, 'take your clothes off and I won't fuck you.' He was wildly waving that knife at me and yelling in this real angry voice. I still refused. Then all of a sudden he ripped the front of my blouse with his knife. After that I did everything he said. So I took off my clothes, laid 'em on the ground like he said to do. Then he pulled his pants down and he did it to me." Schwartz was looking away. "It went on for about ten minutes, then he withdrew his penis. He made me get up and go further into the woods and did it again to me. And no, I don't think he ejaculated."

Following the rape, the masked man ordered her to lay still on the ground while he went back to the car to get something. After three minutes Ms. Schwartz got up and noticed that her assailant had fled.

142

"Do you know where this guy is now?" she said, exhaling a huge plume of smoke.

"No, sorry to say I don't," Joe told her. "But I will find him. I promise you."

"You better," she said. "This guy . . . ," she said, her eyes welling with tears, "he's capable of anything. And I mean anything."

The next three victims were all attacked in their homes. In each case the women were sleeping and awakened by a black man in his early twenties, about five foot eight, who wore a homemade mask and cloth gloves and brandished a twelve-inch serrated knife. He first demanded that the victim give him money, usually by telling the woman to bring him her purse; he then forced her to fellate him for fifteen to twenty minutes and finally he vaginally raped the woman. Throughout the incidents the man spoke incessantly. His rambling, profane soliloquies were a mix of death threats and demands to enjoy the sex. He told Maureen O'Keefe, his second victim, "I'm gonna put my dick in you and you'd better come." Similarly, he told his next victim, "I don't care if I hurt you. You're going to fuck me and like it. You'll have an orgasm or I'll kill you." As Joe listened to each woman painfully recount the rapist's derogatory words, it seemed to him as if their tormentor was following a bizarre script.

With the attack on Millie Redthorne, the fourth victim, the rapist added two new acts to his sadistic repertoire—taping the woman's mouth and attempting to bind her.

"The first thing I remember is waking up and this young man is stretching a piece of duct tape over my mouth while at the same time warning me in a growling voice not to scream," said Redthorne, a thirty-four-year-old civil servant who recounted her experience in a dreamlike voice. "I don't think he was just going to stop with gagging me," she went on. At the mention of duct tape, Horgas remembered young Diane Cho.

"What do you mean?" said Joe.

"Well, after he forced me to do those things to him, he went over to the window and began cutting the cord from

143

the venetian blinds. It was obvious what was going to happen next."

"Tie you up?" interjected Joe.

"Exactly. And so as he turned to cut the cord, I used the opportunity to run out of my apartment."

Antoinette Summers wasn't so lucky. The eighteen-year-old woman was surprised by the masked man as she was getting out of her car. Shoving her back into the car, he ordered her to drive to a remote area on the Alexandria border. Before forcing her out of the car he removed a spool of silver duct tape from his pocket and told her to tape over her eyes. After two hours of agonizing torment, which included not only rape and oral intercourse but repeated anal rapes, the man wrenched Ms. Summers's arms behind her and tied them together with a length of nylon rope. Jabbing the point of the knife into the small of her back, the man walked the young lady around the back of her car, opened the trunk, and pushed her in.

"Several minutes later I smelled smoke," she told Joe. "It seemed like it was coming from the backseat. . . . I kicked and kicked as hard as I could. God must have been looking down 'cause the trunk popped open. When I got out fire was shooting out of the backseat."

The masked man struck once every six weeks through the fall of 1983 and each attack was almost a carbon copy of the ones committed during the summer. Joe was particularly interested in the October assault because of several striking similarities to Hamm. Before sexually assaulting Margaret Page, the man not only bound her feet with nylon stockings but he also lashed her hands behind her back with cords he had cut from the living room venetian blinds. Hamm's wrists had been similarly bound with venetian blind cords; and Horgas remembered that one week before Hamm's murder, the woman who lived just three blocks away, Wilma Thoreau, had come home to find cut venetian blinds on her bed.

The masked rapist's last victim walked into the small interview room on a cold, rainy December afternoon. Marcie Sanders lived six blocks away from Carolyn Hamm and was sexually assaulted on January 25, six hours after Hamm's body was discovered. In fact, the attack occurred while Arlington crime scene agents were processing Hamm's home.

Hearing her side door open, the thirty-two-year-old woman came downstairs to find a black male in his early twenties wearing a homemade face mask and gloves and wielding a serrated knife.

"He said something like, 'OK, bitch, where's your purse?'" said Sanders, a fair-haired woman who wore thick glasses and looked like a prim grade school teacher.

"I led him upstairs to the landing. He took the few dollars I had and dumped the purse on the floor. Then he waved the knife at my face and ordered me to go downstairs. He made me take my clothes off in the kitchen and then ..." She cast her eyes downward, unable to tell Joe what happened next.

"It's OK," Joe said reassuringly. "I have it all down here in the report. I just want to know what do you think made him cut you?"

"He had this dildo and he said, 'Stick it in. Do it to yourself and you better come.' I refused and he went crazy.

" 'What do you mean, no!' he screamed. He punched me in the face four or five times and then cut me right across here."

Sanders rolled up her pants leg to show Joe an ugly four-inch-long scar on her right calf.

"He then grabbed me by the hair and yanked me out my back door. First he tried to get me to suck his penis. He thrust the knife near my eye and so I did it. I was only doing it a few minutes when he said, 'We're going for a ride now, bitch.' That's when I knew I had to fight back. If I got in that car, I was dead. I just screamed and kicked. He punched me a few more times and then jumped over my backyard fence."

A knife and a small pocket flashlight he had dropped were later found by investigators. The dildo and vibrator had been later identified as belonging to Lois Cantor, Sanders's next door neighbor, It was similar to the side-by-side break-ins in the Wilma Thoreau incident. The rapist first broke into Cantor's house—through the basement window—stole some money and the sexual devices and then broke into Sanders's home.

Horgas saw the Sanders attack as positive proof that the rapist was capable of killing his victims. Though he did not tell her at the time, Horgas knew that Sanders was correct when she said she would have been killed had she gotten into the car with the masked man.

Only one of the nine women refused to be interviewed: Cassandra Bennings. Bennings had been attacked in her own bed. She adamantly refused to come in and discuss it.

"It's taken me three years to get over what that bastard did to me and I'm not gonna go through it again," she said.

"But this guy still could be out there and we need to find out as much as we can about him," Horgas pleaded.

"Well, I don't want to help. You said you have other girls coming in to talk. I'm sure they'll tell you exactly the same thing that I would. Listen, I really appreciate what you're doing, but I can't and won't give that guy one more second of my life. I'm sorry." As much as he wanted to speak to her, Horgas couldn't blame Bennings. The pain in her voice was obvious and profound.

I'll do without her, Horgas thought. I've got eight out of nine.

When the eight interviews were complete, Horgas went over the rape case files and the murder case files one more time, comparing these with his interview notes. Similarities, differences. He felt excitement mounting within him. As he closed each case file and opened the next he felt increasingly certain that his gut reaction about the masked rapist's role in the murders was accurate. It was time to try his theory out on the men—again. He convened a task force meeting for Monday, December 21. "With all this," he told himself, "there's no way they can say I'm wrong. No way."

By the time Hill, Spalding, and Chapman had assembled in the conference room, Horgas had it arranged like a classroom. A blown-up map of Arlington studded with color-coded dots showing each type of attack—yellow for rape, green for murder, pink for abduction, brown for attempted rape and abduction—hung on the front wall. On the easel he outlined each attack in Magic Marker, organizing the facts into distinct categories such as date of attack, victim description, location of attack, description of suspect, weapon used, covering on hands, covering on face, sex act performed, items stolen. He detailed extraneous facts at the bottom, such as the presence of the negroid hairs at the Tucker scene—though, of course, Richmond could not confirm negroid hairs at their scene and there was always the possibility that the hairs at the Tucker scene could have come from someone else she'd had contact with prior to the crime.

"You guys ready?" Horgas said with a hint of glee. He couldn't wait for them to hear his speech and immediately admit he was right.

They nodded in unison, each man preparing himself for what he sensed would be another shark attack.

"The first thing that's obvious, this guy did his homework." Horgas spoke like a professor in the lecture hall. "He especially prepared for the assaults on victims in their homes. He had to have cased each victim's home for at least a few nights in a row. Though most of these ladies lived alone, some didn't. And for those that were married or had roommates he broke in when either no one else was home or the other person was sleeping."

Horgas also detailed three sexual assaults over the border in Alexandria, though these had not been handled by the Arlington PD. All white female victims, all midtwenties to early thirties, all attacked by a young masked black man wielding a knife. Fortunately, in each case, the attacker was scared away by bystanders.

Horgas then went back in time to 1984 to describe the Wilma Thoreau break-in, in which a twenty-eight-year-old woman returned home at 1 A.M. to find porno books, a carrot, a vial of white powder, and several lengths of venetian blind cord arranged on her bed—items later found to have been stolen from the house next door. This was less than a block from Carolyn Hamm's home, Horgas stressed, and a mere four days before the discovery of Hamm's body.

"How come you added these two B and E's?" demanded Chapman. "I thought we're only going after a rapist. Besides, how could you even tell who broke into this house? The woman wasn't even home at the time of the break-in, right?"

"Let's look at what we had there," Horgas responded, trying to keep his voice even. "First, you can't deny that our guy knows how to break into houses. Second, you got these cut venetian blind cords just like in the rapes of these two women over that summer. And you also got venetian blind cords, of course, in Hamm. He knew she was a single woman and was just waiting for her to return. The only reason Thoreau is not up on the rape chart, or worse, dead, is that lack of patience got the better of our guy and he left. Plus, there's the location—Thoreau lived one block from Hamm, seven blocks from Sanders."

Horgas then walked over to the map. "And there's not only Thoreau," Joe said as he stuck some blue dots in the area immediately surrounding Hamm's home. "There are these other burglaries which occurred in January right around Hamm's home—on January fourth there were two on Buchannon, another back-to-back like in Sanders, and then on the eleventh on Columbus and on the fifteenth on South Eighteenth Street. Like I said, all of 'em bunched together like grapes."

Silence. Horgas plowed on. "What's really chilling when you look at all of this is that with each rape this guy was becoming bolder and more dangerous. By the end of January, he's taking items from one house and using them in another house. And he's through with threats—he's actually cutting these women. I got no doubt that he would have killed Sanders if she didn't fight back. Who knows with Hamm. Maybe he never gave her a chance."

Horgas put down his marker. He was finished.

Stone silence. All that could be heard were the men shifting position in their creaky chairs and the buzz of the fluorescent light.

"Well, Joe," Hill said finally. "Seein' how you feel that strong about the burglaries, here's two more I found that might interest you." He slid two case files across the table. Horgas eagerly opened the first one dated January 12, 1984.

The complainant reported that his 18 year old daughter awakened him after hearing noises around the house. The

148

complainant checked the exterior of the house and found a broken basement window on the south side and a chip in the basement window on the north side. No entry was obtained. Complainant also found a metal mailbox turned on its end propped up under his bedroom window. The young girl indicated that she was alone in the kitchen washing baby bottles. The kitchen light was the only one on in the house and the window there has no curtains. She indicated that she felt she was being watched and thought she saw some movement in her backyard. At that point she began hearing cracking sounds. The cracking quickly became a banging and she rushed to wake her father.

Horgas noted that the address was one block south of Carolyn Hamm's home. He tore open the next file jacket as if it contained prize money.

On January 14, 1984 at 2255 hours 22 year old Karen Wong reported that a black male between 21 and 23 years old, about 5'10" and 165 pounds, wearing a cream colored jacket, gloves and a home made type mask over his face broke into her home in South Arlington. He entered through a basement window. He surprised her with a knife when she went down to the basement after hearing unfamiliar noises. Ms. Wong stated that the man threatened her with a knife saying, "All we want is the tv set. If you make a noise we'll kill the little girl upstairs." The little girl was the victim's room mate but the victim was not aware how her assailant knew who was sleeping in an upstairs bedroom. The man removed cash from Ms. Wong's purse and fled when he heard another room mate coming down the steps. The investigating officers retrieved a small flash light outside the point of entry. Ms. Wong's home was located two blocks from Hamm.

How could he have missed this one, he thought. This was the case that Hawkins had told him to send a teletype on in 1984.

"Terrific shit. Simply great!" Joe cried. "A similar flash-light was also found in Sanders's backyard."

Spalding and Chapman didn't utter a word. Finally Chapman spoke. "The big problem you have, Joe, is January. From what I remember there were a bunch of rapes from the summer through December. Each time he did about the same thing—threaten the victim with a knife and then rape her. Then nothing happens until six weeks later when someone fitting a similar description breaks into this woman Sanders's home, sodomizes her, and then beats and cuts her real bad. Before that the masked guy always raped his victims and he never cut them. He just made Sanders use a dildo. It's different, Joe."

"So what are you saying? That it's not the same guy just because he didn't cut anyone before?" Joe shouted.

"I'm just looking at the possibilities. According to what you just ran down, the guy changed radically. Not only did he cut one of his victims, but he moved on to killing them," Chapman said. "He may have gotten more violent, but you just don't see guys graduate from raping to murdering," Chapman insisted. "You got your peepers and guys who expose themselves who go on to rape. But to all of a sudden kill, well . . ." His voice trailed off.

"You think more than one guy did those rapes?" Horgas demanded.

"I don't know, Joe. I just don't see it the way you do. That's all." Chapman wished he could see it Joe's way. He was an easygoing man who didn't relish a battle with anyone, least of all Joe. But he had a strong feeling that Joe was wrong about this.

"Just because Joe said it was true didn't make me believe him," Chapman later said. "Some guys will get a theory and they become convinced they're right. Joe's one of those guys. Joe was an immediate believer in his own theory, which was too outrageous for us. No one in my unit believed that one person could possibly have done Tucker, Hamm, and all those rapes."

And if any unit was accustomed to bizarre scenarios, it was the sex crimes unit. They had the guy who got a dog to give him a blow job, and the guy who got a live 50-caliber bullet stuck up his ass. Then there was the man who worked in a lingerie store who would call his female customers at 2:00 in the morning. "It's me," he would say. Thinking the caller was her boyfriend playing a trick on her, the woman would talk to him, and stay on even when the call turned obscene. She would think her boyfriend was being a little kinky, and many would even play along with the request to masturbate in the living room window while the man watched from outside. Too late they would discover that he was not the boyfriend at all.

Some members of the sex crimes squad also thought they knew who the black rapist was. In August of 1987 they had arrested a black male in his late twenties with the incredible name Leroy Lovelace (pronounced "loveless"). Lovelace had a very similar modus operandi to that of the masked rapist. He broke into his victims' homes in the early morning, tied them up, and raped and sodomized them. The detectives could prove Lovelace's involvement only back to 1986, but Ray Harp and Mike Kyle believed Lovelace was a prime suspect in at least several of the earlier attacks.

Spalding, a tall, thin man with a weathered, angular face and wispy blond hair, remained quiet through most of Joe's presentation. But he too was less than enthusiastic. While he wasn't aware of the rapes, Spalding had recalled a rash of breaking and enterings in South Arlington during the latter half of 1983 and early 1984. He didn't feel they had anything to do with Hamm's murder.

"Joe, you know you're talking about a tremendous range in personalities between somebody simply breaking into a home and stealing jewelry and somebody breaking in and raping; and then another range of people who break in, rape, and then murder." Joe's grimace reflected his displeasure at the remark.

"I've never known of one burglary where the burglar hurt the resident," Spalding explained later. "At least eighty-five or ninety percent of your burglaries occur during the day. And the reason they occur during the day is, the perp doesn't want to confront anyone in the house. These guys typically aren't out to hurt anyone and that's why you don't get a lot of nighttime residential break-ins. They don't want confrontation because number one they don't want to get hurt and two they don't want to get identified."

"I haven't worked a burglary in a long time and I've never worked a sex case but I know we're dealing with the same guy," Horgas insisted. "And that's the direction we're going in! OK?" He peered pugnaciously at each detective.

No response. Well, Joe thought again, screw them. With Chapman, especially, it was not surprising. The whole sex squad was dead set against his theory—naturally. If his theory was true, then their failure to apprehend the masked rapist led right to the deaths of Hamm, Tucker, Davis, Hellams, and Cho. When he looked at the shape the files were in, it was doubly obvious that they'd bungled it. He'd never win them over. And besides, he should be used to it. It was the same mentality he'd been hit with in Richmond.

But Horgas did need the support of his superiors. He asked Hawkins and Christiansen to meet him in the conference room that same day, and he laid out the same information for them that he had just presented to his task force.

"Holy shit . . . It's beautiful, just beautiful," were Deputy Chief Arthur Christiansen's first words after Joe finished speaking. "So—who is this masked guy? Vasquez's accomplice, right?"

"That's one of the possibilities, yeah," Horgas said guardedly.

He hoped Christiansen wouldn't ask anymore. He had assigned Spalding—in addition to retrieving files and providing lists of potential suspects—to help Mike Hill investigate each of Vasquez's former associates. Luckily, the Deputy Chief, not intimately familiar with the Hamm case, nodded his satisfaction with Joe's truncated response.

Sergeant Hawkins was far less enthusiastic. With absolutely no inflection in his voice, he said: "That's an interesting theory, Joe." Of course Joe had mentioned the black rapist theory to Hawkins before—back in 1984, right after Hamm's body was found. At that time Joe tried to persuade Hawkins that the Sanders rape and the Thoreau break-in were directly connected to the Hamm murder. Hawkins rejected Joe's hypothesis outright. As Joe unfurled a similar theory almost four years later, he wondered if Hawkins would remember the encounter—particularly that he had strenuously objected to Joe's attempt to insinuate himself into the Hamm investigation.

It was doubtful. Yet the response Horgas was getting now was almost identical. This time, though, Horgas was not about to drop the idea.

Unfortunately, the task force—Chapman and Spalding—was for all intents and purposes disbanded within four days of Christmas. Their assignments were complete, and Hawkins was even beginning to assign new robberies to Mike Hill. He, like everybody else, saw Tucker as simply a single homicide for which a task force was overkill.

The investigation of Vasquez's former friends and acquaintances had turned up nothing. Each individual had been fingerprinted and had submitted blood samples for comparison to the Tucker semen samples.

The first one they checked out was Alan Trenton, who had lived across street from Vasquez in Arlington. Trenton adamantly denied having anything to do with Hamm or Tucker, though he did admit that he'd remained in contact with David during the past four years. A second interview scheduled with Trenton was canceled when it was discovered that his blood type did not match the semen.

Max Zimmer was discounted too. Though Horgas had initially considered him a strong possibility, the reinterview established firm alibis for the Hamm and Tucker murders; then blood typing eliminated him from the pool of potential suspects. Zimmer did provide one piece of potentially useful information, though: one of David's bowling companions had been a young black man, a fact that had not been discovered during the original investigation.

Charles Vandi, David's friend, initially piqued the detectives' interest when he refused to speak to them without his attorney present. After a period of negotiation, though, Vandi agreed to submit his blood. It did not match.

Though Barry Lawson was not an associate of Vasquez, he

was a prime suspect in 1984 because he had a long record for peeping in South Arlington homes and otherwise acting strangely. Hill remembered a rumor during the Hamm investigation that Lawson had been committed to a mental hospital. In mid-December Hill was able to verify that Lawson had in fact been locked in a mental hospital during the period when Hamm was murdered. He had a solid alibi for the Tucker murder as well. All of them did—and nobody's blood matched.

Though none of Vasquez's potential accomplices panned out, Hill remained convinced that Tucker's killer was connected to David Vasquez. Despite being hand-picked and endlessly harangued by Horgas, Hill did not buy into the theory. He simply could not ignore all the evidence that, to him, said that the killer was Vasquez's partner.

Hill, Spalding, and Chapman did not only have a problem with the logic of the theory. It was something much more basic: Joe's personality.

"Joe and I are friends but he's a hard person to work with sometimes," Hill reflected. "He doesn't think of other people too much when he wants to do something or wants something done; he doesn't think about how the people are feeling or anything like that. It's what he wants now and do it now, and he tends to piss a lot of people off the way he comes across."

"Joe's an abrasive personality," Chapman agreed. "A lot of people don't like Joe. A lot of people like Joe. I don't think there are very many people in between."

Hill observed that Horgas had almost made Chapman into an errand boy. "Chapman would bring him the data, and Joe would interpret the data and then not give any feedback. It's human nature—hey, you want to be told that you did a good job, or thanks, or something. It's not like Joe was in a superior position, rank-wise. But if Joe gets an idea in his head he'll run right over you."

Neither Chapman nor Spalding minded doing what they called the donkey work. "Obviously it was his case," Chapman said, "and we can't have him running around on all this extraneous stuff." Still, the way Joe went about asking for information did not exactly help him win converts over to his theory. " 'Please' was not part of his vocabulary," Chapman noted.

Those outside the homicide squad, including the detectives in the sex squad and the detectives in Richmond, were infuriated by what they viewed as a homicide cop going beyond his territory—and telling them they were wrong, to boot. Joe's bluntness didn't help. "It's like they thought I purposely tried to show people that they were dummies," Joe insisted later. "And that's not so!"

The end result was that nobody on the homicide, sex, and burglary squads, let alone the Richmond Police Department, believed Joe was on the right track. He tried not to think about the traditional wisdom, that if a case wasn't solved in the first forty-eight hours it was likely to stay unsolved forever. Forty-eight hours! That was starting to seem like a bad joke. The Tucker investigation had dragged on almost a month already.

But the main problem, of course, was the killer. He was out there, free as a bird. They didn't have the faintest idea who he was. And he was surely getting ready to kill again.

6

JOE STILL HAD ABSOLUTELY NO SUSPECTS. THIS GUY WAS SMART, smarter than any murderer he had ever tracked. Everything was painstakingly planned and executed, then all the evidence was erased. And what was the guy's motive? Robbery appeared to be incidental. Some he raped, some he raped and killed. Why?

He had to get some answers. Only a few days remained before the new year. The blood typing was not going to be enough. Sometimes it was, of course—he'd known cases where the lab could narrow the suspect to 4 or 5 percent of the population, and if everything else fell into place that could convict a man and send him to prison—but he had to get something more definitive this time. Even the fact that negroid hairs were found on Tucker's body wouldn't sew it up. And that was assuming he caught the guy!

A couple of days before Christmas, Horgas opened his desk drawer and pulled out the brochure on Lifecodes, the lab in New York State that did DNA testing. He'd heard about the lab while he was down in Richmond and had seen the glossy brochure with the corporate logo in the shape of a double

**Detective Joe Horgas sitting on his desk in the robbery/homicide
squad room at the Arlington County Police Department.**
[Photograph courtesy of Joe Horgas]

Detective Robert Carrig at his desk in the robbery/homicide squad room at the Arlington County Police Department.
[Photograph by author]

Detective Chuck Shelton sitting at his desk in the robbery/homicide squad room at the Arlington County Police Department.
[Photograph by author]

Richard McCue, the attorney who defended David Vasquez in 1985. *[Photograph by author]*

Henry Hudson, the Arlington County Commonwealth Attorney who prosecuted David Vasquez. *[Photograph by AP/Wide World Photos]*

Mug shot of David Vasquez taken after his arrest for the murder of Carolyn Hamm. *[Photograph by Arlington County Police Department]*

Detective Mike Hill, Joe Horgas's partner. *[Photograph by author]*

Arthur Karp, the assistant Commonwealth Attorney who assisted Helen Fahey. *[Photograph courtesy of Arthur Karp]*

Helen Fahey, the Arlington County Commonwealth Attorney who prosecuted Susan Tucker's killer. *[Photograph courtesy of Helen Fahey]*

Detective Ray Williams of the Richmond Police Bureau, assigned to investigate the South Side Strangler killings. *[Photograph by Richmond Newspapers, Inc. Staff Photo]*

Detective Glenn Williams of the Richmond Police Bureau, assigned to investigate the South Side Strangler killings. *[Photograph by Richmond Newspapers, Inc. Staff Photo]*

Crime Scene Agent John Coale of the Arlington County Police Department, who processed the Tucker crime scene. *[Photograph by author]*

Crime Scene Agent Rick Schoembs of the Arlington County Police Department, who processed the Tucker crime scene. *[Photograph by author]*

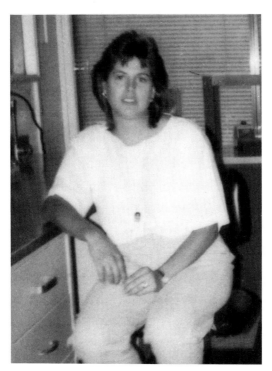

Lisa Bennett of Lifecodes, Inc. *[Photograph by author]*

Deanne Dabbs of the Virginia State Crime Lab. *[Photograph by author]*

FBI Agent Judson Ray in his office in Quantico, Virginia.
[Photograph by author]

FBI Agent Stephen Mardigian in his office in Quantico, Virginia. *[Photograph courtesy of Stephen Mardigian]*

The front of Carolyn Hamm's home in Arlington, Virginia, on the morning of January 25, 1985. *[Photograph by Arlington County Police Department]*

Side view of Susan Tucker's home on the morning of December 2, 1987. A police warning sticker can be seen pasted to the front door window. *[Photograph by Arlington County Police Department]*

Wide shot of the back of Susan Tucker's home. Carolyn Hamm
lived just beyond the ridge of trees in the far background.
[Photograph by Arlington County Police Department]

Basement window at rear of Susan Tucker's home where the killer made his entry. *[Photograph by Arlington County Police Department]*

Basement window at rear of Carolyn Hamm's home where the killer made his entry. *[Photograph by Arlington County Police Department]*

Contents of Susan Tucker's pocketbook as seen by Detective Horgas on December 1, 1987. *[Photograph by Arlington County Police Department]*

Contents of Carolyn Hamm's pocketbook as seen by Detectives Carrig and Shelton on January 25, 1985. *[Photograph by Arlington County Police Department]*

The front of Debbie Dudley Davis's home in Richmond, Virginia.
[Photograph by Richmond Newspapers, Inc. Staff Photo]

The front of Dr. Susan Hellams's home in Richmond, Virginia.
[Photograph by Richmond Newspapers, Inc. Staff Photo]

The front of Diane Cho's home in Chesterfield County, Virginia.
[Photograph by Richmond Newspapers, Inc. Staff Photo]

helix and the slogan: "Lifecodes: Where People Make the Difference." He read through it again. Founded in 1982, they originally did cancer testing, paternity testing, prenatal screenings, and cases of missing persons or unidentified human remains. The use of DNA testing in criminal cases was Lifecodes' most recent venture. DNA testing was $150 per suspect, and $300 per stain. It took ten days just to determine whether DNA typing was possible from a particular sample. Then the actual testing to isolate the DNA pattern took ten weeks longer. Though the process was not as quick as regular fingerprint identification, which took only hours, Horgas liked what he read:

> We at Lifecodes are dedicated to making DNA profiling the most reliable and accurate test ever used for identity purposes. The Lifecodes' DNA-PRINT Test is based on DNA, the genetic material found in virtually every cell comprising our bodies: blood, skin, bone, tissue, semen. DNA in each human being is distinctive (except in identical twins). Therefore, evidence such as blood stains found at a crime scene or semen from a vaginal swab of a rape victim can provide a unique genetic pattern or profile. These results help authorities to make a positive match so they can prosecute the guilty. And protect the innocent.

He especially liked the line:

> Our DNA-PRINT Test makes a rapist's semen the equivalent of leaving a calling card with his name engraved on it.

It was exactly what he needed. With approval from his superiors, he booked a flight to White Plains, a town just north of New York City, on Piedmont Airlines for December 28.

That morning, though, before he left for the airport, he got a disturbing phone call. A teletype had come in from Fairfax County about an attack on a seventeen-year-old girl in her bedroom on December 17. A masked black male in his late twenties had come in through the window, and had just fin-

ished tying her hands behind her back when he was surprised by the girl's sister. He fled. Boy, Joe thought grimly.
Is she lucky.

Horgas flew to White Plains and then drove the hour to
Valhalla. He carried fifteen different samples: blood and
semen from the Tucker homicide, semen samples from several rapes, including two that took place in 1983, and semen
samples from the Hamm murder. He knew that Richmond
had already sent Mary Jane Burton up with samples from the
Davis and Hellams scenes, and Chesterfield had sent samples
from the Cho murder by Federal Express. The case was too
important to Horgas to leave this task to anyone but himself.

Lifecodes was a sleek gray building fronted by a grassy
lawn. People were using high-security access cards to get in,
and everybody had to pass through a lobby receptionist at a
gray half-moon desk. It's more secure than the PD, Joe
thought in surprise. Part of this was probably due to sanita-
tion requirements; people had different high-tech badges and
it appeared that this gave them access to different parts of
the building. Not like the gritty free-for-all atmosphere in the
robbery-homicide squad room.

He first met with Kevin McElfresh, director of forensics
and paternity, a friendly bearded bear of a man. McElfresh,
who had a Ph.D. in molecular biology and population genetics, told Joe DNA testing was the first real breakthrough in
identification technology since fingerprinting. Had Joe heard
of Watson and Crick, the two English scientists who first
identified DNA? Joe had just some vague recollection of their
names from high school biology.

Seeing that Horgas was eager to learn about his world,
McElfresh continued with his science lesson. He brought the
history of DNA analysis smoothly up to the biotechnology
revolution of the 1970s, by which time even high school and
college students were isolating DNA, cutting it up, and comparing the DNA from one organism to that of another—corn
versus fruit flies versus rats. In 1975 a better testing technology became available, and scientists began founding companies to do identity testing, gene cloning, and recombinant
DNA. Companies like Lifecodes and Cellmark in Maryland.

"DNA testing was first used in a criminal case in England in nineteen eighty-six," McElfresh told him. "A Dr. Alec Jeffries used it to identify Colin Pitchfork as the man who murdered and raped two fifteen-year-old girls in central England. To find this killer they took blood samples from almost every adult male in the surrounding villages—about four thousand people, and then found a match in Mr. Pitchfork." If it were only so easy over on this side of the Atlantic, Horgas thought. American law enforcement officers did not have that kind of latitude in investigating a case. In England, the mere fact that two young girls were found raped and murdered gave the Leicestershire Constabulary the power to demand that every male in the county give a sample of his blood to be tested; the Arlington Police Department could require a citizen to submit a blood specimen only if they had probable cause to believe that he had committed a crime. And of course, Horgas still had no clue to the actual identity of his suspect.

"Look around any room you walk into," McElfresh suggested. "Everyone is different. That's all in the DNA. Its component chemicals are called nucleotides—adenine, guanine, cytosine, and thymine—and they're linked in chainlike sequences, their order varying to an almost infinite number of arrangements."

McElfresh led him politely around the facility while he gave Joe this practiced introduction. Joe saw the sparkling clean labs, the scientists operating mysterious machines, the technicians handling body fluids and tissue samples with double rubber gloves and goggles. He knew he was getting a sales pitch, but even so his excitement was all but uncontrollable. This place was going to give him the answer he had been praying for. He was going to prove that the masked rapist was the same guy who strangled Hamm, Hellams, Davis, Cho, and Tucker. They'd all see he was right.

In an animated rush he launched into a description of the case. To his dismay, though, McElfresh's eyes glazed over. It was obvious that, his introduction complete, all he wanted to do was take the samples, log them in, guide Horgas through the requisite paperwork, and give him his receipts.

It's just one more job to them, Joe thought, disappointed. But then they have thousands of them.

Next he met with the goateed, grandfatherly director, Michael Baird. With a Ph.D. from the University of Chicago, he'd been a pioneer in identifying genetic diseases before he'd gotten involved in bioengineering and come to Lifecodes. His role was obviously to explain DNA testing to the customers, and he started right in.

"First we have to make sure we have a sample of sufficient size and quality. It has to be enough for us to isolate the tiny percentage of DNA that differs from one individual to another—the part that goes beyond two arms, two legs, and two eyes and is, in effect, a detailed map of those aspects of the person which are completely one-of-a-kind. And actually all that DNA fingerprinting does is zero in on those areas of the DNA that are most unique to individuals and then we compare them. The good news is that this can come from almost any forensic substance: blood, semen, skin, bone, urine, sweat, hair follicles—anything the body secretes. And the samples can be old, too. Normally we can work with DNA from twenty-year-old bloodstains and four-year-old semen stains. Once the stain is dry the DNA remains stable. The key is protection from humidity."

"Visualize DNA as a twisted zipper," Baird continued. "The sides are phosphates and sugar and the teeth are complementary pairs of bases—adenine, guanine, cytosine, and thymine—paired off in specific sequence. It looks like a complex ladder."

Joe nodded, accepting this without trying to fully grasp it.

"Here's what we do. First we identify the sample, photograph it, then we take the human cells out of whatever medium they're in. Let's say it's sperm on a piece of fabric, like you've got here. We cut it up into square-inch pieces and wash it in a soapy reagent, which floats out the sperm cells. Now we're ready for testing."

"The first step we call lysis. We break open the sperm cells with a mild detergent and spill the DNA into solution. Then we clean up the debris and get a nice clean sample of DNA in something that looks like lengths of twisted rope."

"One individual's rope will have four or five knots, another three, another one hundred. We use enzymes to cut the DNA into sections of this exact length. These are restriction enzymes; they recognize the amount of information in each DNA block, and cut the DNA precisely so each block is separated. And the amount of information or number of blocks between the cuts differs completely from one person to another."

"Now the pure DNA is poured onto a substance like hard Jell-O, which is electrified with a positive charge at one end and a negative charge at the other. The process is called electrophoresis. The DNA fragments migrate toward the positive charge, and this organizes them according to size, because the small pieces can move through the gel more quickly. Then we transfer it all to a nylon membrane, where the DNA is fixed in position—the long lanes and the small lanes."

"I'm almost finished explaining the process," Baird said, noting Horgas's look of concentration.

Horgas nodded. Some of the information was going above his head, but he wanted to hear it all.

"Our next step is to apply a DNA probe to the nylon membrane. The probe is a piece of human synthetic DNA that is made radioactive. The probe seeks out its mate on the membrane: it's like a plug with thirteen to forty-five prongs and it has to find the exact DNA socket to fit in.

"Finally we go through several steps to make what is basically a radioactive picture of the DNA pattern. The film is fixed to the membrane with a material similar to Saran wrap and then it is put into a deep freeze to develop. Where the radioactive probes attach to the membrane, a black spot is produced on the film. The film is called an autoradiograph, or, in DNA parlance, an autorad.

"It's like developing X-ray film. What we're left with is a picture that looks a lot like a supermarket bar code, and that's your suspect."

"Could this bar code be deciphered to find out anything about the son of a bitch? What he looks like?" Joe pressed.

Baird laughed. "Not yet! But you're right: each band of the bar code represents a piece of genetic material that has a certain frequency in the population like eye color and height. We keep databases of all the bands we see, and use population genetics to predict how often you see the band in the population. At this point all we can do is compare samples— tell you we have a match or a nonmatch. We use a computer to calculate the size and weights of the bands, and we digitize the sample so we know the exact molecular weight of the DNA. Then we can give you the margin of error for your match using population genetics. For instance, we could confirm a match and say only one in three hundred million men, for instance, could possibly have this pattern."

"Those are great odds," Joe said, thinking of the 13 percent that was all the state lab could give him on blood typing.

"Of course," Baird agreed. "But it takes time. About two and a half months. We can have a preliminary answer for you before then, but the final results will be ready in late February."

"I need it a lot quicker than that," Joe said doggedly.

"We'll do our best," Baird said smoothly. Clearly he was used to this. "Look, detective," he said, shifting the subject away from the deadline, "this is important work—DNA testing in rape cases. We know rape has the lowest conviction rate for violent crimes, and that something like half of them aren't even reported. DNA can really make a difference. It can match a suspect to a crime, almost beyond dispute."

"Of course I gotta catch the son of a bitch first," Horgas muttered. And then—what if he caught the guy, and the DNA didn't match? A chill shot through him. And what if the DNA test showed that the masked rapist and the murderer were two different men? This DNA business could save his ass, definitely—or it could blow him right out of the water.

During the weeks that Lifecodes was extracting the DNA fingerprint from the crime scene samples, Joe would have only one priority: come up with a suspect.

Though he hated to admit it, he couldn't go any further alone. He'd used every ounce of his training, talent, and experience and come up empty-handed. There was one place left to turn—the FBI's Behavioral Science Unit.

Of course, these were the experts who supposedly told the

Richmond detectives that the killer was probably a white male. Still, he had to try it. Nothing else was left.

The eleven FBI agents attached to the Behavioral Science Unit, or BSU, in Quantico, Virginia, were known as profilers. They were called in only when local law enforcement agencies had exhausted every traditional avenue of investigation in serial murders, child molestation/abduction, arson, bombings, and product-tampering cases.

Joe's usual bulldog confidence gave way to waves of anxiety as he awaited the arrival of special agents Stephen Mardigian and Judson Ray from Quantico. It was December 29, and snow was falling around the Arlington Police Department—twenty-eight days since the discovery of Susan Tucker's body.

He fought down memories of his disastrous meeting with the South Side Strangler Task Force in Richmond, and their breezy confidence in what special agent Judson Ray had supposedly told them back in October: the strangler was in his late twenties, a white male.

He anxiously rose to his feet when they walked in at 9:30 A.M., feeling instantly intimidated. He'd worked with FBI field agents many times on bank robberies and had always been comfortable with them, but BSU agents had a reputation for being cut from a different cloth—and, well, it was true. Ray and Mardigian each had a powerful, important presence. Steve Mardigian wore a rumpled suit and chomped an unlit, half-smoked cigar, while Judson Ray, well built and impeccably dressed, seemed to be intensely aware of everything around him and fixed Joe with a penetrating stare. They sat right down after exchanging only the briefest of pleasantries.

Joe had already laid the bulging Tucker file out on the ACPD conference room table. His plan was to hold back initially any mention of the Hamm murder, the rapes, and even the Richmond connection. He didn't want to pollute their perspective of Tucker. Everything in due time—after they'd reviewed the file. Yet after just several minutes of talking between themselves as they examined the autopsy reports, crime scene photos, witness interviews, and PD 6's (reports of field investigators) Mardigian began firing questions at him. Any evidence of sexual assault after death? Did the victim have a criminal history? What was taken from the victim? Mardigian scribbled Joe's responses to the questions, and also made notes on comments made by Ray, who was gravely reviewing the crime scene photos.

It was completely unlike all his other sessions, in which detectives had always sat passively as Joe explained his theory. These guys were actively searching for answers. Excitement pricked at him. He had planned to let them see it for themselves, but—

"You know," he said hesitantly, "Richmond's got a few of these type killings." Both agents stopped reading and looked up, concern dragging their mouths down.

"I was down there a few weeks ago talking to them about their situation. And you know Tucker looks an awful lot like . . ."

"We're well aware of those cases as you know," Ray interrupted. "But we're not here to talk about that investigation. We really don't want to get into what another jurisdiction is doing."

"I'm not criticizing what they're doing down there but I want you guys to know about the similarities!" Joe insisted. "It's more than just the ropes, entry through a window, no fingerprints, and bunch of other things. The blood typing came back last week and it's identical in all four cases." Joe carefully excluded mention of Ellen Talbot's rape. A discussion of the killer's race was premature.

"Listen, Joe, there's no need to evaluate the Richmond investigation," Ray said.

"Of course not!" Joe agreed instantly, and spread his hands for emphasis. He knew full well that the last thing Ray and Mardigian would want to do would be to say anything about the quality of another jurisdiction's investigation. The FBI's daily bread depended on maintaining good working relations with local law enforcement, and not favoring one department over another.

"OK," Ray continued in a conciliatory tone. "Let's just assume for this meeting that you're right. The same guy killed all these females."

Joe couldn't keep back a smile. This was the first step. "Great! Assume that's true. What does the Tucker murder tell you about him?" Joe asked.

"First off, Joe," Ray said in slow surprise, paging through the grisly crime scene photos, "it does in fact seem that an argument can be made for saying the same guy killed all of them. There are some striking similarities here. Things, Joe, you've obviously noticed yourself."

Joe nodded excitedly, welcoming the first glimmer of support.

"What jumps at me from these pictures is the attention the killer paid to the bindings," Ray continued. "It's something we saw with the Richmond victims too. These were sophisticated jobs. The noose construction in each case was identical—a slipknot tied at the base of the neck. He then ran the rope down the middle of the back where it was tied to another piece that bound the hands. He wrapped the rope four times around each wrist and then he tied it together. This— the excessiveness of the bindings—is the signature aspect of the murders. Such an elaborate noose construction was not necessary. He could have successfully completed the crime by simply strangling them. But obviously he was attempting to satisfy some deeper urge. It seems the ropes probably have some connection to his need for control in sexual situations. And it's clear, as we'll get into a minute, that control was what this guy was all about."

Ray cleared his throat. "Now. He rigged the bindings so he could choke and release his victims, so we're talking about a sadist. Not only did he want to kill these women, he got off on hearing their screams for mercy and seeing their faces contort with pain."

Joe was impressed. The bindings had drawn his attention as well, but he didn't know they held such significance.

Mardigian took over to spin off several other signature aspects of the crime. First, there was an effort to conceal the bodies. Tucker was draped with a sleeping bag, Hellams was stuffed in a closet, Cho was covered with a sheet, and Davis was wearing her shorts. Then, a large amount of pure semen was found on each of the bodies. Also, there was no evidence of a struggle, meaning the women were overcome quickly, and each woman was killed in her bedroom.

"The guy who did this is what we call an organized killer," Ray put in. "These types plan all aspects of the murder from targeting their victims to displaying control at the crime scene. You can really see the planning in the fact that he obviously monitored each victim's movements at least for several days before he attacked—they were not victims of opportunity, they were stalked. He selected women who lived alone or, in the case of Cho, someone who he knew would be alone at the time he attacked. The fact that all these assaults occurred inside the victims' homes tells us that he made a conscious decision to limit his risk of detection. His strategy guaranteed that there would be no witnesses. We know we're not telling you anything new when we say this guy was smart and experienced. Very sophisticated. Very bad."

"Do you have any idea what kind of history this guy would have?" Joe asked, keeping his voice casual. "I mean, we know he knew how to break into houses. What else?"

"Well, just looking at Tucker you can tell this guy's committed who knows how many sex offenses prior to these homicides," Mardigian responded confidently. "His entire MO just screams that he didn't start off raping and killing at the same time. He had practice."

"Yeah, lots of practice," chimed in Ray. "Early on in his career he would have been responsible for some rapes. We're not saying he got caught for them, but he definitely has a sex offender history."

Joe nodded his head with interest as he had done throughout the agents' discourse. Inside, however, he was exploding with excitement. Now it was time to give them a little more information.

"Really, that's interesting," he said almost innocently. "You know, a few years back we did have a very active rapist running around our community and he was never identified." As he finished the sentence he pulled a two-foot-high stack of rape case files from the floor behind him and placed them squarely in front of the agents. "We had nine confirmed rapes and at least seven attempted rape-abductions from the summer of nineteen eighty-three through the winter of nineteen eighty-four.''

The agents' eyes widened. As they eagerly flipped through the files, Joe wove in the next crucial fact. "And right around the time of the last rape we had a homicide of a single female. Carolyn Hamm. She was raped and murdered in her own home. Strangled with a noose. And she lived here," Joe said, pointing to the map. "It's about four blocks from where Susan Tucker lived."

Mardigian and Ray closed the rape files they were reading and leaned forward with great interest. It was Joe's turn. He presented a detailed discussion of Hamm and the rapes that he believed led up to her killing.

As he had done with his task force two weeks earlier, Joe laid out his entire theory in a respectful but self-assured tone. But unlike his task force, the agents, as he went through each rape, became increasingly animated.

"Goddamn, Joe!" Ray said enthusiastically. "You know what you've got here? If you're right about this masked guy being the killer, then these women are your eyewitnesses! They can give you details about the crimes that otherwise you'll never know."

When Joe was finished the agents asked for some time to review the files. As they paged through the victim interviews and studied the Hamm crime scene photos, Joe sat back with a satisfied smile.

Unlike the sex crimes unit, Mardigian and Ray were positive upon reviewing the files that one man committed all the rapes. It was not so much the similarities in physique and disguise, it was the rapist's language that convinced them. One investigation technique the BSU had perfected was applied psycholinguistics. It was a science they relied on heavily in hijackings, kidnappings, bombings, and product tamperings where verbal or written threats and messages were a part of the puzzle. Analysis of word choice and sentence structure told them a great deal about offender intent and personality.

The rapist was an incessant talker. Mardigian and Ray zeroed in on his sex-related comments.

"There's the usual stuff we see in these cases," Ray pointed out. "Things like, 'I want you to suck my dick' and 'I'm gonna have your pussy.' But whenever he was about to commit the rape or during the act of intercourse he gave them angry variations on the following, 'I want you to come, you'd better come.' This phrase was frequently tied to a physical threat. Look." He indicated one of the files. "To his second victim he said, 'If you don't come I'm gonna kill your baby,' and—here—to his fourth victim, 'You'll have an orgasm or I'll kill you.' "

Joe furrowed his brow. "And that tells you—?"

"Aside from the fact that the same person committed all the rapes," Mardigian said, "we know this guy needed to reassure himself of his own masculinity by ensuring that his victims were sexually satisfied. On the other hand, his demeaning verbal insults coupled with the use of a weapon indicates that the dominant motive for the rapes was control. Now there are many rapists who will continue to do the same thing every time they assault a woman. But these types for whom control is paramount will become progressively violent."

"He's what we call an escalating rapist," Ray clarified. "With each new attack, he's modifying his MO based upon how successful he was at the one prior. He's learning criminal behavior—what works and what doesn't. It's kind of like he's climbing a ladder of criminality."

Joe had never worked a rape, and the complexities of a rapist's personality were foreign to him. But their basic point seemed to jump out and hit him in the face: the masked rapist graduated from raping to killing—exactly what Joe had been saying for weeks.

The agents went through the rapes again and pointed out where each one fit on the rapist's learning curve. He was not well organized when he started out; the first assault was an abduction in a parking lot leading to rape in a nearby wood. This first crime was too risky. He learned from it. Except for two other car abductions, the remaining attacks occurred in the victims' dwellings.

With each attack the young masked man also became more proficient in controlling his victims. At first he simply threatened the women with his knife. Later, he began taping his victims' eyes and mouths and tying their feet. By the last attack on January 25, 1984, the rapist had become confident enough to do side-by-side break-ins. In several of the rapes and in Hamm he used venetian blind cord found at the crime scene to bind his victims, but by the time he killed Diane Cho and Susan Tucker he had become much more sophisticated. He brought along his own rope.

The agents stressed to Joe that the rapes, especially the last one, provided a blueprint for understanding the homicides. In almost all the in-home rapes the point of entry was a rear window or door. There was a concentrated effort to avoid leaving fingerprints behind by wearing gloves or thick socks and he always dumped purses after rummaging through them. Tucker's purse—like Hamm's—was found on the floor. It was also clear that the masked man waited inside the residences for each of the victims to return.

"This guy spent an exorbitant amount of time inside each victim's home," Mardigian commented. "We think he used this time to his advantage, most importantly to surprise these women. We can assume that just like the rape victims, Tucker and these other women were accosted coming into the house. Or else he waited until they went to sleep. That appears to have happened with the Chesterfield girl, Cho. Also, it's a safe bet that once he gained control over them, he didn't tie them up right away."

"Now how do you know that?" Joe asked, puzzled.

"Well, go back to even the early rapes. He marched these women around to various places in the residence," Ray explained. "He raped them several times, typically in at least two different places in the house. In Debbie Davis's case, for example, she was found wearing her cut-offs, which meant he made her undress, raped her God knows how many times, made her dress, and then tied her up."

"But why did he just start killing?" Joe interjected.

"Control. It's all about control with these guys," Mardigian explained. "A lot of people think the motivation for sex crimes is sex but it's control, manipulation, dominance. You can see this not just in the type of physical wounds that are inflicted but from the verbal behavior of the assailant. How he interacted with the victim, what he said to her. A rapist that comes in and says, for example, 'Do what I say and I won't hurt you' is differently motivated than a guy who says, 'You don't do what I say, I'm going to kill you.' Look at Sanders, your last known victim. She was very lucky since he had just killed Hamm within the last twenty-four to forty-eight hours. Sanders was like a blueprint for the homicides." He pulled the Sanders file out and began reading from the reports.

> . . . Victim awakened by a noise and went downstairs from her bedroom. In the living room she was confronted by the subject who was armed with a kitchen knife. He demanded money and the victim took him upstairs to her purse. He removed the cash and dumped the contents on the floor. He then ordered her to go back downstairs into the kitchen where he made her undress. In the kitchen he sodomized her vaginally with a vibrator. He also punched her in the face and sliced her calf with the knife. He then ordered her outside into the backyard and forced her to commit oral copulation on him. Eventually she was able to escape and screamed, attracting her neighbors.

Mardigian stopped reading. "Something else happened here to make him go off," he said slowly. "He lost his control. But I don't see why."

"I know!" Joe cried. "You're right—it's not in the file! But I interviewed her again, and she told me after he penetrated her with the dildo she said, 'Enough's enough, OK? You've done what you wanted to do to me, now leave. Get the hell out of here!' Then he screamed at her: 'Quit telling me to leave!' He yanked her by the hair, punched her in the eye, and cut her on the leg."

"It had to be something like that," Mardigian agreed. "He

got angry because she tried to take the control away from him. Her resistance directly threatened his power and the command he thought he had over her. She's very lucky. It seems he was on track for killing her."

"Do you think Tucker tried to resist him?" Horgas asked.

"This is all theory. But if you look at these women who were killed you're dealing with professional types. Tucker was a writer, Hellams a doctor. Achievers. Those types of personalities don't give up control of their lives too easily, especially in a bad situation. As you told us, the forensics suggest they did not physically resist him. They would have likely engaged this guy in a conversation, however. Perhaps they attempted verbally to take back his control. This might have precipitated his anger. It's just one theory."

Joe couldn't completely accept this. It seemed much more likely to him that this masked guy just got a taste for killing and simply couldn't stop. At least that was the only way he could explain the murder of a fifteen-year-old high school girl.

"So from what I've shown you here today you guys are saying that this black rapist killed Carolyn Hamm, am I right?" Joe asked.

"We're not saying anything definitively," Ray cautioned. "But from everything you've presented to us, yeah, it looks like this masked guy could be responsible for Hamm's death. And because of the similarities between Hamm and Tucker as well as the short distance between them, it looks like this black guy also did Tucker," Mardigian said. The agents specifically excluded mention of the Richmond cases.

"I agree, obviously. But if we're right about this masked rapist, we have a problem here—because we have a man who was convicted for Hamm's murder and is now in Buckingham," Joe disclosed. "Here's the file on him. David Vasquez."

As Joe handed the file to them the agents looked at each other with raised eyebrows as if to say, 'Do we really want to get into this?' In silence they paged through the background investigation and eyewitness statements.

Joe continued talking as they read. "Even though this guy pled guilty, our investigators had some pretty compelling evidence that Vasquez was no more than the tagalong. There are two sets of shoe impressions outside the basement window, and Vasquez didn't seem strong enough or for that matter bright enough to pull something like this off by himself. Now I know you guys said that these rapes and murders were one-man jobs, so you can see where the problem is."

"Is *this* the evidence your men had back then to support this guy's involvement in the crime?" Mardigian asked with a grimace, pointing to the file.

Horgas nodded.

"Well, look at this! You realize this Ranser woman didn't come forward to say she saw Vasquez until *after* her brother was called in for a second interview? And that was a full six days after the murder! Why didn't she come forward immediately?" Mardigian narrowed his eyes in reproach.

Horgas cringed with embarrassment. He had completely missed the point. So had everyone else in his department.

"It's not so difficult to see. This Ranser woman's brother was being looked at by the police very closely as a possible suspect. He was interrogated several times. On January thirty-first he submits to a PERK kit and hands over his shoes so the soles could be compared to prints at the scene. At eight A.M. on the following morning, February first, this lady comes forward and offers Shelton and Carrig a suspect. Now, I'm not saying that this woman was fabricating a story, but you have to evaluate her statement on the basis of concern that she may have had for her brother being linked to such a hideous crime."

A sister protecting her little brother, of course, Joe thought. It was the only way to explain why, if she'd had such an intimidating experience with Vasquez, she'd waited almost a week to call the cops. And when the police had interviewed her mother, whom she was visiting the very night of the murder, her mother never mentioned the daughter's harrowing confrontation with Vasquez. One would have thought that Ms. Ranser would have run down the street into her home and told her mother as soon as it happened.

The agents were equally skeptical of the eyewitness account given by Michael Ansari.

"This information was delivered through a police officer, Roger Estes. Estes was friends with Ansari and said he'd received information from him in the past.

"He's the type of individual who repeatedly reports problems to the police department, the kind of guy who is always coming forward, always knows something that's going on in the community. And when something of interest is happening in the environment, he knows about it and he relates that information to the police. I'm just not real impressed by those eyewitness identifications."

Mardigian then drew Joe's attention to a telling document in the Hamm file, a field interview with Ansari conducted several days after Hamm's body was discovered. In the interview, Ansari was asked by a detective to identify a photo of Vasquez and another man. Ansari, according to interviewing officer Cindy Brenneman, "had a hard time recognizing Vasquez."

Ray and Mardigian conceded that it was indeed a major coincidence that two people had independently identified Vasquez. They were not surprised, though. Vasquez was the type who would stand out in any community. He was a visibly troubled person in a quietly middle-class community and thus naturally on the short list of unusual neighborhood characters.

Joe watched the agents turn to the record of Vasquez's interrogation. Their raised eyebrows and slowly shaking heads confirmed that the interrogations were even worse than the eyewitness statements. Horgas knew there had to have been problems with the interrogations because the judge had suppressed the first two confessions. He hadn't concerned himself with the particulars, since the third confession had been accepted by the court.

As they jointly read each succeeding interview page, the agents' dissatisfaction became palpable.

"Joe, they gave the suspect everything!" Mardigian said with obvious displeasure. He was only halfway through the first interrogation.

"How could somebody who works homicide conduct this kind of interview?" Ray chimed in. "We sure would like to have a copy of this for training purposes. How *not* to do an interview!"

Embarrassment, anger, and sympathy raced through Joe as a flashing image of a pathetic Vasquez sitting in prison cut across his mind. Innocent, he thought—that poor son of a bitch. His musings were interrupted by Mardigian.

"Here's a really good example of what we're talking about. They're asking him here what he used to tie Hamm's hands." He read:

> Shelton: Whatcha use?
> Vasquez: The ropes?
> Shelton: No, not the ropes. Whatcha use?
> Vasquez: Ah, my belt?
> Shelton: No. Not your belt.
>   Carrig: Come on, David, think about what you used now!
> Vasquez: I just don't . . .
>   Carrig: Remember being out in the sun room, the room that sits out to the back of the house?
> Vasquez: Yeah, I know—
>   Carrig: The new addition, you remember being out there?
> Vasquez: I think so.
>   Carrig: And what did you cut down?
> Vasquez: A coathanger?
>   Carrig: No, it wasn't a coathanger, it was something like a coathanger. What was it? By the window? . . . Think about the venetian blinds David. Remember cutting the venetian blind cord?
> Vasquez: Ah, it was a thin rope.
>   Carrig: Yeah!

The next example was equally vexing.

> Shelton: Okay now tell us how . . . you did it.
> Vasquez: I grabbed the knife and just stabbed her, that's all.
>   Carrig: Oh David! No David! Now if you would have told us the way it happened, we could believe you a little bit better.

> Vasquez: I only say that it did happen and I did it, and my
> fingerprints were on it . . .
> Carrig: You hung her!
> Vasquez: What?
> Carrig: You hung her!
> Vasquez: Okay so I hung her.

The agents were also bothered by how thin the forensic evidence was. The blood type of the semen extracted from Hamm did not match David Vasquez's. The only thing tying Vasquez to the scene was his hair, the weakest form of proof. Though hairs can be typed according to several factors, there is no lab tech who can definitively state that a hair fragment recovered at a scene belongs to a particular person. The most that the tech can say is that the subject's hair shares certain characteristics with the recovered fragment. And that is hardly enough even for an arrest, let alone a conviction.

Vasquez's involvement was a critical point, though. "How can you dismiss the theory that Vasquez could have had an accomplice?" Horgas asked.

"These are typically one-man jobs. Guys who do these things to women don't usually have a tagalong," Ray asserted. "When two perpetrators are involved you also find a lot more activity at the crime scene. We just did not see enough behavior at the Hamm scene that would suggest more than one person. But almost more important, this fellow was simply not capable of it. The Hamm murder was too sophisticated. It required a higher level of intellectual functioning than David Vasquez appeared to have."

Joe also knew that the logical extension of the "masked rapist turned killer" theory precluded any consideration of an accomplice, for there was no hard evidence of a partner in any of the rapes.

It had turned dark two hours earlier and the meeting was wrapping up. Joe had one final question.

"So if what we've been talking about is true about the black rapist being the same one who killed Hamm and Tucker, what the hell happened to the son of a bitch since

January of eighty-four and what kind of leads can you give me to find him?" This, to Joe, was the main question.

"You have to hold on a second, Joe. Before we go any further we have to tell you there's one big problem with this whole theory," Ray said.

Horgas swallowed hard. Now they're gonna back down—now, after all this?

"Everything seems to make sense except for one thing. Serial murderers, especially those who also sexually assault their victims, have traditionally been white. It's really unusual to have a black person commit these offenses. In fact, the only other one which comes to mind is Wayne Williams, the Atlanta Child Murderer."

There was no way Joe could question this. Both Ray and Mardigian had both worked on the Atlanta Child Murders as well as a whole host of other serial murders. Yet hadn't they agreed that the masked rapist was the killer? Maybe they were hedging because they didn't want to make Richmond look bad.

"We're not saying that your guy isn't black," Mardigian amended, "it would just be extremely unusual if he were. Even with individual rapes and murders, it's typically a white on white and black on black type deal."

"But I have good evidence," Joe said defensively. "And it's not just based on this masked rapist. The crime scene guys found several black hairs on her body and picked a couple off the sink."

"All we're telling you, Joe, is what profiles of these guys usually look like. And we would never tell an agency to completely exclude one race over another! Even if we say you are looking for a white guy, you certainly can't eliminate a black guy," Ray said.

That's not what the Williams boys told me, thought Joe. Hadn't Richmond been told by the FBI to look for a white guy? But there was no reason to press this point. At that time, based on their experience, the FBI did have good reason to think the killer was white. And if Richmond wanted to keep looking for a white guy that was their problem, not Joe's.

"Joe, let's move on to your big question—where the hell is he, right? And why did he stop for three years and then start again?" asked Mardigian, clearly ready to leave the race issue behind.

Horgas nodded eagerly.

"If your man is in fact this masked rapist, then your best bet is to look in the area where the first rape occurred." Mardigian presented this novel idea as if it were a fact of nature. "When a serial rapist starts out he tends to do his first dirty work where he feels most comfortable; usually in his own neighborhood."

"How do you know that?" Horgas blurted. This was something he would never have come up with on his own. And it was obviously something of which his cohorts in the sex crimes unit were also unaware.

"It's just something you see. And when we have gone into the penitentiaries and asked some of these guys where they started out, this is what they tell us," Mardigian said. "If not his neighborhood it can be near the residence of a relative or even around his workplace."

The agents went on to explain that a person starts out in a familiar place in order to minimize his risk of apprehension. In his neighborhood he knows the most traveled streets and the routes the police regularly patrol, as well as the quickest escape routes. A familiar area gives him more control during the criminal act itself. Then this success gives him the confidence to extend the geographic zone of his assaults.

Horgas busily scribbled notes of the agents' advice and then looked up.

"I know the neighborhood in which the first rape occurred, but that still doesn't tell me what happened to this guy for the last four years."

"Joe, there's only two possible things that could have stopped this guy after Hamm's murder," Mardigian responded. "These guys don't take vacations from their crimes. They just don't get up one morning and say to themselves, 'I'm not going to do this anymore.' "

"Well, how about if this guy got married, things go well

for a while, and then something happens to make him start again?" Joe reasoned.

"No way, Joe. No way in hell would a wife or girlfriend stop this kind of person," Ray interjected. "The only way he'd stop on his own would be if he died and you wouldn't be sitting here with Tucker if that happened."

Mardigian and Ray said it had to be one of two things. The first possibility was that he might have moved out of the area. If that had been the case, though, then somewhere in America, between 1984 and September of 1987 there should be a string of similar rapes and murders. Since Joe had received no such indication in response to his teletypes, the agents settled on the theory that the killer was probably arrested shortly after January 25, 1984, the date Hamm's body was discovered. The crime had to have been for something nonsexual, though—not rape. If his arrest had been for rape, he would have been targeted as a suspect back in 1984. Plus, Joe had checked this already; he knew there was no record of any sexual assault arrest during that time frame. Mardigian suggested that since there was ample evidence of the killer's prowess at breaking and entering—and Joe confirmed that he had discovered several burglaries with an entry MO similar to the rapes and murders—this unsub was probably arrested for a residential burglary.

"What you're saying is I have to look for someone who was arrested for a burglary shortly after January twenty-fifth, nineteen eighty-four. And the odds are he lived in the area where the first rape took place, right?" Joe asked, digesting it all.

"Right," said Mardigian. "And he would have been released shortly before September nineteen eighty-seven."

Joe gratefully thanked Ray and Mardigian and the two agents walked to their car through the snow-covered parking lot.

As the agents drove away they both acknowledged that if Joe's theory bore any fruit at all, they had just helped open one gigantic can of worms.

Ray nodded gloomily. Richmond was off in one direction, and now they had just encouraged Joe to take a completely different tack. There was bound to be an extremely embarrassing situation for at least one of the police departments.

And then there was David Vasquez. If Joe was right, an innocent man was in prison. There was nothing they could do about that right now, however. Joe's theory had to play itself out.

Joe raced back to his desk, feeling better than he had felt in weeks. At last he had some meaningful work cut out for him. The dinner hour was long past, but there was no way he was going to stop now. He sent out a national teletype to all police agencies detailing the crime's "signatures" and asking if any similar rapes or murders had occurred between January 1984 and September 1987. He then called Hill and told him to go first thing in the morning to the probation and parole office and retrieve copies of all persons arrested in 1984.

Finally he went back through the rape files and pulled the first one.

It had been the most enlightening day Horgas had had in nineteen years on the job. From the moment he'd first visited Vasquez at Buckingham, he'd known he was on the right track. But now, hearing that the experts agreed with him, the real bigwig cops—he felt exhilarated from his head to his toes.

He poured himself another cup of coffee and cracked open the rape file of Roberta Schwartz, the masked man's first victim.

He felt like king of the hill.

7

IN THE STEELY LIGHT OF THE NEXT MORNING, JOE SAT IN HIS CAR
ON South Oxford Street in South Arlington. Laid out on the
passenger seat was the Schwartz case file. Roberta Schwartz
had been the masked rapist's first victim. As he read the
witness interview for perhaps the tenth time since the evening before, Mardigian's words echoed in his mind: "Wher-
ever that first rape took place, that would be his area of
comfort. Either he lives there or works there. Maybe even he
has a relative who lives within a few blocks. But it's his
environment."

He turned to the incident report, which he had also read
dozens of times in the last twelve hours. "I placed Miss
Schwartz in my cruiser and she told me that a B/M, 20's . . .
had abducted her at knifepoint from a supermarket," it began.

Joe made a mental note of the supermarket's location—
close to two miles away, just south of Route 50.

"The perpetrator had her park on South Oxford. The victim readily identified this location because she was several
car lengths south of an ACPD officer's take home cruiser,"
the report continued.

Glancing behind him at the police cruiser conspicuously parked in front of the officer's house, Horgas thought: God, this guy had one set of huge balls. He had to have been very comfortable with the area since he had her park spitting distance from a marked police car. It took a very bold or very stupid guy to rape a woman near a cop's home. He also noticed that the spot was no more than a mile from the homes of Tucker and Hamm.

"Once they parked . . . he forced her out of the passenger side and led her to an adjacent wooded area." Joe looked to his right. The rapist had made her walk only fifteen yards into the woods. Though Horgas could clearly see through the woods in the dead of winter, in June those same bushes, weeds, and clustered oaks would be in full foliage. At that time you wouldn't have been able to see ten feet inside the woods, even at high noon.

"After raping her the assailant then told the victim that he was going to return to her car, get something and return. He ordered her not to move. She heard him moving things around in her car. When he did not return in three minutes, she exited the woods and noticed he had fled."

But in which direction? Joe asked himself. There were only two choices. To the cluster of modest ranch houses to the left, across the street from where Joe was now parked, or down below the wooded area to the right.

What if he went left, to the ranch houses? That was a neighborhood known as Green Valley, Arlington's only predominantly black area. Joe had worked the Valley since his early days in burglary and over the years he had developed a good reputation among the community's less than desirable elements. If the killer lived here, Joe told himself, I must have run across him sometime. Either that or I'll find someone who knows him.

Joe drove slowly through the area adjoining Oxford Street and peered intently at each modest ranch-style home. He knew there would be no sign stuck in one of the postage stamp front lawns announcing "Serial Murderer–Rapist Lives Here" but at least he could dream. Turning right onto Monroe Street, he headed down to Four Mile Run Drive, through the

Valley's short commercial district. As his car snaked through the narrow streets, he thought of the various people he had arrested over the years for murder, armed robbery, and assorted malevolent acts. He drew a complete blank when he tried to think of just one of them capable of committing the atrocities he had been investigating for the last month. As he stared up at the wooded bluff where the rape had occurred, he fervently wished a name would come to him so he would be saved from what was sure to be a nightmarish document review.

Aside from living near the Valley, the only other identifying suggestion Joe was given by Mardigian and Ray was that the killer was likely to have been arrested on a property-related felony soon after January 25, 1984, then incarcerated, and then released just before the Richmond murders. Despite this specific guidance, Horgas knew that identifying the guy would be an agonizingly painstaking task.

Two things had to be done. The first was reviewing all property arrests made in Arlington and the neighboring jurisdictions between January and April of 1984, then determining the dispositions of each and every arrest. The next step was to review the cases of all those from Arlington and Richmond—the two areas in which the killer was operating—who had been released on probation or parole from June through early September of 1987.

Instead of proceeding directly to the department to start chipping away at this mountain of a job, Joe decided to stop off at his house for a minute. His house was close to the Valley, about the same distance, in fact, as was Susan Tucker's home. It was not that he was trying to avoid the arduous records search. It was that, for the first time he could remember, he felt afraid.

He had been fighting off a deep, personal apprehension ever since yesterday's meeting with the FBI. Most of what Ray and Mardigian had said had been gratifying, even inspiring—but they had also, in effect, suggested that the killer probably lived only a few minutes from his home! He'd felt increasingly uneasy, and now felt only a stop at home would put his mind at rest. David was out of school for Christmas vacation, and he would be home now with Teresa.

As he hurried through the early-morning, wintry, gray neighborhood, he couldn't keep certain disturbing facts out of his head. Three days before Susan Tucker had been killed she had taken an aerobics class at a local recreation center—the same one to which Teresa took David to play basketball. Ray and Mardigian had stressed that the killer preselected his targets, probably stalking them for several days before breaking in to kill or rape. Could this deviant have stalked Tucker at the center? Was he there at the same time as Teresa? And what about the man noticing David, Joe's child, the center of his world? Horgas's mind spun increasingly disturbing scenarios.

Usually Horgas had much more self-control. Homicide detectives, like emergency room physicians, have to distance themselves emotionally from their work in order to survive. They can't look at a dead victim and think, "this could be my wife or my husband or my child." This case, though, was different. Working fifteen hours a day for a month, seeing firsthand the swath of destruction the killer had cut in Joe's own backyard, made it impossible for him not to worry about his family.

Joe knew all too well that Teresa could be just another random victim of the killer. The guy didn't just attack single women. Susan Hellams had been married; but the killer knew her husband would be in D.C. until late. And Joe thought of the fourth rape victim from 1983. She had been married too, but the suspect had known her husband worked the night shift. And then there was the one where he threatened to hurt the victim's child if she didn't cooperate.

Of all of them, Diane Cho's death was the most chilling. He tried to push the crime scene photos from his mind as he entered his own neighborhood, where his son was growing up. These pictures underscored how bold the killer had become. If the killer was so confident that he would risk raping and slowly strangling a young girl whose parents and brother were sleeping in adjoining rooms, he could be expected to strike anyone, anytime, under any circumstances.

As he pulled onto his tree-lined street, Joe slowed down. Teresa's car was in the driveway. As he pulled over to park, Joe noticed that the evergreen bushes in front of the house were overgrown. A perfect place to hide, he thought. Joe made a mental note to cut them back as soon as he was able to take a couple hours off—maybe on New Year's Day.

"Teresa," Joe yelled as he came in the door. "Teresa, David? Where are you?"

He glanced to his right and noticed the kitchen door sitting half open. As he turned to rush upstairs, Teresa walked through the back door with the kitchen trash can in her hand.

"Hiya. What are you doing home?" Teresa said with a smile. It took her a second to see Joe's furrowed brow, flushed cheeks, and tightly pursed lips. "What's wrong? Are you OK?" Her voice was tinged with concern.

"Listen! When you go outside, even if it's for a minute, close the door—and lock it!" Joe cried. "Where's David?"

"Upstairs. And I was just taking out the garbage," Teresa insisted gently. She searched his face and sighed. "OK, Joe. Sure. No problem. I'll lock up next time."

"Thanks," Joe said, relieved. He turned and raced upstairs.

First he greeted David and managed to talk to him normally for almost five minutes as if there were nothing unusual about his showing up at home in the middle of his shift. Then he checked the windows in the rear bedroom and bathroom. Teresa silently watched as her husband meticulously went on to inspect the locks on every window in the house. And when that was done, he rechecked all the lower rear windows as well as the front and back door locks.

From the moment they were married almost fifteen years earlier, Joe and Teresa had strictly adhered to a practice of never discussing Joe's job. Bringing home the tales of human degradation made for great barroom talk but had no place in the Horgas household. Being the daughter of a town constable and the sister of three Pennsylvania state troopers and having numerous friends married to cops, Teresa understood full well that the job could drain the lifeblood of a marriage and family.

"When we first got married I asked him about work and

his response was, 'You don't have to know. It's just work,' "
Teresa later recalled. "I'm glad he felt so strongly about leaving his job at the office. When he goes on shift, Joe's a one
hundred and ten percent cop but at home he's one hundred
and ten percent family man. A lot of detectives like to bring
home not only their war stories but their files. The last thing
I want is for our son to see any of those pictures that might
be left lying around."

Now, however, seeing the naked worry etched into her
husband's face as he made his way around their house forced
her to break with her long-standing practice.

"It's this guy you're looking for, isn't it?" she asked.

Joe took a long deep breath and shook his head despondently.

"He's bad news, Teresa. Really bad news. What he did to
these women . . ." Joe cut himself off. He knew Teresa really
knew very little about the murders—maybe he should keep
it that way. Outside of the police force, almost no one in
Arlington County knew much of anything about the murders.
It was nothing like the hysteria that was going on in Richmond, just 100 miles to the south, where the South Side
Strangler was the biggest, most frightening story of the year.
Here in Arlington the ACPD had made a purposeful decision
to treat the Hamm and Tucker murders as two isolated, un-
connected incidents. The last thing they wanted was for people to think there was a serial killer on the loose, preying on
women. Aside from wanting to keep the county calm, they
wanted to protect the integrity of the investigation. In fact,
shortly after Joe's visit to Richmond, Tom Bell, the press
officer, had issued a release saying that the ACPD was fairly
confident its murders were unrelated to those in Richmond.
Horgas had been bitterly opposed to this. He was equally
certain that it was a mistake for the Arlington press to almost
completely ignore the murder investigation. There had been
virtually no coverage since the day Tucker's body was found.
People had a right to be warned, Joe figured. Christiansen,
however, was dead set against scaring the public. Sometimes
Joe felt like he was the only one who realized how incredibly
dangerous this guy was.

"Teresa," he said now, "I want you to know you have to be very careful until we get this guy. Just be sure everything is locked up when I'm away. Everything! OK?"

"Are you close?" Teresa asked.

"Closer than I was last week but still far away. Really far away."

The next day, New Year's Eve, Horgas invited the Richmond boys—Glenn Williams, Ray Williams, and Lieutenant Robert Childress—to Arlington for a briefing. He hadn't had much contact with them since the initial meeting. Still, especially considering the FBI meeting, he felt they needed to be brought up to date. His idea may have been a wild hunch four weeks ago, but now, with Ray and Mardigian's informal endorsement, it was a fully supportable theory.

Joe did his dog and pony show, easel and all. He tried everything to get them on his wavelength, which was that the black rapist was the killer. He spent a lot of time on the Ellen Talbot rape. He emphasized the matched blood typing, the manner of each death, the signature aspects of the murders, and he tied it all to the masked rapist. He ended by going over Arlington's rapes in 1983 and how they led up to the Hamm murder, all showing the escalating pattern.

Unlike the FBI, who had shot back rapid-fire questions, the Richmond detectives listened in silence. They asked no questions. They hadn't even arrived until close to noon, and soon after they got there they started letting Horgas know they had to get back to Richmond. They still seemed to feel that a commuting serial killer was out of the question. The meeting was a flop.

Joe gave himself a rest on New Year's Day. As a precautionary measure he took an hour away from the football games to trim severely the bushes all around his house. Early the next morning, however, he was at the third-floor conference table sifting through the mountains of computer printouts he had received from probation and parole. He had already called quick meetings with the robbery-homicide squad and the sex crimes squad and briefed them on the profile given by the FBI agents. He had practically begged them for any and all names they could come up with, anybody they could recall who seemed to fit the profile so he could check the applicable dates. This plea received a halfhearted response. The sex squad in particular seemed to feel that Joe was reaching beyond his territory, but nevertheless they came up with several names, including two guys they already had in custody. These led nowhere.

Reluctantly Joe finally sat down in front of the agonizing stack of arrest and release data.

Faced with the dilemma of identifying someone arrested in the Arlington area in 1984 and released in Richmond in 1987, Horgas had originally planned to start with the arrest dates. He immediately abandoned this notion after the first records began to arrive and he realized the astronomical number of arrests he and Mike Hill would have to check. By concentrating on the parole releases he would have to review only those whose arrests resulted in imprisonment and then were paroled in the right time frame. The task would, however, still be like sifting through a haystack the size of a house in search of one very slim needle.

The probation and parole records that stood before Horgas in tall, uneven piles listed only each inmate's name, release date, and length of time he would be on parole. Though the records listed the individual parolee's county of residence, there was of course no grouping of names by county, and so the stack included every prisoner released to Arlington and Richmond in 1987. They first had to identify those who originally resided in Arlington and then, out of all those who were released in 1987, those who were released during the late summer. The final blow was that the records contained no indication of the individual's crime or the day he was incarcerated.

During that first morning Mike and Joe read through over 300 files and located only ten people who had been arrested in January of 1984 and then released in the summer of 1987. To obtain the critical information on each, they ran a background check called a triple—a computerized criminal history that listed the individual's federal, state, and interstate arrest and conviction record. The tedious line-by-line checking was compounded by the fact that each time Horgas and

Hill wanted to check a name they had to leave the conference room and go back down the hall to the squad room where the computer was located.

None of the names they had checked by the following day resulted in anything even remotely helpful. "The only thing that was certain," Joe later remarked, "was that I couldn't do this shit for a very long time. The first day wasn't that terrible. But by the second my vision started getting blurry after just a couple of hours. All I could do was hope that this guy was listed somewhere in those stacks of release records." But it was not just the monotony of the task that made it difficult for Joe to sit hour after hour reviewing the long lists of names.

His concentration was continually interrupted by one thought: Who do I know down in the valley that could have raped those women back in '83? And every time he asked the question, his mind went blank. Frustrated, he even took periodic breaks to drive through the Valley, hoping to stimulate his memory. During each of these drives, he parked for several minutes at the precise site of the rape. Nothing brought him the answer.

At around noon on January 4, Joe was at the computer checking the background history of a parolee. As the information scrolled by on the screen, suddenly—from nowhere—Joe remembered a burglary investigation he had done in the Valley about ten years earlier.

A lady who lived on Four Mile Run had reported that a local teenager, whose name Joe could not remember, broke into her house. He was a real neighborhood problem. During the investigation, which never resulted in an arrest, Joe recalled a rumor that the same boy had set fire either to his mother's car or house. Horgas's mind immediately shot forward to one of the victims, who, after being raped, had been forced into the trunk of her car. The masked man had then set fire to the backseat. Joe beat his brain for the kid's identity, but all he could remember was the name Timmy.

"Hey, Mike," Joe said turning to his partner, "you know any Timmys down in the Valley?"

Hill thought for a moment. "I can't think of anyone off-hand. Could it be Ted? 'Cause I arrested a Ted Nathan a couple of years ago. A real badass."

"No, no, it's not Ted. I'm sure it's Timmy, but I can't think of his last name," Horgas said dejectedly.

"Timmy, Timmy. What the fuck was that kid's last name?" was the refrain Horgas muttered to himself that evening and the entire next day. He spent the next morning of January 5 trying to locate the file on the burglary that had prompted his memory but could not find it.

By morning of January 6 he was so obsessed with recalling Timmy's last name that he had all but abandoned the parole review, leaving the wearisome task solely to Mike Hill. All he could do was sit at the long conference table staring off into space, thinking about the surname.

Joe had just finished his fifth cup of coffee when his eyes widened and he screamed, "Spencer, that's it. Timmy Spencer!" He triumphantly slammed his palm down on the table and leaped out of his chair. The conference room door flew open and Horgas raced down the hallway to the squad room. Hill was at the computer checking several parolee's names.

"Lemme in there, Mike. I got his name!" Joe roared.

Hill gave Joe a puzzled look but quickly made way for Joe's bulky frame.

"Whaddya mean you got his name. How?"

"I don't know. I was just sitting there. I couldn't read another name on those lists. My head felt like it was about to explode. And then all of a sudden it came to me," Joe shouted. His stout fingers nimbly typed SPENCER, TIMOTHY on the blank screen. Since Joe only had a name, he couldn't immediately check criminal history. This required a birthdate, address, and a social security number. To obtain this information he had to first do a Virginia driver's license search.

The computer asked Joe to give a birthdate. Though he did not know the day and month, he did have an approximate age. The rape victims had reported that the black man was about twenty-five years old. That meant he was born around 1959. Joe typed two commas indicating day and month and then "1959." If there was any Virginia driver's license issued to a Timothy Spencer born in 1959 that information should come up on the screen. Joe waited several long seconds for the system to search but the screen remained blank. Crestfallen, Joe typed the same information but this time substituting 1960. No hits. He had similar luck with 1961. He then entered 1962.

SPENCER, TIMOTHY W.
DOB: 03–17–62
SEX: M/ RACE: B
ADDRESS: 1500 PORTER ST., RICHMOND , VA.
SS# 228–11–3436

Joe's heart leaped a thousand miles.

Not only was this Spencer a black male but he was living where the FBI said he should be now—Richmond. With his eyes riveted on the screen, he punched in Spencer's name and social security number to determine if he had an FBI identification number. Bingo: Number 446 345 W2.

Spencer was registered as a felon.

Now the final test—checking the state crime-indexing system, the one he had used to no avail over the last six days. Joe quickly entered the requested information. A red light flashed repeatedly in the right corner of the screen, indicating that the computer was retrieving a file. The light was flashing an inordinately long time, which could indicate only one thing—a long file. Several seconds later the screen lit up in a mass of green lines as Spencer's extensive criminal record appeared.

Spencer's record indicated that he was a burglar, not a rapist. His first burglary arrest occurred on November 20, 1980, in Fairfax County. That charge was dismissed. He was arrested again on a burglary little over a year later and was sentenced to five years in the penitentiary, with three of those years suspended. From this second arrest in January of 1981 through 1984, he was arrested three more times for burglary, once for violation of probation, and once for trespassing.

Joe noticed with interest that Spencer was arrested for a

burglary on December 20, 1982, convicted, and sent to prison. He was released on May 23, 1983, one month before the first rape. Horgas was more interested, however, in Spencer's next and last arrest. Scrolling quickly down the screen, he came to it.

"Here it is, Mike, waiting for me like Christmas dinner!"

01–29–84 PD, ALEX. VA BURGLARY CONVICTED: BURGLARY

"I was going warp speed now," Joe later recalled. "He looked like the right guy but I still didn't know whether he had been locked up and sent to the penitentiary on the burglary."

Horgas searched furiously through the parole records looking for Spencer's name. His name was nowhere.

"There's no way he wasn't locked up for this burglary. Mike, see if you can find his name," Joe said to Hill. Unfortunately, Hill's search was equally unproductive.

"I know it's him but where the hell is he?" Joe asked.

"Since he was last arrested in Alexandria lemme go down to the PD there and pull his arrest jacket. I'm sure it'll tell us where he is," Mike said reassuringly.

While he was enthusiastic about the news he had just received, as Mike Hill drove down the George Washington Memorial Parkway to Alexandria he couldn't help but think it was just too good to be true. "Joe was a solid investigator," he later reflected, "because he had an uncanny ability to put names and faces together. The guy's like a goddamn computer. But this was something different. There was no reason he focused on Spencer's name aside from some vague memory of an investigation. He essentially pulled Timmy Spencer's name out of thin air."

An hour later, as Hill paged through the file he had just been handed by an Alexandria City detective, he saw no evidence indicating that Spencer was in fact the sadistic serial killer. His record read like that of so many Hill had seen over the years. But then he came to a document detailing Spencer's prison history.

"Holy shit," he muttered to himself as his jaw dropped. He raced out of the office.

"I don't know how or why, Joe, but you were right," Hill said as he threw a thick manila envelope down on the conference table. Joe tore open the file as Hill continued. "The guy was never released after he was arrested in Alexandria. He went straight from the lock-up at Alexandria to the penitentiary."

"And he was released!" Joe interrupted enthusiastically, "to a place called Hospitality House, a halfway house at 1500 Porter Street, the same address on his driver's license, on September fourth, nineteen eighty-seven. That's only two fucking weeks before Davis was murdered! Jesus Christ, this *is* the guy. It really is him."

"Joe, you realize the reason he never showed up in these probation and parole records was that he was not technically paroled? The corrections guys still had custody over him when they released him to the halfway house. So we would never have located this guy if you hadn't come up with his name!"

Horgas ignored the compliment. He was flying.

"Now let's look at his last B and E," Joe said.

The point of entry was through a very small rear window which the suspect had broken out. He crawled through the broken window pane. . . . While searching Mr. Spencer I found a large amount of coins—one U.S. nickel dated 1902, two République Française 5 centimes, 14 Eisenhower and 21 Susan B. Anthony silver dollars, 5 Kennedy half-dollars, one Queen Elizabeth the Second Caribbean coin, and more. Several of the coins apparently taken from another home were also in his pocket. I located a pair of black socks in his coat pocket. A screwdriver and a small flashlight were also found on Mr. Spencer.

"When they searched Spencer's car back then they also found a five-inch folding knife," Joe added, studying the reports. "Mike, you think it's just a coincidence that several of the rape victims reported the masked guy wore socks on his hands and threatened them with a folding knife?" Horgas asked gleefully. "Or what about the fact that point of entry in Hamm and Tucker was through a rear window almost the same size as in these burglaries?

"And what do we have here? A burglary into an empty house three blocks away reported the next day. This must be the one they referred to in the first report. 'The method of entry—through a rear door by breaking a six-by-eight-inch pane of glass—and time frame match a similar offense at 1508 Mt. Eagle Place.' Surprise of surprises!"

Horgas went back to the description of the collector's coins confiscated from Spencer by the police. These were not regular, circulated coins; they were commemoratives, easily traced. It was these, matching those taken in the burglary, that led to Spencer's arrest and conviction. Horgas's mind flashed back to the commemorative coins strewn about Tucker's spare bedroom. Of course! They were valuable, but Spencer had learned from this previous arrest not to take them. It was just like the FBI said; from crime to crime you could see his learning curve.

Perhaps the most critical part of the arrest report for Joe, though, was the line that listed Spencer's home address on South Four Mile Run Drive. His home was located no more than 200 yards down the hill from the first rape and only three-quarters of a mile from Tucker's and Hamm's homes.

Looking back at his early history, they saw that he had also been out of jail during the summer and fall of 1983, when the first string of attacks by the masked rapist occurred. In fact, he had been released only days before the first rape, of Roberta Schwartz, on June 27, 1983.

Now, in 1987, Spencer had been out of prison all through the fall and had been living at the halfway house. The next step was to see if Spencer had been signed out of the halfway house on the dates of the murders. "I'm gonna call down there to check these dates!" Horgas exclaimed.

"You sure you want to do that, Joe? What if they tell him you called and he gets spooked and splits? We haven't even told Richmond about him. Maybe we should call Williams and get some guys to go watch the house."

"No! I want to find out where he was on the days these women were killed," Joe insisted.

He nervously picked up the phone and dialed the halfway house. He had to take the risk that Spencer would be tipped off. Before he'd be able to go to his superiors and request that Spencer be placed under surveillance, he needed to have some proof of Spencer's whereabouts around the times of the homicides.

Alan Artegan was the halfway house director.

"Is this Mr. Artegan?"

"Uh-huh."

"Hi. This is detective Horgas from Arlington. Are you familiar with Timothy Spencer?"

"Yes sir, I am."

Horgas detected some hesitancy in Artegan's response. He shifted uncomfortably in his chair.

"I hope we're talking confidentially," Joe said.

"Yes, sir. Oh, yes, sir. Confidentially."

"In other words are you gonna tell him that anyone was talking to you about him?"

"No, no, sir. We're confidential."

"OK. Now all I'm looking for are the dates he was furloughed."

"Well, that'd be on the weekends. But he does work every day also from eight to five."

"I'm just interested in the weekends."

"Well, his sign-out time is seven P.M. Friday till twelve midnight Sunday."

"How's he get around?"

"He told me he takes the bus, like if he's going to Arlington."

"Just one thing before I get to these dates. Where does he work?"

"Pine Factory Furniture in Ashland. He makes furniture."

"How in the hell does he get all the way from Richmond to Ashland?"

"He rides with a coworker. And he's been there since December eighth. Was at another job before that—the Virginia Precast Corp."

As Horgas was jotting notes, he was beginning to put to-gether a mental map of how he could use the information that was streaming in over the phone lines. Could he have gotten any of the rope from his workplace? Horgas thought. Or did he use a knife at work? Who is this guy who drove him to work? Did Spencer ever borrow his car?

"I'll give you a date and you just tell me if you have a record when he signed in and out," Joe directed. As he spoke he quickly scribbled the dates of the homicides on the left side of his yellow pad and drew a line down the middle of the page. First, the date of Debbie Davis's murder. "How about September the eighteenth?"

"On that day he was signed out at five-twenty A.M. and went to work. His return was three-thirty P.M. that day. He signed out at seven-fifty P.M. to go to the store and he signed back in at twelve midnight."

"What about September eleventh?"

No one was murdered on the 11th. But on the chance that Spencer might become aware of his inquiry, Joe wanted to throw in a variety of dates so as to not tip him off.

"Let's see. He left at seven-oh-five A.M. and signed in at ten-twenty A.M. Then he left at nine and returned at midnight."

"October fourth?"

This night, Horgas was told, he signed out at seven-thirty P.M. and returned at two A.M. on October 4th. It was ample time to kill Dr. Hellams.

"November first?"

"November first. I don't have a record for that date."

Horgas bit his lip. That was the night Ellen Talbot was raped. She lived no more than a mile from Davis. Spencer had to have been out that night.

"Are you sure he wasn't out?"

"Well, I can't verify it. I'd have to do some more checking."

"What about November twenty-first?" This was the date of Diane Cho's murder.

"He left at seven-fifteen and returned at eight-twenty-five A.M. on the twenty-second."

"Now, let's see what other date," Joe said, trying his best to sound nonchalant. He was ready to hit the Tucker murder. "Thanksgiving. Was he there Thanksgiving?"

"No. He went back to Arlington. Left at seven A.M. on the twenty-fifth and returned on the twenty-seventh at midnight."

Yes! "Just one more question. What times does he normally come home from work?"

"I'd say about five-thirty P.M. Say, is he in some sort of trouble up there?" Artegan wanted to know.

"I have no idea. I'll tell you what, all we're trying to do is rule him out. This is confidential, right?"

"Oh, absolutely."

"Thanks. Just one more thing. You don't happen to know when he's next scheduled to come up here to Arlington?"

"Well as a matter of fact, this weekend."

Joe nervously hung up. "Shit!"

Initially he had only been worried that Artegan might run to Spencer and tell him about the call. Now, he thought, I find out the son of a bitch will be here in two days! It was 6 P.M. He had to act quickly. Joe punched in Deputy Chief Christiansen's extension.

"It's Horgas. We found him! The guy who killed Tucker. Name's Spencer, Timmy Spencer," Joe blurted triumphantly. Still he could not keep the edge out of his voice.

"Terrific, Joe! Congratulations! Where is the bastard?" Christiansen inquired excitedly.

"Richmond. In a halfway house. We need to keep an eye on him for a while. We need to check out a few more things like his availability around the time of Hamm. I also gotta speak to Helen to see what she wants to do." Joe knew that the police department couldn't take any major steps in a case of this importance unless Arlington County's Commonwealth Attorney was consulted.

"But we got a problem," Joe continued. "What I'm worried about is that we gotta get Richmond to put some plainclothes on this guy right now. Not only 'cause of what he may do tonight, but the halfway house counselor told me that Spencer's put in for an Arlington visit for this weekend. He takes a late afternoon bus from Richmond on Friday. So we really gotta get with Richmond to coordinate surveillance."

"Before I do anything, Joe, you have to tell me that you're sure *this is the guy.* I mean, you're sure you're right? 'Cause if it ain't and I go to all this trouble contacting Richmond, making them mount a whole surveillance operation . . ."

The deputy chief let a couple of seconds of silence speak for themselves. He didn't have to spell out the consequences for Horgas if Spencer was the wrong guy.

Horgas sucked in a breath. "It's him, Chief. You can go to the bank on it," Horgas declared, his voice heavy with resolve.

There was no answer at the homicide squad when Christiansen called Richmond late that afternoon. Everyone was out on a call.

A twenty-nine-year-old woman had been murdered in her apartment. She was strangled to death. Not only was she nude but her hands and feet had been bound. And a preliminary examination indicated she had been raped.

8

WHEN RAY AND GLENN WILLIAMS WALKED INTO THE THIRD-FLOOR apartment of twenty-nine-year-old Rena Chapouris on the morning of January 6, 1988, both—despite everything they'd seen—were overcome with despair at the sight splayed out before them. The partially clothed, dark-haired woman was faceup on her blood-spattered double bed. The arms of a pink sweater were wrapped tightly around her neck and, like Dr. Hellams, she was nude below the waist. Her hands had been bound behind her with a section of venetian blind cord. Another length of the cord had been tied around one ankle. Unlike the other victims, however, Chapouris had been repeatedly beaten across the forehead with a blackjack that now lay on a bedside table.

Subsequent background interviews revealed other disturbing similarities. Chapouris worked as a lab technician in the Department of Neurosurgery at the Medical College of Virginia—the same department in which Dr. Hellams had worked. She also held a part-time job as a waitress at O'Toole's, a South Side bar frequented by Hellams and Debbie Davis.

If she was killed by the Strangler, though, her death indicated a disturbing change in the killer's pattern. The killer had now resorted to viciously beating his victim. Also, the location of Chapouris's apartment indicated he was on the move. Chapouris was not a South Side resident. She lived across the James River in the fashionable Fan district on Richmond's west side.

Within several hours of finding the body Richmond police were called to a suicide, a man named Michael St. Claire. St. Claire, the detectives quickly discovered, dated Chapouris's sister and once rented a room from the victim. Several months earlier Chapouris had evicted St. Claire from the apartment. Crime scene techs found spattered blood on St. Claire's sweatshirt, Rena Chapouris's blood. Later in the day they discovered fibers from that very same sweatshirt on Chapouris's body. Before the day was out the Williams boys had concluded it was a classic copycat killing. St. Claire had strangled Chapouris and then beat her with the blackjack after she was dead.

Glenn Williams was still reeling from the shock of Chapouris's copycat murder when he received the late-night phone call from Horgas.

"I've located your killer," Joe boasted.

"Bullshit," Glenn retorted. "Bullshit!"

"It's not bullshit and I'll tell you all about it tomorrow morning."

"What do you mean?" Glenn was puzzled.

"We need to coordinate surveillance," Joe said. "My deputy chief called down earlier to speak to your people. It's already been approved. I'm even buying you guys lunch!"

"Where is this guy? How'd you locate him?"

"He's right down there with you. Lives in some kind of halfway house," Horgas said.

Late the next morning, January 7, Horgas and Hill met the Williams boys and Lieutenant Robert Childress at the Fredericksburg Holiday Inn, located halfway between Arlington and Richmond. Joe's last meeting with them was painfully fresh in his mind as he strolled toward their table in the hotel's restaurant. He could still see their bored faces, listening to his dog and pony show on that snowy New Year's Eve in Arlington, absolutely ho-hum positive he was wrong.

He remembered being in the third-floor conference room and telling them they had to look for somebody who was arrested about January 25, 1984, and then released sometime around the beginning of September of 1987.

"First, how could you have a commuting serial killer?" Childress had interjected. "How could he kill in Arlington and live in Richmond?"

"Well you're down in Richmond," Joe had said defensively, from his easel. "I don't know what kind of halfway houses you have down here, but it'd be a good idea to check them out." The FBI had given Joe this advice several days earlier.

"I had no idea at the time that Spencer was actually going to be in a halfway house in Richmond," Horgas later said. "I was just following what the FBI told me. But my advice to them went bang!"

Now, walking toward them in the restaurant, Horgas knew the New Year's Eve meeting had changed nothing. They had still thought he was full of it. But that didn't matter now. He didn't have to convince them of a thing. He had his man, Spencer, and they had orders to watch him.

The Richmond contingent listened in stunned silence as Joe confidently explained how and why he had targeted Timmy Spencer. In broad strokes, he reminded them of his theory and then handed around the halfway house furlough records, which demonstrated Spencer's availability to commit each crime.

Though it did not look like the Richmond detectives had any resistance to going ahead with the surveillance, they were clearly dumbfounded by Horgas's disclosure. Sure, Spencer had been available on those nights and was only one mile from Hellams's house, two miles from Davis's. Yet Spencer was black, and the man they were looking for was white. Not only had they had been told this by the FBI but a prominent forensic psychiatrist, Dr. Park Dietz, told the local media that the killer was white.

During the course of the South Side Strangler investigation,

Dietz, a nationally known expert on sexual homicides, a respected professor at the University of Virginia and a consultant to the FBI's Behavioral Science Unit (Dietz had *not* been retained by the FBI on the Strangler case), had told the *Richmond News Leader* on October 7, 1987, "Absolutely [the killer is a man]. And he is white. It's extremely rare to find a black sexual sadist. And in those cases they don't cross racial lines." He had also aired his views on a local television newscast.

But the real topper was Horgas's explanation of how he came up with Spencer's name. It was as if he'd pulled it out of the air. And the Richmond detectives were not the only ones who had difficulty with this.

Deputy Chief Christiansen had given permission for Joe to go forward with the surveillance plan but did not authorize him to arrest Spencer. Both he and recently elected Commonwealth Attorney Helen Fahey believed that there was insufficient probable cause for that. Also, Christiansen hated the tension that was growing between Horgas and Carrig, tension that started almost as soon as Joe began reviewing the Hamm file and putting around his theory that the man who killed Carolyn Hamm—the masked rapist—had never been caught. Christiansen remembered the morning of December 30, the morning after Horgas's long meeting with Ray and Mardigian. Horgas had walked into the squad room and announced to one of his fellow detectives, "The FBI was up here last night. They told me I was right. Vasquez was innocent. Carrig got the wrong guy." Carrig had not been in the room at the time, but word traveled fast in the eight-man squad. He was livid when he heard Joe's accusation, but he refused to confront him.

Christiansen sighed. Still, catching the killer was more important. He had to give Horgas's theory every possible chance.

It was compelling, Joe's theory. But it was basically a tour de force of deductive reasoning. Joe had no eyewitnesses, no fingerprints, no physical proof. Not even for the rapes. In the rapes only cash had been taken, no property. The only way to link Spencer firmly to the murders was going to be through his blood. With a sample of his blood, Lifecodes could compare his DNA to that found in the semen at the crime scene. But this was not like the Colin Pitchfork case. They were not in England. Short of arresting him, the only way Joe could get Spencer's blood would be if Spencer voluntarily gave a sample. And that was not a likely scenario. Even if Horgas managed to get Spencer's blood, analysis would take months. Lifecodes wouldn't even be finished with the crime scene samples for weeks. And what was going to stop Timothy Spencer from snuffing out more women in the meantime—if he *was* the killer?

That was why Commonwealth Attorney Helen Fahey and the others had been willing to mount the surveillance, Horgas knew. If he was right about its being Spencer and they didn't stop him from striking again, no explanation would ever satisfy the public as to why this demon hadn't been taken off the streets. There would be hell to pay if they let him take out another woman.

Richmond went along willingly with tailing Spencer. It made sense. And it was a smart precaution in case Horgas might be right.

Joe's immediate agenda, though, at the highway restaurant in Fredericksburg, was to coordinate surveillance for Spencer's visit to Arlington, which loomed menacingly on Saturday, January 9. They decided that two detectives would board the bus with Spencer in Richmond and that the bus would be tracked by plane and two unmarked cars. At the Fredericksburg stop, Arlington would pick up the tail.

He drove straight back from Fredericksburg and reported to the deputy chief. Christiansen immediately called together the tactical team to coordinate the surveillance in Arlington. Up to now the investigation had been him, alone, with little support for his hunches. Now that he had identified a suspect, everybody was in. Of course, he also knew that the stakes were now too high to permit him to make decisions on his own—especially with Spencer's impending visit to Arlington. Still, support was support. He'd take it.

Horgas's last meeting that day, Thursday, and his first meeting Friday morning were with Helen Fahey. In routine felonies the detectives obtain arrest warrants on their own, but in ongoing, major felony investigations—like Tucker— the police go through the Commonwealth Attorney.

At that Friday morning meeting, January 8, they covered the minute-by-minute plan to track Spencer upon his arrival in Arlington the next morning. Fahey was a diminutive woman with shoulder-length auburn hair. She listened patiently as a superior officer from the tactical squad explained that they would not apprehend Spencer *until* Spencer was halfway into the window of a home.

"So you're going to allow him to actually get halfway into some woman's house?" Fahey asked in a tone of staggering disbelief.

"Yes, ma'am. We'll be on him so closely that he won't get an inch further inside before he's stopped," the officer promised.

"Well, what if he's quicker than you?" she demanded. "What if he gets in there and kills somebody?"

"That's not really a concern of ours. We know he spends a long time with his victims before killing them." A defensive edge was creeping into the officer's voice.

"What happens if you're wrong? It is possible he could lose the surveillance team—isn't it?"

Horgas, listening, sat silent, his body feeling for the first time in that warp-speed day like it was made of stone. Fahey was probably right. Spencer had more than demonstrated his skill in avoiding those who were tracking him. He was like the king stag, slipping through the moonlit forest with only the faintest crackle of dry leaves, just twenty paces ahead, and then suddenly gone. Dead silence. No. Eluding the tactical squad was not outside the realm of Spencer's possibility.

"The longer we talked about the surveillance," Fahey later said, "the more I realized that it was not like television. You can't watch anyone twenty-four hours a day. You can sort of keep track of someone, but there's no way you can say . . . he will not be able to lose us and commit another murder. And if he came up to Arlington, who were we going to have trailing him down in Green Valley? A whole bunch of white cops hiding around the bushes? The surveillance as a means of protecting the community was really of very, very limited value."

Fahey's concern about the surveillance went beyond the work. It was personal. She was a single professional woman about the same age as Tucker. She had even lived in the Fairlington complex up until September of 1987 in the same type of town home as Susan Tucker. Fahey had toured the crime scene with Horgas several days after the body was discovered. She remembered now the eerie feeling she had had, seeing her own rooms with different furniture, different decor, and a woman much like herself murdered. She pushed those disturbing images out of her mind and focused on Horgas and the tact squad officer outlining their plan. Damn. There just was not enough evidence to arrest him.

Joe felt he had enough evidence for probable cause. He knew, moreover, that the surveillance could be a dangerous waste of time. As he had been trying to do for the past month, Horgas would have to convince Helen Fahey he was right.

Then, all of a sudden, late Friday afternoon, a Richmond intelligence officer called Horgas. Because of a huge snowstorm, Spencer was not coming up to Arlington the next morning. An audible sigh of relief coursed through the conference room as Joe broke the news.

That day, though, Saturday, was not without surprises. Around three that afternoon Joe's home phone rang.

"We stopped your man a few hours ago." It was the raspy, two-pack-a-day voice of Ray Williams.

"What! Why?" Horgas exploded. "What the fuck happened?"

Williams calmly explained that the surveillance team followed Spencer and five of his friends to the Cloverleaf Mall. The detectives observed two of the women shoplift several items from a department store and then arrested them as they got into a green 1979 Chevrolet Impala. The car belonged to one of the women, but the driver was none other than Timothy Spencer.

"You sure he was the one behind the wheel?" Horgas probed.

"No doubt about it. One of 'em had a record, too," Williams added. "So we could have arrested Spencer for a parole violation for consorting with known lawbreakers. But we let him go. He told us some bullshit that he was married to one of the boosters. Spencer ain't married, is he?"

"No," said Joe. "The woman is probably his girlfriend. But it definitely looks like he's got wheels—and that's a real problem. He can go anywhere he wants. He doesn't need a bus now. Anything else? You guys didn't interrogate him or nothing, did you?" His exasperation was obvious.

"No. But our men did observe Spencer do something pretty weird. After the unit pulled away, a backup surveillance unit noticed that he got under the car and crawled from one end to the other and back. There was at least three inches of snow on the ground and here he is crawling on his back under the chassis."

"What the hell was he doing?"

"It seemed like he was checking it for bugs or something. Maybe he thought we planted something when we were checking the car."

"Shit!" Joe yelled, slamming down the phone when they were finished. Why did they have to stop him for such a meaningless reason! He'd be on to them. He'd flee. Still, Horgas had to admit, the incident had produced some critical information. It proved he knew the Cloverleaf Mall.

Most of the victims had been preselected, the FBI thought. Followed for perhaps days prior to the homicide. And Cloverleaf Mall was an ideal place to troll for targets. Debbie Davis had worked part-time at Waldenbooks; Susan Hellams had shopped at the mall; Diane Cho had lived directly across the street. And also Horgas had learned—and this was infinitely more disturbing—that Spencer had access to a car.

At least he knew the killer's identity and where he lived—Timmy Spencer, in a halfway house on Porter Street in Richmond. Finally, Joe didn't have to worry anymore about protecting Teresa and David. The last week had been awful.

"Joe was paranoid," Detective Steve Carter said later. "He was possessed about getting this guy off the street. He'd go home four, sometimes five times a day to check up on Teresa and the boy." Joe knew that when Spencer came anywhere near Arlington, his department would be watching his every move. Joe would make sure of that.

Of course, there was still the problem of David Vasquez.

Now that he had found Spencer, Horgas knew beyond a shadow of a doubt that Vasquez was innocent. It was a subject he now felt compelled to raise in his frequent meetings with Deputy Chief Christiansen.

"It's a hell of an injustice that Vasquez is behind bars when I know this guy Spencer killed Hamm," Horgas had declared a few days before.

"Listen, Joe, your goal is to arrest this guy, then prosecute him," Christiansen responded testily. "David Vasquez can wait." David Vasquez might have to wait for a long time, though, Joe thought, fuming, because prospects for the immediate arrest of Timothy Spencer seemed to be getting dimmer each day.

It was after the identification of Spencer that Horgas began to feel he was losing control of the investigation. His superiors would not let him go to Richmond to gather intelligence or assist in the surveillance. Short of monitoring Spencer when he came to Arlington, Horgas would have to leave all the critical next steps to Richmond. And he knew the Williams boys did not really have their heart in the surveillance.

Joe became unbearably anxious. In the days after they pulled Spencer over at Cloverleaf Mall, Horgas called Williams three times a day for updates. By the morning of January 13, one week after Spencer was identified, Horgas could tell that Ray Williams and his colleagues were getting very impatient.

"He hasn't done anything to really excite us," Ray complained.

"What do you mean? What's he been doing?" Horgas shot back, doing his best to control his anger.

"[He leaves the facility and] gets into a car with three other people." Ray sighed. "He takes a bag with him and they drive to a house up on Church Hill. That's where the projects are. He goes in there and stays the whole damned night. We been with him twenty-four hours a day. We even had the plane on his ass. Everything."

Of course he's not going to do anything out of the ordinary! Horgas thought. After being stopped at the mall he's going to be very careful. But Williams had a different perspective.

Williams made it very clear that Spencer had done absolutely nothing to indicate he was a serial killer. They had expected him to be walking the streets scouting out potential victims, but he never did that or anything even remotely similar. At the end of the conversation, Williams lowered the boom. He informed Horgas that because the surveillance consumed significant manpower he and his superiors were discussing how long they could maintain the effort.

"You've got to put your manpower and your resources where you feel they are most important," Williams said. With a frightening lurch Horgas knew that the surveillance effort would now be short-lived.

Then Friday, January 15, Williams informed Horgas that his department had reached the conclusion that Spencer was not a good suspect. Spencer did not justify the manpower of such an intensive surveillance effort, Ray explained. The department felt that their time would be better spent watching other people. Williams reiterated that Spencer wasn't doing what they thought he should be doing. No prowling the streets looking for targets. No peeping. Spencer was acting completely normal. The surveillance would be removed within the next couple of days.

Of course he's not doing anything out of the ordinary, Horgas thought. After the Cloverleaf stop, Spencer undoubtedly knew he was being followed. He was too smart even to jaywalk, let alone peep in a window. It would take Spencer only a few days to realize the surveillance had been taken off him and then he'd do it again. There will be another victim, Joe thought with terrible clarity.

A somber-faced Horgas dashed straight to the third-floor conference room and relayed Williams's message to the department brass and the Commonwealth Attorney.

Helen Fahey was deeply affected. Her distress was palpable to everyone in the room.

"How would it look? We take the surveillance off and he kills someone." Helen peered intently at each of the men seated at the oblong table. No one responded.

Then the meeting turned to a subject the group had been hashing out. How could they get Spencer's blood to compare it to the semen found at the scene? The answer was the same.

"There is no legal way short of arresting him to get his blood and there's no way in my opinion that we can arrest him because we have no probable cause," Helen said firmly.

Horgas clenched his jaw again.

"What about parole revocation?" asked Hawkins. "We can get his parole officer to yank him in and get a blood sample."

"We can't. There's no basis for it. He hasn't done anything. Just like we can't pull his prison medical records." Despite Spencer's criminal record, he still had a constitutional right against a warrantless search and seizure.

Another detective raised the possibility of having Arlington police chief "Smokey" Stover call Richmond's chief and simply request that the surveillance be continued. Helen offered her concern that Richmond might respond by stopping Spencer and asking him for his blood, a practice they had been doing with other suspects since October. Fahey felt that the practice was illegal. If Spencer was the right suspect, Richmond could blow the case out of the water by doing that.

"Well, you all know how I feel," interjected Joe. "Absolutely, Spencer's the right guy. If it was up to me, I'd go right downstairs to the magistrate, get a warrant, and go get him."

There was an uncomfortable silence. Horgas continued: "And the longer we talk about this, the more likely Spencer is going to kill someone else."

Another long moment, and now everyone shifted in their seats.

"Joe, I think we all feel you have a solid theory, but it seems like you got the name out of thin air. It's sound," Helen continued, "but it would never be admitted in court. If we arrested him, he confessed, and later some judge decides that there wasn't probable cause—you know."

Fahey knew, however, that something had to be done. It was a race against the clock until Monday, when Richmond would be pulling the surveillance. While Joe's scenario wasn't sufficient for an arrest warrant, it would probably convince a magistrate to issue a search warrant, to obtain Spencer's blood. Then, she hoped, the DNA analysis would yield evidence for an arrest warrant. She realized it was equally possible that DNA could also eliminate Spencer.

Horgas left the office immediately after meeting with Fahey and his superiors. He shook his head in frustration as he pulled out of the parking lot. Now there would finally be some real movement against Spencer, he thought to himself, but they still don't completely believe my theory. As he entered his driveway a few minutes later, he did his best to push all thoughts of Spencer and the investigation out of his mind. This was Friday night and he had a long-standing engagement to take David and Teresa out to dinner.

On Saturday morning at 10 A.M. Horgas was hunkered down in the third-floor conference room writing the search warrant. Helen poked her nose through the door.

"How ya doing?" Helen asked, her arms brimming with file folders.

"All right, I think I can have the search warrant written by noon. What are you doing here?"

"We're getting ready for the grand jury. They convene on Wednesday morning."

Horgas's eyes lit up.

He saw the opportunity for an end run.

"Grand jury, huh? I know you had problems with me going to the magistrate for a warrant, but if a grand jury found probable cause and indicted Spencer—wouldn't that solve your problem?"

She stopped to think. It was a novel suggestion. The grand jury decides if there is probable cause to indict an individual. And their decision, unlike that of a magistrate, is almost immune from later challenge.

Helen couldn't help but be moved by his passionate, brimming concern to catch this guy. She put the folders on the table, sat down, and over the next few hours went point by point over how he could approach the grand jury. The more they talked, the more Helen became persuaded by the idea.

Seven Arlington County citizens sitting as grand jurors could decide whether there was sufficient evidence to arrest Spencer. Helen left the meeting telling Joe she would give him her final answer on Monday morning.

Horgas arrived at 7 A.M. on Monday the eighteenth for the first of several meetings with his superior officers. Everyone had expected Horgas to discuss the search warrant he had written over the weekend.

"Joe, you know they're pulling the surveillance today," Christiansen said, removing his glasses, his face showing the strain. "When are you planning to get the search warrant? We need to move fast."

"Well, Chief, I spoke to Helen on Saturday. I don't know about the search warrant now. Helen is thinking about letting me go into the grand jury day after tomorrow."

"What the hell are you talking about?" Christiansen was flabbergasted. "She said there wasn't sufficient probable cause."

"All I know is that she's gonna tell me this morning what she wants to do," Joe said matter-of-factly. No reason to let the deputy chief know it had been his idea to go to the grand jury.

Twenty minutes later Helen Fahey opened the conference room door and walked to the head of the table. Conversation halted.

"On Wednesday, January twentieth, at ten A.M., Joe Horgas is going into the grand jury and make his case for why Timothy Spencer should be indicted for burglary, rape, and capital murder," she announced. "Like many of you, I have been concerned about whether we have sufficient probable cause. However, considering the crisis we now face, this is our best alternative. If Horgas gets the indictment, we'll take Spencer's blood and then find out if Spencer is our man."

A slow smile crawled up the sides of Joe Horgas's jowly cheeks.

Close! He was close. If the grand jury returned the indictment, Horgas planned on arresting Spencer that very same day. Joe was not immediately concerned that Spencer would kill before Wednesday. He counted on the probability that Spencer knew he was being watched. And he counted on its taking Spencer several days to realize the surveillance had been pulled.

And when he did bag Spencer, what about interviewing him? Joe was a skilled interrogator. Several Arlington defense attorneys had nicknamed him Joe "Confession" Horgas. Joe felt sure Spencer would deliver the goods within a few short hours of his arrest.

On Tuesday morning Horgas and Hill drove down I-95 to Quantico to meet with the "miracle workers," as Horgas had recently dubbed them. Steve Mardigian and Jud Ray had led him to Spencer. Now they were going to show him how to get Spencer to confess—providing, of course, that the grand jury gave Joe the ability to bring Spencer in.

"Be very patient with him," Mardigian said lighting his second cigar that morning. "Looking back at his nineteen eighty-four arrest, you can see he willingly talked to the police about the burglary. In fact, he would have told them almost anything, as long as they didn't ask him about the Hamm homicide or any of the rapes. He's probably thrilled to tell them about the burglary because he knew it was small compared to the biggie. Our thought is he just might do the same thing this time—that's why we're advising you to begin with the burglary. Don't tell him about the other warrants for rape and murder. Maybe he'll give up the burglary and that'll give you a great way to get in on the other charges." Mardigian paused to let his words sink in. "But regardless of what you do," he said, puffing his cigar, "don't expect him to confess. These serial killers seldom confess, but if he will, this is the way to do it."

"To pull this off, Joe, you have to get a separate indictment and bench warrant for burglary and murder," Ray interjected. "If he knows he's being arrested for murder, then there's no way he's going to talk. Hold back on telling him about the murder and rape. Maybe he'll let his guard down and you'll get something."

"And another thing," Mardigian concluded. "Be nice to him. Let him talk."

Joe slept very little on Tuesday night. All he could think about was the next day, which would go at breakneck speed. In a few short hours Timothy Spencer would be his. Though Helen Fahey and his superior officers steadfastly believed that a DNA match was critical to a conviction, Horgas allowed himself the confidence that the case would be over before Spencer even gave Joe a blood sample. Timothy Spencer was going to confess to the murder of Susan Tucker before midnight tonight. They'd see he'd been right.

Wearing his favorite gray suit and maroon sweater vest, Joe exuded certainty when he entered the grand jury room at 10 A.M. Wednesday morning. He laid out his theory as he had done for his task force, the FBI, Richmond, and Helen Fahey. A half hour later the foreman returned "true bills" on murder, rape, and burglary.

It was a simple one-paragraph statement but one Joe had been dreaming of since that cold, rainy December evening when he had first seen Susan Tucker's body.

IN THE CIRCUIT COURT OF ARLINGTON COUNTY
January 20, 1988

The Grand Jury charges that:

On or about the 27th day of November, 1987 in the County of Arlington, TIMOTHY WILSON SPENCER did either break and enter or enter without breaking in, in the nighttime, the dwelling of Susan Tucker located at 4801 South 27th Road, Arlington, Virginia.

Horgas clutched the document and raced upstairs to the chambers of Senior Judge William Winston. Winston was the same judge who had sentenced David Vasquez. He read the indictment and then signed an arrest warrant for Timothy Spencer.

Horgas exited his chambers, breathless. He rushed back to his office to perform his last task before leaving the building.

"Williams, it's me, Horgas."

"Hey, what's going on?"

"I'm coming down there in about three hours."

"Why the hell for?" Ray asked.

"I was just in before the grand jury this morning. They indicted Spencer in the death of Tucker. I'm coming down to arrest him and bring him back here."

There was a moment of stunned silence on the other end.

"You're shittin' me," Williams said finally. "How'd you get an indictment?"

"I just went in and gave 'em my theory." Of course he's flabbergasted, Horgas thought. They didn't even think there was enough reason to continue the surveillance and now I have an indictment.

Williams contained his astonishment and told Horgas he'd meet him at police headquarters to coordinate the arrest. Williams also agreed to maintain the surveillance until the arrest was completed.

Horgas and Hill had to make one more stop before jumping on I-95 for the drive down to Richmond. They had to visit Timothy Spencer's home.

Prior to his 1984 arrest Spencer lived with his mother and his younger half-brother, Travis, in one-half of a two-family brick home. Spencer's grandmother lived on the other side. The house, which Horgas had driven past numerous times in the last three weeks, was located at the end of a cul-de-sac just off Four Mile Run. It was just down the hill from where the first rape had occurred in the summer of 1983. Susan Tucker's home was about a ten-minute walk across Walter Reed Drive.

Mrs. Spencer, a fifty-year-old woman with large tired eyes, sat on the living room couch patiently listening to Horgas. Her mother sat next to her. It was obvious to Joe that she had had conversations like this before. She nodded slowly as Horgas explained he was investigating an area burglary that had been committed over the Thanksgiving holiday. Someone had seen Timmy in the vicinity of the break-in and now Joe wanted permission to look around the house. He had no search warrant but if he saw no stolen items, then it would help exclude Timmy as a suspect.

Mrs. Spencer could have slammed the door in Horgas's

face, or demanded he come back with search warrant. But she was open and cooperative.

"I can't remember if Timmy was here for Thanksgiving but I'm sure he was here on Christmas," she said assuredly.

"I know he was here back then because he gave me some glassware as a present along with the receipt for its purchase." She paused for a moment, gazing soberly at Horgas. "I don't accept presents from him anymore unless he gives me a receipt."

Horgas was moved by her forthrightness. It had to have been difficult to discuss her son in such tragic, telling terms.

Horgas knew he was taking a serious chance coming to the house, because Mrs. Spencer might call her son as soon as Joe left. Though Horgas had called Hospitality House before going into the home to make sure that Timothy was working, there was the very real possibility that Mrs. Spencer would call her son at work. The risk was worth taking. Horgas felt there was a chance Tucker had been bound with newly purchased rope. Perhaps the remaining spool was somewhere in the house, along with tape, a cloth mask, or a knife. If he found any of these items, they would give him immense leverage during the interrogation.

After a twenty-minute discussion in the modestly decorated living room, Mrs. Spencer gave Joe and Mike permission to search both houses.

They searched the house for half an hour.

"The only thing we found was a roll of duct tape, which only mildly looked like the stuff that had been used on Cho," Horgas later said. "Other than that, zip."

Horgas and Hill were accompanied to Richmond by Detective Steve Carter and tactical squad sergeant Henry Trumble. Following the arrest, Horgas and Trumble would take Spencer back to Arlington while Hill and Carter would search his room and do follow-up interviews with other members of Hospitality House as well as Spencer's girlfriend.

A light rain began to fall as they made their way down I-95 through the dark brown, lifeless January landscape. Horgas was uncharacteristically quiet. He pondered every detail of what he was going to say and do after he had Spencer in custody. His concentration was momentarily interrupted as they drove past the Quantico exit. He smiled and quickly saluted his miracle workers, in the direction of the FBI headquarters.

When Horgas and his entourage walked in to see the Richmond homicide squad at about 5 P.M., an uncomfortable silence fell over the room. The Williams brothers were cordial, and offered their guests the usual high-octane coffee. Still, it was obvious that the detectives, especially Ray Williams, were not very happy to see Horgas.

Arresting Spencer in their jurisdiction was the ultimate slap in the face. Richmond had perfunctorily dismissed Horgas's theory from the start. Now the burly detective was in *their* office with an arrest warrant. To exacerbate the wound, the court order Joe held in his dense fist required Richmond to assist him in the actual arrest. And then—the inevitable avalanche of questions and criticisms the arrest would generate to feed the hungry local press.

"So when are we going over there?" Horgas wanted to know. He had been in the squad room for less than five minutes.

"Relax, Horgas," Ray said lighting a cigarette. "We've been following this guy for two weeks. We know his schedule. We got information that he's returning from work at six P.M. to attend some kind of meeting."

"Why do we have to wait till then? Let's get him now!"

"We're gonna wait, Joe. That's it," Ray said.

Horgas couldn't be held down. "You guys know it's him, don't you?" he shot at Ray gloatingly. "I told you three weeks ago it was him. Remember?"

Ray and Glenn ignored the remark. They just kept shaking their heads in disbelief.

"You know, I'm not too sure you guys really know where he is or we would have arrested him as soon as we got down here," Horgas taunted.

"Bullshit," Ray retorted. "We told you we know where he is. If it'll make you happy, I'll call up there just to find out."

After briefly speaking with Spencer's counselor Ray said, "Just as I told you. He's gonna be back at six P.M. There's some group therapy he's gotta attend. We'll go up at five-thirty."

Horgas felt each minute of the next half hour drag by agonizingly. At 5:25 he could finally stand up. He announced, "Let's do it!"

Joe drove with Glenn Williams. They were followed by a long procession of unmarked detective cars.

They crossed over the James River into South Side by way of the Robert E. Lee Bridge. The halfway house was located in a predominantly black, low-income neighborhood just over the bridge. Porter Street was only a twenty-minute walk across Semmes Avenue to Hellams's home on Thirty-first Street and from there, another fifteen minutes to Debbie Davis's apartment.

Williams and Horgas made a left on Porter, a street lined with dilapidated two-story frame homes. They pulled up to the curb about a hundred feet from the halfway house. Glenn Williams and Hill parked just past the halfway house on the opposite side of the street.

Horgas anxiously looked at his watch.

5:45. He'll be here in fifteen minutes, he thought.

5:47. "Let's just you and me take a drive past the house. I wanta see what's going on," Joe insisted. Glenn nodded and slowly pulled away from the curb.

When they got within ten yards of the three-story dilapidated brick house, Joe saw a thin black man about twenty-five years of age get out of a brown Chevy that had just pulled over to the curb. In a momentary mental flash Joe remembered the rape victims' descriptions of their assailant. He envisioned the wiry young man wearing a homemade mask.

"That's him. That's him. That's Spencer," Joe cried. Williams yanked the mike from its cradle. "Suspect has arrived. Suspect has arrived. Everyone move."

Williams slammed on his brakes in front of the halfway house. Seven other cars screeched up closing off the street and the adjoining alley; one cut off the brown Chevy's exit.

Horgas's large body flew out of the passenger door and up the creaky wooden steps. He reached out and grabbed Spencer's left shoulder just as Spencer slipped into the vestibule.

"Timothy Wilson Spencer, I'm Detective Horgas from Arlington. I have a burglary warrant for your arrest."

Spencer turned with a dazed look on his face. He didn't try to run or resist in any way at all. As Horgas fixed the handcuffs around Spencer's slender wrists, he was surprised at the young man's build. Horgas had expected the killer to have a powerfully developed upper body; Spencer, however, had a slight frame and appeared to weigh no more than 140 pounds. Horgas was also struck by this Spencer's seemingly calm demeanor. Horgas had never arrested a serial killer. Nevertheless, he had anticipated seeing evil or anger in Spencer's eyes, something that would hint at the horror within.

But no, Horgas only saw a meek, compliant, astonished young man.

After Horgas showed Spencer the warrant, the young man with short-cropped hair and a pencil-thin mustache asked, "How much is my bond?"

"Three hundred fifty thousand," Joe said.

"Three hundred fifty thousand for a burglary?" Spencer said incredulously. It was not his first burglary arrest. And he had never had a bond even a quarter this amount.

"Jeez, I don't why it's so high." Joe was playing dumb. "Judge just looked over the case and set the bond. That's all I know."

"You sure this is a burglary? Why all the cops if it's just a B and E?" Spencer asked suspiciously.

"I really don't know. I'm just here with a couple of guys. When we leave the jurisdiction, rules say we gotta bring two cars," Joe lied. He wanted to do everything possible to dissuade Spencer from thinking the arrest had anything to do with the murders or rapes.

"Man, with that bond I ain't coming back soon. Can I take my stuff with me?"

"Where is it?"

"Up in my room."

"OK!" Horgas agreed instantly to this welcome surprise. The arrest warrant gave Horgas the right only to search Spencer's person. By requesting to go to his room, Spencer had in essence given Horgas permission to search all areas of

Spencer's room. And if any of Spencer's "stuff" proved to be evidence from the crime scene, Horgas had the right to confiscate it as evidence. To be sure that Spencer understood Horgas's intentions, Horgas asked Spencer to sign a "Permission for Search" form. Spencer willingly complied. Another lucky stroke.

Spencer shared his second-floor room with another man. Like the rest of the house, the room was dilapidated, with peeling paint and a well-worn wooden floor. The walls were adorned with those posters one finds in service station garages: scantily clad young women promoting automobile products.

Spencer watched calmly as Horgas dumped his meager worldly possessions into a large trash bag. Much to Joe's chagrin, nothing stood out as being connected to any of the crime scenes. There were no trophies, no items taken by the killer to remind him of the victim, but Horgas noticed several highly suspicious articles. The two screwdrivers, one a foot long, were not used for chores around the halfway house but rather were tools commonly used to break into homes. It did not escape Horgas's memory that at the time Spencer was arrested in 1984, a screwdriver was found in his jacket pocket. Spencer explained that the folding five-inch buck knife they found in his pocket and the smaller pocketknife were used for protection; he had no explanation, however, for the box of .25 caliber bullets found in his dresser—a clear violation of halfway house rules, to say nothing of his parole. Possession of a ski cap and a pair of gloves would normally be considered appropriate winter attire but they took on an ominous meaning for Joe. In his mind Horgas saw the beige knit hat with eye slits cut out, pulled down over Spencer's face, the black-leather-gloved hands busily constructing an ornate noose.

Before leaving the room Horgas decided to search one more place. He lifted the mattress on Spencer's bed and all he saw was the bare metal box spring. But on the underside of the mattress there was a crudely drawn insignia he had seen once before—an infinity sign or the number eight lying sideways.

Joe waved to Glenn to join him. "Hey, Glenn," he whispered, not wanting Spencer to hear, "isn't this like that sign that Chesterfield found on that Korean girl's thigh?"

Glenn bent down to examine the mattress.

"Jesus. Seems like it. The one on Cho was drawn in nail polish. I can't tell what this was drawn with." Glenn looked a little perplexed.

"You draw this?" Joe said to Spencer.

"Never saw it before," Spencer responded nonchalantly.

No one knew what to make of the figure at the time Cho's body was found, and its significance now was equally unclear. The only clue Horgas had was that Spencer lived in room number eight.

According to their plan, Hill and Carter remained in Richmond to interview Spencer's counselors and roommates; Horgas and Trumble took Spencer back to Arlington.

From the moment Trumble pulled out of Porter Street and traveled over the Seventh Street bridge to I-95, Spencer was composed. And, unlike many seasoned criminals, he wasn't telling Horgas to fuck off. Quite the opposite: he willingly engaged in cordial conversation.

Horgas spent the first half hour trying to gain Spencer's confidence by discussing people he thought they both would know from Green Valley—petty crooks and drug dealers. Spencer did not bite.

Somewhere around Fredericksburg, Horgas turned to Spencer and said matter-of-factly, "When we get back to the PD I'd like to get a sample of your blood. Do you have any problem with that?"

Spencer smiled but did not respond. Several moments of silence went by and then Spencer turned to Horgas and said, "Does this have anything to do with a rape?"

"Rape? Why the fuck are you thinking about a rape?" Joe shot back excitedly. "Man, I told you, we're talking about a burglary here. Reason we want your blood is lots of times people cut themselves on broken glass breaking into a house."

"No, no, no, if you want my blood it's got to have something to do with a rape because I didn't cut myself going in

219

no house. I didn't cut myself on no fucking broken window," Spencer responded assuredly.

Trumble and Horgas exchanged knowing smiles through the rearview mirror. The brief interchange showed the first chink in Spencer's armor.

Spencer shifted uncomfortably and turned his gaze out the window.

"Where'd this burglary happen anyway?" he said staring at the darkened landscape.

"Fairlington," Joe said perfunctorily.

Spencer thought for a moment and looked at Horgas.

"Does this have anything to do with that murder?"

Horgas could taste the first bite of Spencer's confession. It took an immense effort to control his thrill.

"What murder? What do you know about a murder?" Joe volleyed, feigning confusion. "I'm just here to ask you about a burglary."

"Well, I'm from the area up there, I read the papers, I know what's going on," Spencer answered as if Horgas had asked a stupid question.

Susan Tucker's death was not reported by the Arlington media until *after* Spencer would have returned from his Thanksgiving pass. And it was only reported in Richmond after Horgas had made his first visit there on December 8, and even then not given much play in the press.

Horgas wanted to pursue the conversation but remembered the FBI's advice. Don't push Spencer on the murder. Get him talking about the burglary and then go to the murder. Spencer, however, was unwilling to discuss anything about a burglary. He kept pumping Horgas for more information on the homicides, but Horgas stuck strictly to the FBI's advice. It was a cat-and-mouse game that continued until Trumble pulled into the parking lot across from the Arlington police department at about 10 P.M.

Spencer was escorted past the third-floor conference room where his capture had been planned and into the interview room where, just a month earlier, Horgas had talked to eight victims of the masked rapist.

Over the years Horgas had developed an interrogation technique that had gained him the admiration of his squad. It was a twist on the age-old practice of offering the arrestee a cigarette to get on his good side. The first thing Horgas typically did after taking a seat at the interview table was ask his prisoner for a cigarette. Horgas believed the opening accomplished two crucial goals: it made the prisoner feel important and it laid the groundwork for the prisoner to give Horgas something else much more important—his confession.

The cigarette trick didn't work because Spencer didn't smoke. And even if he did smoke, Horgas felt it would have been unlikely that Spencer would have given him a cigarette. After all, he was not giving anything else up.

No amount of cajoling would work. As he had done in the car, Spencer refused to discuss the burglaries. Instead, he continued to pump Horgas for details about his arrest and how it related to the Arlington homicide. Abandoning the FBI's advice, Horgas tried a new tack.

"Listen, lemme tell you a little theory of mine," Horgas said, switching tactics. "After I finish tell me what you think."

"OK," said Spencer with a smile on his face and a glint in his eyes that said, This could be fun.

"Let's just suppose there was this woman who was murdered back in nineteen eighty-four. She's choked to death by a noose and all bound up. Now right before this lady was killed there was a bunch of rapes by this masked guy in the same neighborhood. The guy not only rapes these women, he also ties some of them up and takes their cash. Never anything but cash."

Spencer was on the edge of his seat, eager for more details.

"Now three years later four other women are found murdered, one in Arlington and three down in Richmond. And in Richmond, right in the same neighborhood where these women are murdered, a woman is raped by a masked black man who tries to tie her up."

Horgas paused to let his short speech sink in, then he made his next move.

"So you know what I think? I think the same guy who

raped those women back in eighty-three killed that woman in eighty-four and all the women in eighty-seven."

Spencer slowly nodded his head in agreement. "Yeah, yeah. I can see why you think it's the same guy," Spencer said supportively. It was as if he were another detective giving Horgas feedback. "And if it is the same guy, he's pretty slick. And he wasn't no dumb dude. If he took anything but cash it'd be traced back to him."

"But there's a problem," Joe said solemnly. "Back in '84 another guy who was not too swift admitted he killed that first woman. Now he's in Buckingham. That's a real bitch, huh? An innocent guy in jail."

Ignoring Horgas's remark, Spencer continued to pump Horgas. It was obvious there would be no appeals to his conscience.

"How many rapes were there again?" Spencer asked voyeuristically. Sensing Spencer's utter fascination with the rapes, Horgas gave him some general information but no details. Under no circumstances did he want a repeat of the Vasquez arrest. Perhaps this—and not the burglaries—was the way to get Spencer to discuss the murders. Maybe he'll start bragging about his crimes, Horgas thought, just like countless others who had sat in this very same chair had done over the years.

Spencer leaned forward, absorbed in the things Horgas told him. He was clearly enjoying it, relishing hearing about his handiwork. The irony of Spencer's intense interest was not lost on Horgas. In essence, Horgas had just laid out an abbreviated version of the theory he had been trying to sell over the past six weeks to his department and his counterparts in Richmond. Now his most avid listener was the killer himself. Much to Horgas's chagrin, however, he, not Spencer, was the one doing all the talking.

Finally, at 2 A.M. Horgas called it quits. Since Spencer seemed interested in talking, Horgas felt he would have at least one more opportunity to interview him prior to arraignment. Before going home Horgas asked Spencer one more question: would he submit a PERK kit and give a sample of his blood? Spencer willingly complied. Horgas was amazed.

Though the evening had convinced Horgas that Spencer was the killer, Spencer's easy consent to submit blood was cause for great concern.

As Joe drove home that night, he was preoccupied with why Spencer so easily gave evidence that could send him to his death. Joe's first thought was that since Spencer did not cut himself, he legitimately did not believe that the police had anything to tie him to the crime scene. Spencer probably did not know about DNA fingerprinting, but could he have also been so ignorant as to not know that his semen could be typed? Or maybe, if he was aware of blood typing, he knew that a match by itself was insufficient to convict him of the murders. Or did Spencer willingly give a blood specimen because he knew he was innocent? Horgas dismissed this last option because it was simply unacceptable that he might have been wrong all this time.

At 8 A.M. the next morning, Horgas was sitting at a long black lab table with Deanne Dabbs. Spencer's PERK kit and two vials of his blood sat between two long racks of test tubes. He also had some of Spencer's clothing and personal effects.

"I know this is the guy," Joe said. "But I need these results as quick as you can get them to me. I'm interrogating this guy in the next day or so and I'd like to show him what I have."

Shaking her head in dismay, Dabbs looked out among a sea of blood samples, swatches of clothing, and other items waiting to be analyzed. "I can't promise anything, Joe, but let me see what I can do."

Horgas spent the remainder of the day tracking down Spencer's employers and the places he had worked since his release the previous September. Despite Spencer's obvious savvy, perhaps he had given some hint of his crimes to a coworker or friend. But Horgas could not give these tasks his undivided attention. He was simply too anxious about the outcome of the blood typing. In fact, Horgas was so preoccupied, he was not even bothered by an article in the late edition of the *Richmond News Leader*. The page one story was headlined, CONVICT IS ARRESTED HERE IN ARLINGTON STRANGULA-

TION. After giving the details of Spencer's arrest, the reporter wrote,

Joseph Weaver, director of the halfway house described Spencer as a . . . clean cut guy [who] never gave us any problems. He was one of our better behaved residents. He changed jobs a couple of times but kept on working. He was quiet. We had no problems with him.

Horgas was not surprised to see that Weaver's perspectives were also shared by the Richmond authorities:

Richmond Commonwealth Attorney Aubrey Davis Jr. declined today to discuss the Arlington case. "I'm the Commonwealth Attorney of Richmond, not Arlington. We had a murder arrest in Richmond last night. That's the only one I'm interested in," he said. Davis was referring to the unrelated arrest of a Richmond man in connection with the August 18 murder of a man in Fonticello Park. . . . Warren Von Shuch, an assistant Commonwealth's Attorney in Chesterfield said, "Chesterfield has not obtained warrants for [Spencer] and has no immediate plans to do so."

By Friday morning, it was all Horgas could do to stare at his brown desk phone. At 8:15 it rang. Horgas picked it up before the first ring was finished.

"Horgas!"

"It's Deanne. We've got first-level results."

"So quickly? Last time it took like a week. Are you sure you did it right?"

"Relax, Joe. I did it right. I spent all night preparing the samples." A wave of gratitude went through Joe. "Like I said before," she continued, "all we have is the first level. The rest will come later today. The blood type of semen samples recovered from Susan Tucker's nightgown, the blue sleeping bag, and her blanket were from an O secretor. Timothy Spencer is an O secretor.

"Holy shit, I was right."

"Now don't jump to any conclusions yet. We still need to wait for the other results. I'll call you later."

"When?"

"In a few hours. Joe, just relax."

Horgas leaned back in his chair and cast a confident stare around the busy room.

"Dabbs says he's an O secretor. Anyone want to bet ten bucks he's a PGM one or a PEP A one?" Horgas asked with a smile. He had no takers.

It was impossible for him to take Dabbs's advice and relax. He called her every hour until lunch.

"Joe, we're not gonna know anything for a few more hours. I told you, I'll *call* you," she said sternly. Horgas paced the squad room like an expectant father.

At 3:45 P.M. Deanne called.

"The Tucker samples broke down to an O secretor, PGM of one, PGM sub-type of plus one, and a Pep A of one. Only thirteen per cent of the population has blood with these characteristics and your Mr. Spencer is one of them. Congratulations, Detective. And by the way, the hair samples found on Tucker's body and in her sink have the same characteristics as the pubic hair samples you delivered to me yesterday."

Horgas had no words, simply a hearty laugh that echoed throughout the squad room. "Before I got the results I knew I had four aces," Horgas later reflected, "but when I got those blood results, it was like raking in the pot. I knew what I was holding all along and now everyone else did too."

At least one person did vehemently disagree with Joe: Spencer's mother. The day his blood came back, Thelma Spencer told a reporter: "They've got my child locked up for nothing. . . . Just because he had a burglary conviction doesn't mean that they can pin everything on him."

Although he was now flush with the success of the matching blood type, it was still not easy to wait until Sunday, January 24, to show Spencer his hand. It had been decided that Ray and Glenn Williams would come up from Richmond to observe this session. The look on their faces when they heard it and saw it was something Joe would relish almost as much as Spencer's confession itself.

Ray and Glenn arrived at 9 A.M. that Sunday, January 24. Spencer agreed to talk, despite his experience with cops. Another slight surprise, though Joe was getting used to Spencer's contradictions.

Horgas sat across from Spencer. Listening from an audio monitor in an adjoining room, Hill and the Williams boys could hear every word spoken by Spencer and Horgas. However, they could not see what Spencer saw: the absolute satisfaction on Joe's face.

Joe first read Spencer his rights. It was not the first time in his life that Spencer had been told he had the right to remain silent. Spending long hours over the years in similar interview rooms had taught him a valuable skill: how to talk for hours on end without giving up anything substantive but, in the process, discovering how much his captors knew.

"We got the results of your blood work back," Horgas said accusatorially.

"You did." Spencer appeared indifferent.

"Yeah." Joe beamed. "And I got a big question for you. Why'd you give it to me?"

"What you mean *why'd* I give it to you?" Spencer retorted, as if Horgas had asked a stupid question.

"Because I can't figure it out. The results told me you're an O secretor, PGM of one, a PGM subtype of plus one, and a PEP A of one—all of which is what we're looking for."

Spencer did not appear to appreciate what Horgas had just told him.

"And that typing fits in with what we got down at the crime scene," Horgas elaborated.

Spencer shook his head in disgust. "I knew I shoulda never done that."

"Well, you knew we would have gotten it sooner or later. Right?"

"Yeah," Spencer agreed. "That's right."

"Now, because this all matches up, I've got to make sure what put you there."

"Put me where?" Spencer asked as if he had no clue to what Horgas was talking about.

"At the crime scene. It's possible that you could have been

226

there and not be the man we're looking for. I got to rule out
the possibility that you had a girlfriend up here, you visited
her, and after you left somebody broke in and killed her.
That's what I gotta rule out."

"I don't know what the fuck you're talking about, man."
It was the first significant break in Spencer's otherwise
calm demeanor.

"You don't have no girlfriends up here then?"

"I do have a girlfriend up here."

"White or black?"

"Black."

"Well, that's not her because the one who was killed was
white."

"Ain't no goddamn way my blood is on no goddamn crime
scene!" Spencer shot back.

"You know that, huh?" Horgas asked skeptically.

"I know it," Spencer insisted. "Everybody in my family
know where I was at the whole Thanksgiving weekend."

"Well, they didn't know when we spoke to them," Horgas said.

"Well, they'll remember."

"I figure when you gave us your blood you knew that we'd
come back saying it was the right blood. You had to know
that. You gave us your hairs too, and they also matched."

Shrugging his shoulders, Spencer spat, "Well—that's
stupid!"

"So you never left your family that entire Thanksgiving
weekend?" Horgas asked.

"I went out with my two uncles to see a friend of
theirs. . . . The whole time I was in Arlington I was in the
eyes of my family. You can check it out."

"We will!"

Horgas was quickly losing patience. He tried turning up
the heat.

"What do you think we're checking your blood against?"

"I don't know."

"Well, we're not checking your blood against blood." He
watched his opponent carefully.

Spencer's face took on a perplexed look. "What are you checking it against then?"

"You thought you were so fucking slick," Horgas hissed. "You covered your fucking fingerprints up, you covered your face up. But you left your fucking sperm behind! And that's what we're checking it against!" Horgas smiled ear to ear.

"Is that so?" Spencer retorted.

"Yeah, that's so! Everybody slips up."

"Well, you ain't got my sperm," Spencer said confidently.

"Hey—you ever jack off?" Joe queried.

"No, never in my life!"

"Come on. Everyone jacks off. You know, you take a sex book into the bathroom and jack off. Everybody does it." Horgas thought he could draw Spencer out. Now I can see he's lying, Horgas thought, studying the young man's face. Because those were big, pure semen stains, and Spencer definitely masturbated over his victims. I can't believe that he's actually saying he's never done it! Especially considering he was in prison for the last four years.

"I never jack off," Spencer insisted again.

Ray and Glenn Williams, who had up until this point been riveted to the audio monitor, now snickered.

"What we have now ain't one hundred percent sure so we gotta send your blood up to New York for another test and that's gonna tell us one hundred percent."

"You must be leaving something out. You just can't say it's me because of some test."

"Oh yes we can," Joe said confidently. "One hundred per cent." Spencer cast his eyes down and shook his head in despair.

"Now I'm just trying to find out whether you have any fucking good in your heart at all because there's a man in prison for killing this first girl," Horgas continued. "I told you that the other day."

"You shouldn't have arrested him. You need to get him out if you put him there," Spencer said confidently.

"I didn't arrest him, someone else did. You're the man that killed that girl and you can clear that innocent man. And so I'm just waiting to find out if you have any good in your heart!'' Horgas roared. It was the first time since the interview began that he had lost his calm. "The shit is all gonna hit the fan! It's all gonna come out in court and that's gonna be your judgment day. . . . Are you religious at all?''

"Yeah.''

"You believe in God?'' Joe asked the man who he knew was a serial killer.

Spencer nodded.

"You read the Bible and the Gospel and all that kind of stuff. It says confess your sins, am I right?''

"I didn't do nothing wrong to confess,'' Spencer asserted.

"Your cooperation would be important. Let's say you're the fucking judge and some guy comes before you saying he didn't kill this woman.''

"I'm the judge?'' Spencer asked incredulously.

"Yeah, you're the fucking judge. You see that the evidence is overwhelming but this guy denied everything right up until he came into your courtroom. Right up to judgment day. What are you gonna do with that guy? Are you gonna be easy on him or hard on him?'' Horgas raised his voice even louder.

"I'll be easy on him because I know he didn't do it,'' Spencer answered respectfully.

"What if you knew he did it and the evidence was overwhelming that it couldn't have been anyone else?''

"I'll still be easy on him. I'll believe him,'' Spencer answered, demonstrating his skill for handling detectives.

"OK,'' Joe conceded. "Then compare it to a guy who says he's guilty and admits that he knows there's an innocent man in prison for one of his crimes. Which one are you going to be easier on?''

"I don't care who the fuck is in jail,'' Spencer replied angrily.

"I know you don't because that's how I got you labeled— a real hard-ass, a real hardened criminal,'' Horgas bellowed.

Spencer didn't respond; he just shook his head and smiled.

"You don't give a fuck about nobody but you,'' Horgas continued, disgusted by Spencer's last remark. "You're a criminal and you probably deserve every fucking thing coming to you."

"You're wrong 'cause when this New York shit comes back you'll see," Spencer maintained.

"You know, I can understand you not wanting to tell me you did this or you did that because you think it'll send you to the penitentiary. I can understand that. But I think there's more to this."

"Yeah? What's that?"

"It's that you can't stand the fact that your mother's gonna read about this in the paper. She's gonna know this and that about what you did."

"I ain't worried. She already knows."

"She don't know those girls died."

Spencer exploded. "I didn't kill no one!"

"Oh, yes, you did and you're worried about what everybody's thinking about you!"

"Yeah, you know about me," Spencer said contemptuously. "What else do I think?"

"I don't know, but the time is gonna come when you have to make a big decision."

"I don't think so."

"You're living in a fantasy world! The test is gonna come back saying you're the guy. You know as well as I do that's gonna happen. You got a pair of fucking deuces and I got a full house and now you're trying to raise me. . . . I got your sperm!"

"No you don't," Spencer insisted. "You're wrong, wrong. I got nothing to hide."

"Oh, you got a lot to hide!"

"No I don't. What am I hiding?"

"There's a lot of stuff. Only you know. A lot."

"I didn't do no crimes you're talking about! I know that."

Spencer had the final word. Uncharacteristically, the prisoner had gotten to Horgas. Hill, who had been listening from the next room, could not remember the last time Horgas had lost his composure with an arrestee. It was as clear to Hill as it was to Horgas himself that Joe had lost control of the interview; nothing more would be gained from continuing the interrogation now.

Joe lumbered out of the room, his eyes downcast. "That motherfucker is lying to me. I know it! Never jacked off in his life. Did you hear that line of bullshit? You try him, Mike." Joe heaved a huge sigh of discouragement and he lumbered into the monitoring room and sank into a chair.

Mike Hill pulled his thoughts into order. This Tucker investigation was not his first exposure to the black masked rapist. On the same evening Marcie Sanders had been assaulted back in 1983, her next door neighbor Lois Cantor reported that someone had broken into her home. The Sanders investigators had concluded that the dildo the masked man used on Sanders was stolen from Cantor. Hill had been assigned to investigate the Cantor break-in and determine if in fact the dildo belonged to Ms. Cantor. Upon being asked about the dildo, the woman became very defensive, denying ownership of it.

"I would know if that was my dildo," she emphatically told Hill. "I have eight of them and none are missing." And to prove her point she brought out the eight dildos and laid them on her couch. Cantor clearly felt guilty about her neighbor's having been sexually assaulted by one of her dildos. After being assured that the assault would have happened even if Cantor had not owned a single dildo, she finally admitted that the one used on Sanders had belonged to her. Hill had never had a more uncomfortable moment in his entire career than that discussion with Cantor, her eight dildos in a neat row on the couch in front of them. And now he sat face to face, in the brightly lit interview room, with the man who probably had stolen that dildo and used it to violate Marcie Sanders.

"What do you think of someone who'd do the things we told you were done to these women?" Hill asked, after reintroducing himself to Spencer.

"A motherfucker who do this shit gotta be a crazy motherfucker," Spencer said.

"What do you think should happen to a person that does things like this?" Hill asked.

"I don't care."

"You said he must be crazy, right?"

"Must be."

"Well, what do you do with a person like that?"

"I don't know. It ain't for me to decide. He's gotta have a problem if he's killing people. He ain't no ordinary normal motherfucker."

"I'd say he's normal except for one missing part," Hill insisted. "One part's just not right. I wouldn't say he's crazy. I'd think of crazy as someone who shits on the floor and eats his shit. That's crazy. But this guy is normal except for one little thing in his background that went wrong."

And what was that one little thing? Joe asked himself, on the other side of the glass. Damn! Whatever it was, it was not obvious. Joe had been over the correctional reports again and again with a fine-tooth comb. There were psychological summaries, commissioned by the Department of Corrections, and reports on his family background and childhood and adolescence, prepared as part of the sentencing process in his earlier arrests. His background may not have been privileged, but it looked better than what a lot of kids had. Both his parents had completed several years of college. His parents had divorced (the mother complained that the father had wanted to be a "playboy") and his father had gone to live in D.C. Timmy claimed to have had no contact with him from age seven on. His mother had continued to work steadily, though, as an accounting technician, and Timmy had lived with her and his little half brother, Travis, who was nine years younger. Then the mother became engaged again and her fiancé, a college graduate who worked as a bricklayer, came to live with them. Both Timmy and his mother insisted there were no family problems and everybody got along.

But Timmy started getting in trouble young. At age nine, he set a fire in his school and committed petty larceny. In reviewing this first arrest, Joe noted that the date corresponded with his memory of first hearing about "Timmy." Spencer was arrested again for larceny at age eleven, and then it was breaking and entering at age fourteen. At fifteen he was brought in for joyriding and hit and run, and he was committed to a juvenile learning center. That was it for school. He dropped out in tenth grade, saying later he was suspended for skipping too much school.

At eighteen he was arrested for possession of a concealed weapon and breaking and entering; at nineteen a probation violation and a nighttime breaking and entering. From 1980 to 1984 it was more of the same: burglary, burglary, burglary, burglary, trespassing, violation of probation, burglary. In the early eighties, when out of prison, he lived with his grandmother, Mrs. Elizabeth Esau. She told correctional authorities that she believed he was making a genuine effort to overcome his criminal behavior. He did make on-again, off-again efforts to study for his GED. In addition, though, she wanted him to make a "sincere commitment to the church." I doubt he ever did that, Horgas thought wryly.

Horgas had taken special interest in a psychological report done in January 1983 during Spencer's three-year sentence for burglary and trespassing. The report noted that he regarded himself as being closest to his mother, grandmother, and brother; he had never married, never fathered a child, saw several women, denied ever having had a relationship with a man. He had drifted from one job to another—bricklayer, janitor—and usually left jobs within six months, of his own volition. The psychologist found him to be mentally intact, not suffering from delusions or hallucinations, and a regular consumer of alcohol and marijuana who nevertheless regarded himself as not having a substance abuse problem.

Psychological testing suggested that Spencer had "a tendency to disregard rules, was uninhibited, and easily led." Based on his own observations and Spencer's behavior in jail the interviewer elaborated that the young man was "very uninhibited and tends to set his own limits as compared to following those set by others." What an understatement, Joe thought grimly.

And then there was the matter of his IQ. The psychologist had scored his IQ as 89—in the "dull average" range. Wrong. Spencer was anything but dull average. The careful execution of the murders, the improvement in his criminal technique from one offense to the next, the cat-and-mouse game in the car from Richmond to Arlington—no, Timmy Spencer was not "dull." He was very, very sharp.

How could they have missed so much with this guy? But then, Joe reminded himself, the corrections system had been mainly interested in evaluating his potential as an escape and disciplinary risk so they could decide what type of unit to place him in. And there really wasn't anything obviously wrong with his manner or his behavior, even now. Just as nothing stood out in his background.

"It's got to be more than just background," Spencer was retorting to Hill. "I wouldn't go goddamn out and rape no goddamn body. I ain't no damn rapist or ain't no motherfucking killer. . . . I don't need to do no shit like that." For the first time, a ripple of agitation seemed to disturb Spencer's glass-smooth exterior.

But Horgas didn't buy it. He sat in the other room shaking his head at Ray and Glenn. "What a bullshit artist. He really expects us to think he's legitimately disturbed by these killings. Jesus Christ!"

"Listen, Horgas. How about me and Glenn going in there for few minutes to talk to him?" Ray asked.

"Be my guest."

"You remember us, Timmy, we're from Richmond," Glenn said as he and Ray walked into the interview room. "We just want to sit in here and talk with you for a little while."

Ray took a completely different tack from Horgas and Hill. "Did you ever talk to a serial murderer—or know any of 'em?"

"Nope."

"Heard anything inside the joint about them?"

"Nope."

"If you were looking for the guy that killed these women, what would you suggest we do?" Ray asked.

"Be hard to say, man, because I wouldn't know who he was. I wouldn't know what to do." Spencer was not playing their game.

"Let me ask you one question. Why are these guys so interested in you?" asked Glenn.

"The way the other guy explained it to me when I came up to Arlington, somebody got killed. And he said the murders didn't start in Richmond till I got to South Side. But I know Richmond's got the highest crime rate in the whole motherfucking world."

Ray and Glenn responded with a hearty belly laugh. "Thanks for telling us," they said in unison. Horgas grimaced as he listened to this apparently friendly interchange. These guys aren't getting anywhere, he thought.

After about a half hour Horgas asked Ray and Glenn to come back into the monitoring room, and Hill resumed his interrogation.

"You know what I told my partner when we arrested you," Hill said with a faint, friendly smile, "I like that guy. I do, I really like you. Most of the guys in here I don't like 'cause they're such dickheads. I like you. It bothers me that you feel that I am trying to screw you."

"Man, I'm not—"

"Listen to me, listen to me," Hill interrupted loudly. "It also bothers me that you would think that I would try to railroad you!"

"I don't see how in the fuck I got mixed up in this shit," Spencer said, shaking his head. "Way I look at it you guys want to close this case and—"

"I don't want you to think like that, Timmy," Hill bellowed. "God be my witness, I am not that kind of person. I wouldn't let it happen to you. . . . I can't put myself inside of Timmy but I can sure as shit sit here and hold his hand. I can see what you have gone through. I read your background reports. It's seriously fucked up. But you gotta let it come out." Hill moved his chair around the table and placed himself eye to eye with Spencer. "I don't want to see you fucked," Hill continued, his voice laden with emotion. "I want you to look into my eyes and want you to know I won't let anybody fuck you."

"Well, something's wrong here. Papers down in Richmond say I'm a psycho." Spencer's eyes welled and a tear moved slowly down his left cheek. He quickly wiped it away. "I don't want to fucking cry in front of nobody," he moaned.

"Timmy, I cry all the time. It's OK," Hill said softly as he put a comforting hand on Spencer's shoulder. "And I want you to know I don't think you're crazy or a psycho. It's not Timmy Spencer's fault." Spencer's tears flowed freely. He was unable to speak.

Horgas came to life. He was on the edge of his seat, waiting for Spencer to finally give it up. Hill, who had been skeptical about Joe's theory from the beginning, thought to himself, this is my glory day! Me, a junior detective, I'm going to get this hard-core serial killer to confess!

"I didn't kill nobody," Spencer announced firmly, dashing Hill's hopes. "I didn't rape nobody and I don't need to take no pussy like that."

"I'm saying it's not your fault," Hill insisted.

"I know it ain't my fault. I didn't do it!'

In the next room Horgas removed his trump card from his coat pocket—a letter-size envelope containing three Polaroids. "It's time to turn the heat up on this son of a bitch," Horgas said to Ray and Glenn as he walked out of the room. He knocked twice on the interview room door and gave Hill the envelope.

"I know the Timmy sitting here now is not that person that could do anything like this," Hill said, removing three gruesome crime scene photos. Spencer stared intensely at each photo. "Can you see what I'm saying?" Hill urged emphatically. "I don't want to see you go to the chair!"

Hill was trying to suggest the possibility of a split personality. But Spencer wasn't getting it. "Whose picture is this?" Spencer asked in a barely audible voice.

"This is the woman we're talking about!" Hill hollered into Spencer's face. "That's Susan!"

"Oh no, oh man," Spencer said with a shocked expression.

What an odd reaction, Hill thought. He probably didn't realize what happens to a dead body after three days in a room heated to 70 degrees.

"You think the person that did the things in those pictures isn't gonna go to the chair!" Hill demanded.

"I didn't do this," Spencer pleaded. "This is bad. Real bad. I know somebody's out to get my ass if they said I did some shit like that. . . . You're all looking at me like I have two sides. Like I'm some kind of Jack the Ripper or Dr. Jekyll and Mr. Hyde. Like I turn into a mutant killer or something like that. I can't do no shit like that, man! That's as low as you can go to do that!"

"You didn't do it," Hill repeated.

"There ain't nothing wrong with me," Spencer said. "I had nothing to do with this murder."

Hill shook his head wearily. He pushed his chair back from the table and left the room. "I thought I had him, Joe," Hill said apologetically. The interview had taken its toll on Hill. Sweat streamed from his forehead.

"It's OK. Don't beat yourself up over it. He's not going to give anything up," Horgas said. "I'm going down to Richmond tomorrow afternoon. I'm going to stay for a couple of days to check out the halfway house, check out Spencer's friends, and talk with his coworkers. Maybe he bragged to somebody."

Though he left the interview room convinced that Spencer killed Tucker, Hill had mixed feelings about Spencer himself.

"Timmy," he later reflected, "was a likable guy, a pleasant fellow. I even felt kind of sorry for him after he broke down." It was a sentiment shared by others in the department. Steve Carter, who assisted in Spencer's arrest, said Spencer had impressed him, a veteran detective, as a "nice guy."

"You could sit down and talk to Timmy. You could probably be comfortable with him anywhere, in any type of situation—at a bar or party. The thing is just don't leave your wife or your girlfriend around him. He's got a problem, this sexual type of thing, and he's a killer," Carter later said.

But Ray Williams still thought they were all on the wrong track. He left Arlington that Sunday afternoon believing that Spencer was not the South Side Strangler and had nothing to do with the death of Susan Tucker. Upon his return to Richmond he called Ernie Hazzard, the Chesterfield detective in charge of the Cho investigation.

"I was just up to talk to Spencer," Ray began, "And I'll tell you what, I don't think he did it. He's not the type. I want you to go up and talk to him and give me your opinion."

Hazzard went to Arlington the next day and talked to Spencer for three hours.

"You're right, he didn't do it," Hazzard told Ray upon his return. "He was just as cooperative as could be. He told me he'll be glad when the DNA tests come back because they will prove he's innocent."

Though Spencer did not confess, the daylong interrogation had a completely different effect on Horgas. It had so thoroughly convinced him of Spencer's guilt that he paid a visit to Helen Fahey on Monday morning, the twenty-fifth, to discuss the other half of his investigation.

"I'm going down to Richmond this morning to check out a few things, but there's no doubt he's the right guy," Joe said confidently.

"Seems that way, Joe. But we need the DNA results," Helen reiterated.

"Right. But you know as well as I do that if Vasquez was going to trial now, without even the DNA, there's no way in hell a jury would convict him," Joe challenged.

"What are you saying, Joe? That we should do something about Vasquez now?" Helen asked.

"Yeah. I mean, the guy's innocent! And it's not only me saying that. You know the Behavioral Science guys said the same thing."

"Listen, Joe, we have to wait for the DNA results. We have to be sure. But if there's a match with Spencer, you don't have to worry. We'll be able to get Vasquez out in a half hour," Helen assured him.

"Then it's gotta be the first thing we do when we get those results back."

When Joe got to Richmond and reached the neighborhood of the halfway house, he drove around clocking off the distances to the various crime scenes. He was stunned to see that Ellen Talbot's place was only four-tenths of a mile from the bar O'Toole's, and O'Toole's was around 800 yards away from Debbie Davis's house. In fact, Debbie Davis's and Ellen Talbot's apartments were both corner units, and the kitchen window had been used by the perp both times. The halfway house sat two and a half miles from Davis's home; but if you went on foot, through the park, it cut off half a mile. How could they say the Ellen Talbot rape was unrelated to the homicides?

Horgas's interviews with the halfway house employees revealed little more than the interrogations. As they had told the newspapers, the halfway house employers were unanimous in their opinion of Spencer. "He was a friendly guy who kept to himself." Though he moved from job to job during the five months he was in Richmond, his employers portrayed him as a "quiet, respectful fellow."

Only one detail drew Joe's attention. Several halfway house personnel observed that Spencer had a strange habit of frequently washing his sneakers. He had been seen meticulously scrubbing them more than twelve times in the past two months. Though they'd interpreted this simply as Spencer's affinity for clean sneakers, Horgas saw the behavior as an effort to erase any residue that might connect Spencer to the crime scenes.

While Horgas had not expected Spencer to open up to coworkers or roommates, Horgas had hoped for something positive from Spencer's recent girlfriend, Terry Dawson. Horgas visited Dawson on Tuesday evening at her home. Carter and Ray Williams had searched the home the day of the arrest but found nothing to implicate Spencer.

"You're sure that he did all these things the papers said he did?" Dawson asked Joe as they sat at her dining room table. She really can't believe it's home, Horgas thought, watching her shake her head in amazement.

"I'm afraid so," said Joe.

"Do you have fingerprints or something?" she asked.

"Oh yeah, we got a whole bunch of stuff," Joe boasted.

"So I guess he won't be out no time soon?" she asked wistfully.

"No, no. Not for a long time. When did you meet him?" Joe probed.

"In October. I was with my cousin. And ever since then I've seen him every weekend."

"So you're boyfriend and girlfriend, right?"

She nodded.

"And, uh, there's nothing wrong with that," Joe stammered. "Did he ever, uh, when—uh—you were making out with him, did he ever put on a mask or anything like that?" Joe asked uncomfortably.

"No!" she shot back as if it was a crazy question. "He ain't never done any of that stuff that the papers said he did like try to tie me up or force me to do stuff. None of that kinky stuff. That's why I can't believe he ever did anything like the papers said."

Horgas took a deep breath. "Did he ever tell you he wanted you to come, though?"

"What? Come, what do you mean?"

"You know—come," Horgas asked uneasily. Twenty years of police experience simply had not prepared him to ask this question.

"You mean while he was making love to me?" she asked. "No, he was gentle with me. He didn't try to hound me or rough me up or anything like that."

"Never brought any dildos over, did he?"

"You mean one of those things you stick up in you?"

"Yeah," Horgas replied with a nervous laugh.

"He never tried to do that," she said firmly. "Everything was normal. We had a nice, sweet relationship. We didn't argue. I just can't see it in him. That's why I don't believe he did it," she insisted.

"OK. Let me ask you this. Did he ever talk about the South Side Strangler?"

"No. In fact, he was over here once and there was a TV news story on about that Chinese girl who was killed when the guy went through the window. He didn't act funny or nothing."

We're not going to find shit on him, Joe thought as he drove back to his hotel. He's too goddamn smart. Joe had known this since the moment he'd stepped into Tucker's home. If he was smart enough to wipe down the washing machine, he wasn't going to wear a mask when he screwed his girlfriend.

Before returning to Arlington the next day, Horgas had been asked to attend the weekly meeting of the Strangler task force. Despite Spencer's arrest, it was business as usual. Discussion concerned suspects who had been identified in the last week and the need in the immediate future to concentrate more heavily on doctors and other health care professionals.

Much to Horgas's chagrin, Spencer's arrest was regarded as irrelevant. Horgas received a testament to Richmond's opinion of the arrest shortly before the meeting ended.

"Joe, we have a little something for you," Lieutenant Childress, Ray and Glenn's superior announced. He held out a plain package. Joe removed the brown paper and found a glossy hard-core porno magazine. "You told Spencer that you liked to jack off in the bathroom so we got you this present," Ray and Glenn said in unison. Everyone howled. Horgas laughed along with them but just below the surface he seethed. In that daylong interview the only thing that those guys remember was me talking about this one thing, he thought furiously. They really think I'm dead wrong about Spencer.

Ray Williams was especially sure that Horgas was wrong. He was so sure that in the days following the arrest he told his fellow Richmond officers, "I'll kiss Joe Horgas's ass on Main and Broad at twelve noon if the DNA says it's Spencer." Horgas later learned that Ray bragged to others he would perform additional sexual feats on different parts of Joe's anatomy, all in public and in broad daylight, if Spencer was the killer.

Joe knew his case was strong. Still, the conviction would come down to forensics. The DNA would either send Spencer to death row or turn him back out on the streets—the thought chilled Joe to the bone—based on the findings of lab techs, not the hard work of detectives. Without the DNA match Joe would never get Spencer convicted. And he would never get David Vasquez, who now appeared to him no more than a hapless pawn, out of languishing the rest of his thirty-five-year sentence in Buckingham.

9

HORGAS WAS STILL SEETHING WHEN HE SWUNG HIS CROWN VICTORIA onto I-95 and headed back toward Arlington. The thin wintry light was dissolving into dusk. Not much traffic. Damn them! He eased into the left lane and settled into a cruising speed well in excess of the posted limits.

He glanced at the porno book on the passenger seat atop his stack of files. Big joke! I wonder how hard they'll be laughing the day Spencer is convicted.

Horgas's wry smile turned to a frown. In one sense the Richmond guys were right. He did not have enough to convict Spencer.

The thought kept bouncing in his head like a ball on an elastic string. Not enough. Not nearly enough.

The girlfriend had given him zip. Well, she had been telling the truth, anyway. Horgas knew liars, and she wasn't lying.

But you, Spencer, you're lying through your fucking teeth! For an instant Spencer's blank, opaque face hung in front of him, the intelligent eyes, the faint smile—you liar!

I'll prove you murdered them, he swore to himself for the hundredth time.

How?

He needed help. DNA.

It was a painful thought. He had never needed help in the silence of the forest, no matter how large and how powerful the buck was; and some of them were enormous. And none of *them* had gotten away, but now . . .

Spencer might. He might walk out of there a free man, because the goddamn case was too weak without a more definitive way to tie him to the murders.

He saw the sign—Arlington, 100 miles—and tried like hell to focus on the road. Spencer was never going to confess. That was obvious now. And nothing in his room, no trophies, nothing. Goddamn it! Then there was the forensics; the guys had done a first-class job. Though they could not lift any usable fingerprints, they had recovered the hairs and the critical semen evidence. He changed lanes and told himself to slow down a little.

While Joe had initially been elated by Deanne's news that Spencer's blood type matched the semen found at the Tucker scene, he knew the result was not enough to obtain a conviction. Still, Joe could not have been happier with Deanne's efforts.

Usually she maintained a removed, objective demeanor. But Joe had won her over with the passion and conviction he had displayed when he first visited her in December with the crime scene samples. It was not the way he told her that he couldn't convince anyone in his own squad of his theory—though that had aroused her sympathy. It was his obvious drive to track down this killer and take him off the streets forever that moved her. Deanne was as vulnerable as any other woman. And she could see that by some miracle, Joe cared about bagging this guy more than cops usually cared about anything, even the biggest cases of their careers.

She had tried to explain to him exactly what she was going to do with the evidence he had delivered to her, every step of the process. He had cut her off. "I don't give a shit how it works, Deanne, I just want to know the bottom line." And of course, she thought grimly, he wants it to hold up in court.

This case had been unusual for her too, because she cared.

"Typically, I never make a judgment in a case; I just do the experiments and tests," she said later. "I don't reach an opinion as to guilt or innocence. I just do my job." But she still remembered her excitement, even the day she did the first of many complex steps to analyze and type the semen on the nightgown. She had cut out a sample of the fabric, mounted it, and turned off the room lights. She flicked on the black light and trained it on the sample. Semen would have a special shine under the black light; it would be iridescent. Yes! The stain was semen. She remembered how her heart had skipped a beat when she saw it. And how she had told herself to be calm, take it a step at a time, just do her job.

In addition to the analysis of Spencer's blood, both Deanne and Joe had especially high hopes for the analysis of Spencer's clothing and possessions. These were things he might possibly have had with him during the murders if in fact he'd committed them, things from which she and her staff might be able to raise some evidence: Spencer's gloves, jacket, tennis shoes, pocket knife, buck knife, a roll of tape, a knit cap, a homemade cap, loafer-style shoes, and another jacket. Deanne had received these items with uncharacteristic excitement, especially Spencer's jacket.

When Joe had been in Richmond he had interviewed Spencer's employers. Anything special he always wore, he had asked them. Yes! they had all answered immediately. He always wore that camouflage jacket.

How often did he wear it?

Every day, they said.

That had gotten Joe excited. A jacket he wore every day was a jacket he probably wore when he went out at night to rape and murder. A jacket that was going to have something in it or on it, some evidence they could use.

Of course, if Spencer had cleaned out his jacket the way the guys in the halfway house said he cleaned his sneakers, there might not be much left.

The jacket went to Joseph Beckerman, a senior forensic scientist. Beckerman's academic background was in geology, and his specialty was trace evidence—especially soil, minerals, glass, building materials, safe insulation, and botanical comparisons. He had done glass comparisons hundreds of times at the Northern Virginia Forensic Lab, and testified many times in court on those comparisons. The camouflage coat was nothing new to him.

First Beckerman cleaned his very large white table and covered it with a fresh length of white paper. He then scraped down the coat with a tool that looked like a cake spatula, paying special attention to the insides of pockets. The type of debris he was most interested in was soil—for comparison to soil outside the points of entry at the crime scene—and glass fragments, since a windowpane had been broken by the perp at each crime. Deposits of bloodlike material were also a possibility.

All the material he was able to scrape off the coat was temporarily stored in small plastic pillboxes, then examined bit by bit under a low-power microscope to see if useful materials like glass particles might be present.

Beckerman did have what he termed the "known glass" for comparison with any fragments found—that is, glass from the broken window at the crime scene point of entry. In fact, he had the entire remaining pane in its frame.

It was a small, thin frame and most of the glass was still intact. Some pieces were missing, but only from down in one corner. This was uncommon. Usually, in a broken window from a crime scene, there was a clear area of impact somewhere near the window's center. Most often, people used objects to break windows, objects like bricks and rocks and hammers, and when they broke windows they aimed at the middle. In this case, there were pry marks instead along the broken corner of the frame. A tool with a thin, quarter-inch-wide blade had been stuck in the corner of the frame and twisted. It looked like this was what broke the glass. He went back and checked the breakage pattern of the glass. Right. The glass had not been broken by impact but by the strain of the tool inserted along the edge.

This would change what happened to the fragments, he knew. When glass was broken by impact, particles would fly back at the source of the impact, sometimes as much as ten feet. A window that was broken by prying, as this one was, would not shower particles out nearly so far. The force would be much more contained.

Beckerman had been told that the frame came from a sliding basement window. Now he understood the entry. The killer had broken out a small piece of glass from a corner of the frame, and then reached in and removed a dowel that had been inserted in the window track to keep it from being slid open. Then he had opened the unlocked window and gone in.

Beckerman had been given several large shards too, some a few inches across, that had been found by the window.

The first thing he did was try to fit the larger pieces of glass back into the frame, to confirm that the broken glass indeed came from it. The larger pieces fit perfectly, not only in shape, but according to the packle marks, the minute, irregular pattern of breakage along each shattered edge. He checked the packle marks by fitting the pieces together under the microscope. Yes, these pieces of glass appeared indeed to have been broken out of this windowpane.

But there was a much more precise method of making sure: an analysis that measured refracted index and dispersion. First he would measure two pieces of the "known" glass, a shard that had presumably been knocked out of the window and a piece of glass that he himself broke out of the frame. These were mounted on separate slides in an oil that had been calibrated by the National Bureau of Standards so that its optical properties were precisely standardized.

Basically, the procedure looked at the optical properties of the glass and compared them to the optical properties of the oil, which were well known. A phase contrast microscope with a Mettler Hot Stage could raise and lower the sample temperature to a tenth of a degree centigrade. A monochromator changed the light bathing the oiled sample from pure white to the blue end of the spectrum and then gradually all the way to the end of the reds. Beckerman dialed in several different temperatures and allowed the sample to equilibrate and become stable at each temperature, then went gradually through the light spectrum until he found the precise setting that brought the glass particle to a complete match with the properties of the oil. At this point the glass particle seemed to disappear under the microscope. Each time this happened he would record the refraction number.

The shard matched the glass he'd broken from the frame; their optical characteristics were indistinguishable. Beckerman noted the refraction number: 1.5170. His method was precise enough to note discrepancies to the fourth decimal place.

Beckerman then turned to the debris he had scraped from the coat. In it he had found, under the microscope, two tiny precious particles of glass. He carefully washed them in detergent, rinsed them in alcohol, and mounted them on slides in the calibrated oil.

He put the first one up on the microscope, and quickly dialed in the temperatures and light settings that had brought him to a perfect match with the known samples. He leaned over the eyepiece—but the particle had not disappeared! It was still there. He tried the next setting. No. And the next. Finally he just dialed through the spectrum until he found the refraction numbers that were correct for the sample, though they did not match his known glass, and noted these in his log. It was window glass, but it was not a match. The suspect had gotten this glass shard in his pocket from some other source.

He took up the second glass particle from the camouflage coat. It was a long, pie-wedge-shaped piece maybe a tenth of an inch on its longest side. The other piece had not matched, so he didn't have much hope for this one. As he took the slide and placed it on the microscope he recalled Deanne's urgency about these samples and the crime scene from which they came. He hadn't thought much about this crime, tried not to think about the crimes, just processed the samples and wrote up his reports and always took the greatest, most exacting care to—

He blinked. He had dialed in the first setting from the known glass and the fragment had disappeared in the oil. He did it again, just in case he had made a mistake. It matched. He went on to each of the other settings. Yes—each one matched. He did every one over again. He always allowed himself a 2 percent margin of error with window glass, but barring that, there really wasn't any doubt in his mind. This fragment he had combed out of the camouflage coat had come from the windowpane he had here.

He repeated it again.

It matched.

On January 29, 1988, Horgas flew back to Lifecodes with samples of Spencer's blood in hand. At this point there was no way he was going to entrust these precious vials to anyone else. He wanted a perfect chain of custody, completely above reproach. No one would be able to say these vials of blood had been out of his sight for so much as an instant to be contaminated with the blood of anyone else.

He met again with Michael Baird.

"This is completely objective, right?" Joe queried. "When you get a match it's totally certain?"

Baird raised his eyebrows. "Why do you ask?"

"It's just that a lot of people don't think this is the guy," Joe said defensively. He held up the blood. "But it is the guy. There is not any doubt at all. None whatsoever. Still, it's gotta hold up."

"I understand," Baird said supportively. "I am objective until the data comes in but once I declare a match, I declare it against all odds."

This was becoming a very exciting case. Lifecodes had done scores of court cases, but they had never had a serial rape–murder. The trial would surely put DNA fingerprinting to the test. "Why don't I take you to see Lisa Bennett?" Baird suggested, when they had finished with the paperwork. "She's the technician analyzing your samples."

"Great!" Joe cried, a little surprised to hear that someone whose name had not yet even been mentioned to him was doing the analysis. But of course he should have realized Baird wouldn't do it, nor would McElfresh, the guy he'd met on his first visit to bring the crime scene samples. They were the suits.

Lisa Bennett turned out to be a fresh-faced girl in her late twenties, chin-length light brown hair and an open, friendly smile. She had a B.S. degree and had started out at Lifecodes in cancer research before switching to forensics. Even in forensics she didn't get involved emotionally—to her it was all numbers. The clients, whom she never met, were voices over the phone. Something would come in, a piece of evidence, and it immediately became a number. She would process it and report back.

But she had never met anyone like Joe. He came in like a tornado, his enormous hands nevertheless bearing up the vials of his suspect's blood as if they were the holy chalice. He ran down the case to her with his characteristic excitement, and she listened very attentively. It was not just his passion. It was the match she had already seen in the crime scene samples, the ones Joe had brought up a month earlier and the ones they had gotten weeks before that from Richmond.

Seven days earlier, the 22nd of January, she and her co-worker Lorah had been sitting across from each other in the lab. "You're working on that Virginia case, aren't you?" Lisa asked.

"Uh-huh," Lorah responded.

"I'm working on the rape-homicide from Arlington. What's your file number?" Lisa had asked casually.

They compared file numbers; Lisa's (5824) was more than 2,000 pieces of evidence earlier than what Lorah was working on (7835). Separate cases, separate jurisdictions, no orders to compare the two.

But they took out their files and started talking.

"I have a band between marker ten and eleven, do you?" Lorah asked.

"Yes."

"And then go to probe two, do you have a band there?"

"Yeah, I do!"

Lisa looked up and grinned in excitement. Neither of them had ever seen anything like this before, two unrelated cases looking like they matched. Lisa got up and walked over to Laura's desk and they put the autorads together. Visually, a perfect match. Band by band by band. They hadn't put them through the computer yet. "Let's run these," Lisa said.

But they already knew what the analysis would yield. The same person who killed the women in Richmond had killed the woman in Arlington. And did the local jurisdictions even know it?

"Baird has to see this," Lorah said, and Lisa nodded. He wouldn't want to release it right away since there was no authorization from the police agencies to do so.

Now, sitting in the lab with Joe, Lisa resisted the temptation to tell him. Instead she went over what she would do with his evidence. "The samples you already brought up here are in the dish gel."

"The crime scene stuff?"

"Here it is. This stuff." She slid the log across the table to him.

7033	Semen stained bathrobe	Carolyn Hamm
7034	Sleeping bag stain	Susan Tucker
7035	Semen stained pants	1983 rape
7036	Semen stained mattress cover	1983 rape
7145	Blood stain	Susan Tucker
7146	Semen stained nightgown #1	Susan Tucker
7147	Semen stained nightgown #2	Susan Tucker
7148	Semen stained nightgown #3	Susan Tucker
7149	Semen stained nightgown #4	Susan Tucker
7150	Semen stained brown blanket	Susan Tucker
7151	Semen stained terry robe #1	1983 rape
7152	Semen stained terry robe #2	1983 rape
7153	Thigh swabs	1983 rape
7154	Vulva swabs	1983 rape
7155	Vaginal/cervical swabs	1983 rape

"These are already prepared and in dish gel. Now let's log in the samples you brought today."

7535	Vulva swab	1983 rape
7536	Vaginal swab	1983 rape
7537	Semen stained blue jeans #1	1983 rape

7538	Semen stained blue jeans #2	1983 rape
7539	Sanitary pad	1984 rape
7540	Blood sample	Timothy Spencer
7541	Blood sample	Timothy Spencer

"What we can do," she said, completing the log, "is put Spencer's blood in the same gel and do it, so that everything comes out at the same time. Or we can put it in different gel, and you would know the outcome of the original samples first, before you know the outcome of his blood. But the goal of keeping it in the same gel is, if you have them on the same autorad, there'll be no mistake. See?"

Horgas didn't see, not fully, but he told her he had to trust her to do it correctly, the same thing he'd told Baird. She said she'd put it in the same gel. She knew as he walked out that he'd be calling her for the results—every day he'd probably call her, if not every hour.

In fact, the first call came in the next day.

"Lisa, is it done yet?" he asked nervously.

"Joe! I told you it would take weeks. Relax. I'll call you as soon as I know anything."

But then the next day he called again. "Look, Lisa, I know it's not done, but how's it going? Can you see anything at all?"

"No, Joe," she said gently. "It's too soon."

"OK," he said, crestfallen.

And then the next day he would call again. She got used to it, though she always had to tell him the same thing. No, it's not ready, it's too soon, I promise I'll call you the instant I know. OK, he would say. It's just that everything's riding on it.

Joe's phone rang on the morning of February 4. Hoping it was Lifecodes calling, he snatched it out of its cradle.

"Joe, this is Ray. I got some really bad news." Williams's voice lacked its characteristic snap; it was sad and weak.

"What's wrong?" Joe asked.

"I can't believe it, but last night Glenn killed himself. Shot himself in the chest in his bedroom."

Horgas was stunned. For the first time in a month, Joe stopped thinking about Timothy Spencer.

"Jesus, Ray. I'm really sorry," Joe said softly.

Despite their differences on the case, Joe liked Glenn very much. Horgas knew that Glenn didn't agree with his theory but Joe didn't cross swords with him as he did with Ray. Unlike his partner, Glenn was reserved and had a very mellow personality. Though Glenn had been under significant strain because of the South Side Strangler investigation, Joe discovered that the cause of the suicide had been problems Williams had been having at home. Like many cops, Glenn kept everything bottled up inside of him. A man who had dedicated his life to helping others tragically couldn't ask for help himself.

The next few weeks dragged on and nothing happened. Spencer still didn't talk. And Richmond investigators continued their search for a white suspect.

It was not until March 16 that Joe got the call he'd been praying for.

He picked up the phone with his usual shout: "Horgas!"

"Joe, it's Lisa."

"Yes?" Instantly he was on the edge of his seat.

"I have the results but I need to call you back in twenty minutes."

"Are these final results?"

"Yes, final."

"Are they good or bad?"

"They're good."

Horgas bellowed a laugh.

"OK," she said. "Stay by the phone. Twenty minutes."

For the last six weeks he had busied himself with tracking Spencer's movements since his arrest in 1985. Joe uncovered no useful evidence. Everyone said the same thing. In prison or out of prison Timmy Spencer was a loner who had done nothing to suggest he was a vicious killer.

During those minutes waiting for Lisa's return call Joe's bulky body seemed to be weightless, floating somewhere four inches off his chair. He fiddled with pencils, pushed file folders back and forth, listened to the hammering of his heart. The other detectives were all around him in the squad room, going about their business. Twenty minutes! He was finally going to get it.

It was an eternity before the phone rang.

"Horgas!" he yelled.

"It's me. I don't have all the calculations done—what I can tell you is visual. You have a match with a couple of things."

"Yes?" His pad and pencil were ready. The Tucker file rose in front of him like a skyscraper. At last. At last.

"OK, 7540 is Spencer, Spencer's blood. Then we have item 7033, that's semen from Carolyn Hamm's bathrobe. No DNA. Then number 7034, it's a semen-stained sleeping bag from Susan Tucker—and you have a match with your suspect."

Joe closed his eyes and tilted his head back. Thank you. Thank you.

"Next is number 7147, a semen-stained rose-colored nightgown, Susan Tucker. It is a match."

Horgas scribbled furiously, his smile spreading from ear to ear. "Now we have 7150," she said, "a brown semen-stained blanket; not enough DNA. Then item 7151. This is a semen-stained terry cloth bathrobe from a 1983 rape. It is a match with your suspect."

Yes! That meant two matches from the Tucker scene and one match from the '83 rape. Yes. "Have you matched these against the homicides in Richmond?" he asked.

She paused. "We have looked at it visually. But I don't know if I can give it to you because it's another department."

"We're working with Richmond! We're trying to help them. Besides, I brought you Spencer."

Another long pause. Clearly, she was thinking it over. "OK," she said at last. "Visually, your suspect 7540 matches with sample 5869. That's from Debbie Davis. It also matches number 5872. That's Susan Hellams."

"Lisa, I was wondering if you had any idea what the odds were that Spencer's blood would match the DNA pattern in the crime scene samples?"

"That's not really my area, Joe," Lisa confessed. "Dr. Baird usually gives those calculations. But I can tell you that the odds that somebody else has the same genetic pattern are very, very slim.''

"Lisa, I don't know how I can thank you.''

"No problem,'' she answered. "I hope this has given you what you need—that everything has worked out for you.''

"It has now,'' he said, meaning it. He thanked her again and they signed off. He put the phone down.

The room seemed to be spinning.

All the detectives were in and out, at their desks—none of them had any idea. Who should he tell first? The boss. A minute later he stood outside Deputy Chief Christiansen's office. "Chief?''

Christiansen put a sheaf of papers down and waved him in. "Joe—hey, look at that smile! You got something?''

"Got the DNA back.''

"Is it Spencer?''

"Ya damn right!'' They both hooted and high-fived.

"They got a match with Tucker?'' Christiansen breathed, eyes wide.

"They got a match with Tucker all right, and with one of the 1983 rapes, and''—he paused for effect—"with Davis and Hellams!'' He cleared his throat. "I'm not sure if I'm supposed to know that yet. But it's him, Chief. I was right.''

"What kinda odds we talking?''

"Let's see—what did they say?—there's maybe one in ten million it's somebody else with the same DNA pattern. Maybe a hundred million.'' He grinned. "Tell ya the truth, I don't remember.''

"And this is the final?'' Christiansen pressed.

"Yeah—they just called me. Letter will go out in a couple days.''

"Congratulations, Joe,'' Christiansen said sincerely.

"Hey, Chief''—Joe's eyes twinkled—"can I tell Richmond?''

"Sure, Joe,'' Christiansen nodded. "Go ahead.''

Joe couldn't remember a task he'd savored more. It was better even than getting Lifecodes confirmation letter, which came on March 18.

Then, on March 22, Lifecodes reported to Richmond by telephone that Timothy Spencer's blood had been definitively matched to semen found at the Davis and Hellams murder scenes, as well as to semen found at the Tucker scene. The same Timothy Spencer who was in custody in Arlington. Boy, Horgas thought, that must have stuck in their craw when they heard it.

On March 23 Richmond authorities issued arrest warrants for Spencer in the murders of Debbie Davis and Susan Hellams. Even though Spencer was already in custody in Arlington, Richmond technically had to arrest him also as a prelude to charging him and trying him for murder.

But Richmond had known, ever since getting preliminary work from Lifecodes on the DNA match, that Spencer was their South Side Strangler. On the 21st of March Aubrey Davis, the Commonwealth Attorney in Richmond, had announced he would seek an indictment against Spencer for the murders of Debbie Davis and Susan Hellams.

The next day Ray Williams called Joe and read him the Commonwealth Attorney's press release:

I have reviewed the investigative reports and the forensic test results and I have concluded that the same person is responsible for the deaths of Dr. Susan Hellams and Miss Debbie Davis. The Bureau of Police conducted an intense and extensive and thorough investigation into both homicides. 600 plus interviews were done, 300 suspects were investigated, a large number of suspects were surveilled and 25 suspects were eliminated by blood tests. The investigating officers and I have met at least once a week since the homicides to discuss the evidence and met with police officers from other jurisdictions with similar crimes as well as the FBI. We have focused in on one suspect that we believe may be responsible for the crime. I am satisfied that the person responsible for the homicides of Ms. Davis and Dr. Hellams is in police custody in another jurisdiction and is no longer a danger to the public. Evidence will be presented to the Grand Jury in the near future and indictments sought in both cases.

Horgas was not surprised, somehow, to hear no mention of his name, the Arlington County PD, or of the fact that he and his theory had been completely dismissed by Davis and the rest of the Richmond law enforcement community just a few weeks earlier.

Richmond had its own backlash to deal with. As soon as news of the South Side Strangler's identity hit the streets, the public reacted with outrage. On March 24 the *Richmond News Leader* ran a story in their evening edition with the screaming headline, RESIDENTS QUESTION TACTICS USED TO INVESTIGATE CITY SLAYINGS.

> People who live in the Forest Hill Park neighborhood knew exactly what kind of man police were seeking in connection with two stranglings in their area last fall. Police were looking for a white man with blond or light brown hair who was about 30 years old, lived in the area, and was physically fit. The man against whom prosecutors plan to seek indictments in the case is a 25 year old black convict from Arlington. . . . Some people in the [neighborhood] would like to know what went wrong. . . .
>
> Immediately after the [first] killing police said they were not sure whether Ms. Davis's residence had been broken into. They also said there was no sign of a fight and there was evidence of recent sexual activity. That left the impression that Ms. Davis was killed by someone she allowed to enter her apartment, someone she knew. . . . Cecil Creasey, another area resident, said police had not discussed their special concern, and neighbors did not take extra precautions until after the second killing. "If they had acted that way after Debbie Davis was killed, Susan Hellams would have thought twice before walking into her house," he said.

Taking the heat of public criticism was not easy. Once Spencer had been nailed by the DNA, Richmond refocused its efforts on going back and proving his guilt. Suddenly the priority was to investigate Spencer's background, and to that end a task force was appointed. Photo spreads were made of Spencer and circulated to every single person the force had interviewed. They didn't learn much. After all the interviews, they were able to find two people who could identify Spencer; they said they had seen him on a bus that went back and forth from Cloverleaf to Richmond. This was important since the link to Cloverleaf Mall had been one of the compelling clues in the case. But despite its efforts the task force was never able to find anybody who could positively put Timothy Spencer near any of the victims.

In addition to combing the community for witnesses, the Richmond task force delved deep into their subject's life. They spoke to hundreds of people and located reams of records. Nothing seemed out of the ordinary. The only thing they found that might have been relevant was a woman they located whom Spencer had dated. She was a prostitute. She discussed his sexual life in detail and said one thing that interested them: Timothy had reportedly told her, "Hey, you don't have to worry if you're dry, just slap some Vaseline on that thing and stick it in." He also told her that he "got a kick out of jacking off." It was interesting but hardly definitive. Plenty of people used Vaseline and jacked off.

In all these efforts they got no help from Horgas. He had spent weeks developing his theory, and now the DNA match had proven it; he didn't see the need to go any further. "I've got mine cleared," he said to them. "I wish you all luck." He did not mention Ray Williams's promise to kiss his ass and more on the corner of Broad and Main in Richmond at twelve noon.

Richmond had enough embarrassment and anger to deal with. The finger pointing began. Some said it was Joe's fault for not telling them he had good reason to believe the killer was a young black man. Horgas heard this through the grapevine and burned with indignation. Of course he had told them about his theory—at the first meeting. And what had they said? How many murders a year you get up there, dumb hick? Four? Five? Don't tell us what's what. We get seventy-five! It was more than Joe's theory. They had known as far back as the 31st of December about the negroid hairs, though of course they could have speculated that a victim could pick up these hairs someplace else. Plus, Deanne and Mary Jane had spoken on the phone—he knew that from Deanne—and

Deanne was sure that early on in the investigation she had told her counterpart in Richmond, Mary Jane Burton, that numerous negroid hairs were found on the body of Susan Tucker.

The FBI was also a target of some in Richmond's law enforcement community. Commonwealth Attorney Aubrey Davis seemed particularly irked. He later commented, "Originally the FBI portrayed [the killer] as a white male and then of course the information was developed on Spencer and obviously it wasn't a white male. I made a policy to rib them right heavily after it was over. . . . They dropped the ball in my opinion. That's not to say it was an intentional dropping of the ball, it's just that, you know, when you're dealing with cases, you want to look at all the angles. There's nothing wrong with them. I'm not being critical of them, because that [a mistake] could happen in any case. You go in a lot of different directions." Davis also said, however, that, "the FBI is the most difficult agency to work for in the nation. [Of] all the law enforcement branches of government—the federal government—they are the worst to work with, as far as cooperativeness is concerned. They cooperate to the degree that it's advantageous to them."

According to Aubrey Davis, the FBI directed their attention to a number of young white males who lived in Hellams's neighborhood. "Probably it put us in an area where maybe [we] wouldn't have gone—or maybe we would have anyway, because of the fact that some of those folks had past histories of Peeping Toms, and various and sundry other things, that would direct one toward them anyhow. We really didn't have anywhere to go at the time. [The FBI] gave us something to work on."

Lieutenant Childress, though, disagreed. "We were *not* confining ourselves to white people," he insisted, "because, see, we had the negroid hair. The FBI was up front. They said it probably is a white guy but we don't know for sure. And saying that Spencer was the guy . . . I didn't feel that we were in a position to say that Spencer was the guy until we knew for a fact he was."

"Nothing can be worse in the world than to think you've

got a good case, and then the evidence falls through on you, and then you've already indicted a guy," Childress continued. "Then you look like stupidity number one!"

Horgas couldn't afford to spend too much time worrying about Richmond's public relations problems, because even though he had Spencer and he had the DNA matches, his job was not done. The trial still lay ahead. And David Vasquez still sat in Buckingham, serving a thirty-five-year sentence.

10

No time was wasted. The Commonwealth Attorney's office flew into high gear for the trial within hours of Lisa Bennett's momentous March 16 phone call to Horgas. Yet, ironically, there was little left for Horgas to do. Aside from interviewing a few witnesses and gathering more background data on Spencer, his role in the trial preparation was almost over.

The sensational case was now in the hands of Helen Fahey and her first assistant, Arthur Karp. The prosecution would not build their case on Joe's theory; rather, the star witness in the case of the Commonwealth of Virginia versus Timothy Wilson Spencer would be deoxyribonucleic acid.

The fact that he would have a limited role in Spencer's prosecution actually pleased Horgas. Now he could focus on his other priority: getting Vasquez released. From the moment he had left Buckingham Penitentiary after his first visit with the ill-fated, confused man on December 8, Horgas knew he had to get Vasquez out of prison. And when the DNA test had finally come back, proof positive of Spencer's guilt in multiple murders and rapes, he felt sure this also indisputably proved Vasquez's innocence.

The day after getting the March 16 results, Horgas made an appointment to see Deputy Chief Arthur Christiansen. Now, he knew, Christiansen would take action on Vasquez. He was full of confidence as he took the elevator down to the deputy chief's office on the second floor.

"Chief?"

Christiansen waved Horgas in.

"Now with this DNA evidence against Spencer, I think we definitely have enough to get Vasquez out." Horgas permitted himself a satisfied smile.

Christiansen leaned back in his chair. "Joe, you're right. We *do* need to do something about Vasquez. In fact, I've just ordered a complete, formal reinvestigation of Hamm. I want a clear separation of duties, so I'm giving the reinvestigation to Carrig and Shelton. You stay on Spencer. Get the case ready for trial."

Joe closed his eyes for a millisecond and ordered himself to stay calm. "Chief!" he cried. "There's almost nothing for me to do on Spencer now. And Vasquez—I'm the one who's come up with everything. I've been doing the reinvestigation all along! That's how I discovered it was Spencer!"

Christiansen furrowed his thick eyebrows and leaned forward.

"You stay the fuck away from Vasquez! Carrig and Shelton are working the reinvestigation. Not you!"

Horgas bit down hard on his anger.

"I want two separate investigations because I want to be assured that whatever decision we come to in Vasquez is a decision that's completely independent of Spencer," Christiansen continued. "You got to see the big picture. Now, you did see the big picture with Spencer—that's true—but this is different." Christiansen went on to enumerate what he wanted done, and by whom.

The reinvestigation was critical because Lifecodes had been unable to extract any usable DNA from the Hamm case semen samples. They had degenerated over time and could not therefore be compared to Spencer's blood. There was nothing concrete absolutely to prove Vasquez's innocence. In fact, before moving for Vasquez's release the department had to resolve the number one question of why Vasquez ostensibly pleaded guilty to a crime he *supposedly* didn't commit. And despite the FBI's analyses the department still had to come up with a reasonable explanation for why two people independently identified Vasquez as being at the scene of the crime.

Horgas remained silent through Christiansen's lecture and then left the meeting, infuriated. I put in all this work and now they're throwing me away like an old rag, he fumed to himself on the way back to his office. I'm the one who's invested everything—and all he does is give those guys a chance to cover their asses!

Still, it was gratifying on a certain level to have his *entire* theory, the Vasquez part as well as the Spencer part, acknowledged by a full-blown reinvestigation. Before March 16 nobody had wanted to spend too much time thinking about the Vasquez problem. All the focus had been on Spencer. But when the DNA came back, making Joe's theory a reality, the department not only had a major win in the apprehension of Spencer but potentially a major embarrassment in the arrest and conviction of Vasquez. Of course, the Arlington Police Department had been but one cog in the system of justice that had sent him to prison. Still, they knew that the public blame for Vasquez's incarceration would be placed squarely on their shoulders. Arlington officers, like police throughout the nation, grudgingly but silently accepted the unfortunate reality that *they* were the whipping posts for the criminal justice system. If the Vasquez story hit the headlines, outrage would not be directed at the Commonwealth Attorney's office who sought the indictment, the defense attorneys who urged Vasquez to take the Alford plea, or the judge who admitted the third confession and accepted the plea bargain. So while Joe's superiors hardly relished a reinvestigation, it was not something they could afford to ignore.

Despite Christiansen's explicit instructions, Horgas couldn't resist. As soon as he got back to the squad room, he made a beeline for Carrig.

"I was just down to speak to Christiansen. So tell me, what are you guys gonna be doing?"

"Command's instructed me not to talk to you about the reinvestigation," Carrig said perfunctorily.

"What the hell does that mean? I investigated the fucking case! Just tell me what you plan on doing," Joe insisted.

"Sorry, Joe. I can't," Carrig said, turning away.

Yet Horgas knew it would be impossible for them to shut him out completely. He was sure that Carrig and Shelton would have to come to him for information, if for no other reason than because he had developed all the leads that drove the reinvestigation. Moreover, it was very difficult to keep any secrets in an eight-man squad. In fact, just a few days later, Horgas saw the departmental memo that set forth Carrig and Shelton's marching orders. The five-page summary of the Vasquez investigation highlighted "leads which were not followed up then but should be followed up at this time."

During the investigation it was learned that Vasquez had a "best friend" in Manassas. Bill Kluge, White Male. Kluge brought Vasquez's mother to the station [the night of Vasquez's arrest]. Detective Carrig spoke with him briefly, but Kluge was released. There is no factual evidence to link Kluge to the Hamm murder except to say that he was a close personal friend of Vasquez. . . . After the plea Det. Shelton learned from Vasquez's defense attorneys that Kluge had gone to a bar in Manassas and attempted to get the bartender to verify that Vasquez and Kluge were in the bar on a particular night. The bartender refused to set up the alibi. The bartender was not interviewed by the A.C.P.D.

The memo stressed what was a major sore point for the Hamm investigators, the failure to pursue Vasquez's connection with Bill Kluge.

Det. Shelton contacted the Sarasota Police to relay information on Kluge for intelligence purposes. Det. Shelton advised [a superior officer] that Kluge had been located in Sarasota and that someone from Arlington should confront

Kluge in Florida. Detective Shelton's request was not acted upon. Some months later Det. Shelton learned that Lieutenant Minnich and others were going to Florida on business. Shelton requested that while Lieutenant Minnich was in Florida he look up Kluge with the assistance of the Sarasota Police. Arrangements were made between Shelton and his Sarasota Police contacts to assist Lieutenant Minnich. Upon Lieutenant Minnich's return it was learned that no interview was attempted.

The memo further noted that during his investigation of Tucker, Detective Horgas had discovered Kluge to be presently living just outside Cleveland. It concluded by recommending that Vasquez, Kluge, and the Manassas bartender be reinterviewed along with the two eyewitnesses.

On March 18, while Horgas was at his desk preparing a detailed packet on Spencer for the Commonwealth Attorney, Shelton and Carrig were interviewing David Vasquez. Hoping they could get Vasquez to make a positive ID, they brought along a photo spread that included Timothy Spencer's picture.

"How have you been?" Carrig extended his large square hands across the table to the slight, hunch-shouldered inmate.

"Not bad. Well, not too good either," Vasquez responded.

"It was sure a pretty drive down here," Shelton interjected. "These mountains are pretty beautiful this time of year, aren't they?"

"Drive down from where?" David asked with a puzzled expression.

"Don't you recognize me, David? I'm Chuck Shelton. Me and Carrig here arrested you in nineteen eighty-four. You do remember us, don't you?" Shelton knew his voice showed his exasperation.

Vasquez scratched his beard. "You guys look a little familiar but I don't know who you are."

"David," Shelton said emphatically, "this is really important. You got to pay very close attention. Watch my lips. We arrested you for the murder of Carolyn Hamm and now we got another guy that we think killed her. But we need your help.''

As he had done almost four years earlier, Vasquez crumpled in his seat and cast his eyes downward. His nervous look told the detectives that he was afraid of getting into trouble all over again.

''You got nothing to be worried about. We're here to help you. David, if you can tell us right now you were in Arlington back then peeping in windows we might be able to get you out of this prison within a week or so.'' It was a promise Shelton couldn't keep but he felt it was the only way to coax the truth out of David. The question also reflected Shelton and Carrig's new theory of the case. They accepted that Spencer killed Hamm, and that he probably did it by himself. But they rejected Joe's theory that Vasquez was not in the neighborhood when it happened. They had no explanation for why David was in Arlington or even how he got there from Manassas but they felt sure he was in the neighborhood the night of the murder. ''You got a guy who may be sneaking around peeking in windows,'' Shelton later explained, ''and he looks in [Hamm's] window and sees this sight. Christ, he gets zoned out! The sight takes him into the next galaxy. That would [even] scare the shit out of me.''

''No, I would never do that, sir,'' Vasquez insisted. ''I would never peep in somebody's house.''

Shelton sighed. ''David, you got to understand how important it is that we get the truth. I'm telling you that's what you were doing in that neighborhood!''

Still, David refused to change his story.

Carrig then laid out six pictures in front of David. Vasquez looked them over but showed no emotion. ''Do you recognize any of these guys?'' Shelton asked.

Vasquez shook his head. His puzzled demeanor suggested that not only did he not recognize Spencer, he didn't seem even to understand why he was being shown the photos. Shelton and Carrig left Buckingham as frustrated as they had been after their original interviews with this hapless soul.

Two days later they returned to the prison to obtain fresh samples of David's blood and hair. In early January, Horgas had found a lab in California that did DNA analysis on hairs. Since the only forensic evidence that tied David to the crime scene were a few small hairs found on Hamm's body, it was believed that this DNA analysis, which Lifecodes did not perform, might possibly exclude David and inculpate Spencer.

This alternative DNA fingerprinting process called polymerase chain reaction, or PCR, was performed by Dr. Edward Blake of the California-based Forensic Science Associates, a privately operated DNA lab. The PCR test differed from the Lifecodes procedure in that it required only a small sample of body fluid or hair. In PCR testing the DNA from the sample was replicated using genetic engineering techniques, creating enough duplicate DNA to be tested.

After taking the samples, Shelton fixed his eyes on Vasquez.

"David. Now I'm asking you again. Please just tell us you were standing outside and peeping in the window. Give us something to help you get out . . . I mean, tell us you were just standing there looking in there. You saw the nude body. Tell us something that can justify why you were there!"

Again Vasquez denied he was a peeper, and denied he was in Arlington. Remarkably, though, he also never said, "I didn't do it. I didn't kill Carolyn Hamm."

Horgas knew the next phase of the reinvestigation was Kluge's interview. Since Joe had been the one to find Kluge, he asked Christiansen's permission to accompany Shelton to Cleveland. Much to his continued chagrin, Christiansen immediately and soundly refused. The deputy chief did, however, permit Hill to accompany Shelton since Hill had helped discover Kluge's whereabouts.

Kluge was cooperative. He told a different story, however, from the one Shelton had originally heard.

In 1984 Shelton had been told through Vasquez's defense attorneys that, following Vasquez's arrest, Kluge supposedly went to the bar where he and David commonly drank. Kluge reportedly said to the bartender, "You know they locked up David."

"Yeah, I read about it," the bartender responded.

"Remember we were in here the night that woman was killed?" Kluge asked.

"Wait a minute, let me check your tab." The bartender then pulled out a pad and said, "No. You guys weren't in here that night."

"Yes we were! And if anybody asks you, we were in here that night," Kluge supposedly insisted.

Now, four years later, Kluge had a slightly different story. He told the detectives that he had been asked by David's mother, Imelda Shapiro, to lie. "She wanted me to say that David was with me on January twenty-third, the night of the homicide—but he wasn't. I told her, 'I ain't lying for no one.' " Nervous that he might be caught up in the homicide, Kluge had fled Virginia for Florida.

The Kluge interview was a critical step in the reinvestigation, but if anything it clouded the matter of Vasquez's participation in the whole affair.

The reinterviews with Muriel Ranser and Michael Ansari, which had also been done at the outset of the Tucker investigation, did not make matters any clearer.

Ms. Ranser was as adamant in 1988 as she had been in 1984. David Vasquez was definitely loitering in front of Hamm's home on Saturday evening, January 23, 1984.

"We don't care what you said back then," Carrig told her. "We don't care if you were lying back then or maybe you now think you were mistaken. We're just trying to get the facts straight here." Ranser still refused to budge. David Vasquez was there. No doubt about it.

Mr. Ansari was interviewed later that day. And he was equally sure Vasquez had been in the neighborhood the night Hamm's body was discovered.

The reinvestigation was over at the end of April. Carrig and Shelton had reinterviewed more of the same people they had four years earlier, pursued the identical leads. And as far as they were concerned nothing had changed during that time. They were not persuaded by Mardigian and Ray's theory that Ranser came forward in an effort to protect her brother or that the second set of shoeprints outside Hamm's basement window was left by a uniformed officer who had been inspecting the point of entry. They had known four years earlier that David didn't kill Hamm—at least, not alone—because his blood didn't match the semen stain extracted from the scene and he was simply not smart enough to pull the rape-murder off by himself. But they still felt he was definitely inside or outside Carolyn Hamm's home that night.

"I always felt and I still feel to this day," Carrig later explained, "that David Vasquez was there. . . . Whether he was peeping in the window, whether he was in the house masturbating, whatever you want to say, I still feel to this day that he was there."

Horgas was keenly disappointed when the reinvestigation did not produce the kind of results he had anticipated. He had expected Ranser or Ansari to recant their stories or at the very least to have Kluge provide a positive alibi for David. The DNA analysis of Vasquez's blood and of the Hamm hair sample was equally disappointing. Unfortunately, it was impossible to replicate the DNA obtained from the crime scene hair sample.

While the similarities in all the crime scenes appeared to tie Spencer to the Hamm murder, Helen Fahey had to conclude that the reinvestigation had failed to provide sufficient proof to exclude David Vasquez unequivocally from the crime scene.

Without such proof it would be very difficult to free Vasquez, especially because Spencer had not yet been convicted of Tucker's murder. But once that happened—and given the DNA results, it seemed practically a foregone conclusion—it would be much easier to get Vasquez out of prison. With Spencer safely behind bars, the public would no longer be at risk, and David Vasquez would be made a free man. Helen was convinced of this outcome.

Vasquez's release wasn't the only thing that bothered Joe. He still smarted over the fact that his pattern-rapist-turned-murderer theory had been so insultingly dismissed by the Richmond PD back in December. Now that he had been proven right, he hadn't noticed anybody from Richmond coming around to apologize, let alone extend to him their thanks for solving one of their worst crimes in recent memory. Toward the end of April, Joe couldn't resist an opportunity to set the record straight. He agreed to be an anonymous source for a story on Spencer's arrest.

Horgas revealed to the *Richmond Times-Dispatch* that DNA fingerprinting had definitively linked Spencer to one of the 1983 serial rapes that had preceded the murder of Carolyn Hamm. Let the public get wind of that one, he thought with satisfaction, proof of the escalating rapist. And let Ray Williams explain why it wasn't acted on! "Just as you could look at the Tucker homicide and see the similarities between [the cases in] Richmond and Tucker, you could also see the similarities between Tucker and . . . the rapes and the homicide in 1984. There's a distinct similarity in the MO and everything in the rapes and homicide in 1984 as well as the Tucker murder in 1987," he told the reporter confidently. And, he thought, if they hadn't been so hardheaded, they would have seen it themselves.

On Saturday morning, April 30, Christiansen burst into the office in a whirlwind of fury. "Who's been talking to the press!" he shouted.

He eyed each man in the squad one by one.

"I dunno," someone said.

"You didn't do it, did you, Joe?" His look was sharp and accusing.

"No!" Joe cried, rather too quickly.

Christiansen stomped out. Joe sat at his desk feeling terrible. He shouldn't have lied. He was a person who never lied. He jumped to his feet and trotted to Christiansen's office. "It was me, Chief," he said through the cracked door. "Sorry."

"Goddamn it, Joe!" was all the red-faced deputy chief would say at that moment. Later, he suspended Joe two days' leave, noting in the disciplinary action memo that "any further violations of this nature will result in more severe disciplinary action." Joe felt bad about it, but it was almost worth it to see the headline that ran in Richmond: TESTS SAID TO TIE STRANGULATIONS TO RAPE IN 1983.

Joe awaited the trial eagerly. The prosecution of Timothy Spencer would be the first use of DNA fingerprinting in a criminal case in Virginia and the first time it would be used in a rape-murder case in the United States. It was critical that Commonwealth Attorney Helen Fahey present this complex new technology in a compelling way to the jury. It was not enough to tell the jury that Spencer's blood had the same DNA as the semen found at the scene. She had to be able to explain the entire process.

This would not be easy. Not only did Fahey have no scientific background, the last time she had studied anything even remotely related to biology or chemistry was in high school.

Fahey was lucky, though. Her first assistant, Arthur Karp, was uniquely suited to the task. Karp had studied physics and mathematics at M.I.T. and had spent twenty years as a systems analyst in the Navy. He not only relished crunching numbers but, with his flowing white hair and bushy beard, he actually looked like a scientist. From March through the trial in July, Karp prepared for trial as if it were the most important science test in his life. He poured over reams of scientific literature, spoke to scientists around the country, and even traveled several times to Lifecodes.

Though they were thoroughly prepared, Helen and Arthur became very nervous the week before trial. With the DNA weighing the trial's outcome so clearly in their favor, they felt the defense hadn't a chance—so why hadn't they been approached for a plea agreement? Time was running out. Maybe their case was not as airtight as they thought. "We panicked the night before jury selection because we thought they knew something we didn't," Karp later said. "It was like they had a secret weapon and were going to zap us as soon as we walked into the courtroom."

There was no secret weapon. In fact, defense attorneys Carl Womack and Thomas Kelley felt their case was so weak they didn't even have enough leverage to bargain; therefore, they didn't approach the prosecution about a plea. Their investigation of Spencer's activities failed to turn up any solid alibi for the Thanksgiving weekend. Even more important, they were unable to find any expert to refute DNA analysis.

Womack and Kelley not only visited Lifecodes and inspected their procedures, they also commissioned Cellmark

Diagnostics Inc. of Germantown, Maryland, the other major U.S. DNA testing lab, to analyze and compare Spencer's blood to the semen samples taken from the crime scene. Much to their chagrin, Cellmark confirmed the DNA match. Womack didn't call any Cellmark witnesses to the stand for obvious reasons—the conclusions of one DNA lab were bad enough. It was a bad day [when the DNA] results came back," Womack later reflected. "From then on I never worried about the case because I was in a totally no-win situation . . . I have a tendency to get close to my clients. I didn't want to get close to Tim, because I knew what was going to happen to him." He knew what the prosecutors knew: that according to DNA statistics, the chance of his client's DNA being confused with that of another North American black person was one in 135 million. With those odds, prospects for anything but a guilty verdict were very, very slim.

The trial began on the unusually hot Monday morning of July 11, 1988. Despite the fact that one of the most infamous criminals in the history of Arlington was about to go on trial, few citizens were seen sitting on the oak benches in the public gallery. Court officials took no unusual security precautions such as installing metal detectors. Timothy Spencer worked alone, and it was highly unlikely that any confederates would try to break him out.

The trial was presided over by Judge Benjamin Kendrick. With his hair parted down the middle, wearing a floppy red bow tie, and peering out over those assembled through a pair of antique wire-rim glasses, Kendrick looked like a judge out of the nineteenth century. Though he affected the look of Oliver Wendell Holmes, he was about to hear a case that would be decided on twenty-first-century scientific principles.

In her opening statement, the diminutive Fahey passionately told the eight-woman, six-man jury,

> There are no eyewitnesses in this case. You don't have eyewitnesses in situations like this. But you will have evidence which is even better than an eyewitness because the defendant left something of himself behind at the murder

scene—his hairs and his semen. . . . He also took something from the murder scene with him—a small piece of glass from Susan Tucker's broken basement window.

The opening statement took a little more than eight minutes, unusually short for a capital murder case. Yet with the DNA proof it was unnecessary to make it any longer. Carl Womack's statement ran only half that time. And for good reason. With the DNA results there was little he had to say as well.

From the moment he entered the courtroom, Horgas kept his gaze fixed on Spencer. He looks like a real gentleman sitting there with his tie and jacket, Horgas thought. Spencer showed no emotion during the opening arguments. He just stared off impassively at the prosecution's first witness, Reggie Tucker, tearfully recounted in his thick Welsh brogue how he discovered his wife was dead. Spencer seemed to remain uninterested through the next three witnesses. The testimony of the next witness, however, riveted his attention.

As Helen Fahey asked officer Rick Schoembs to identify each of the eight-by-ten glossy photos of the Tucker crime scene, several jurors turned away in disgust. Even Judge Kendrick was visibly repulsed by the photos of Tucker's body, especially the close-ups of her bloated, oozing face. Because Spencer was sitting to the left and slightly behind Schoembs, he could not see the pictures. This did not stop him from craning his neck and squirming to try to get a look at them.

Man, this guy's got one set of balls, Horgas thought as he watched Spencer straining for a better vantage point to inspect the pictures. What could he be thinking about, doing something so stupid like that in front of the jury? Horgas shook his head. It seemed to him that Spencer desperately wanted to see what his handiwork looked like after three days. Spencer's fascination made even his own lawyer uncomfortable. "I could see him trying to see the pictures and [said] to myself, I wish he wouldn't do that," Womack later recounted.

Horgas testified on Tuesday afternoon, July 12. His testimony was very limited. First Helen asked him to identify a number of sealed plastic bags containing evidence from the Tucker crime scene.

> A: These items ... I transported in a sealed condition to Deanne Dabbs at the Northern Virginia laboratory.
> Q: Now sometime in January did you have occasion to go to Richmond to arrest the defendant?
> A: Yes.

The only other testimony Horgas gave was a description of the conversation he'd had with Spencer during the drive back to Arlington. His thousands of hours of investigation were distilled into a mere half hour of straightforward, almost sterile testimony. None of the hard work and ingenuity that went into identifying Spencer was made known to the jury.

The final leg of the race to bring Spencer to justice would be run by the experts in the white lab coats.

Arthur Karp called Michael Baird to the stand at 9 A.M. on Wednesday morning. Baird anchored the Commonwealth's case by delivering a simple but informative class on DNA. Using charts and a pointer, Baird spoke as if he were conducting a high school science lesson.

He carefully explained the eight-step process used to extract DNA from tissue samples. Toward the end of his testimony he used an overhead projector to compare the autorads obtained from the semen found in and on Tucker's body to the autorads obtained by analyzing Spencer's blood. Even to the neophytes on the jury the supermarket bar code–like markings seemed identical. Baird concluded his testimony by informing the jury that the likelihood another black American would have the DNA found in Spencer's blood was one in every 135 million.

Baird was followed by Lisa Bennett and a succession of non-Lifecodes experts, such as molecular biologist Dr. Richard Roberts of the Cold Spring Harbor Laboratory of New York, who certified the reliability of DNA fingerprinting, showed the jury that it was a generally accepted scientific principle, and attested to the reliability of Lifecodes' findings about Spencer. Kenneth Kidd, a renowned population geneticist and professor at Yale, was asked a series of hypothetical questions by Karp concerning the likelihood of one DNA sample's matching another.

Q: Let's assume that the DNA print tracks in [sample] #7540 [Spencer's blood] were made from DNA extracted from the blood of a person we'll call Mr. A. Also assume that the DNA print tracks labeled 7034 and 7147 [semen stains from the crime scene] were made from sperm cells from a second person we'll call Mr. B. Do you have an opinion, which you can state to a medical certainty, as to the identity of Mr. A and Mr. B?

A: There are two possible conclusions. These patterns are identical so either the two individuals are in fact [one person] or two individuals have shown by chance coincidentally to possess the identical pattern. And that latter alternative is an extraordinarily unlikely coincidence.

Q: What I would like you to do is answer this next question [using] your most conservative estimate, an estimate so conservative as to be unrealistic. Based on [these patterns] how many adult black males are there in the United States with the pattern shown in these autorads?

A: I would estimate between one and two.

Karp sat down; Womack rose to cross-examine.

Q: The study assumes unrelated people, doesn't it?
A: Correct.
Q: If the people are related then the odds would increase that you might get an identical pattern between two people?
A: That's correct.
Q: Nothing further. Thank you.

On Thursday afternoon, after Lisa Bennett testified as to the specific steps she took to analyze the samples of semen and blood, the defense began its case. It was a simple defense composed exclusively of Spencer's relatives. The thrust of

Spencer's mother and grandmother's testimony was that Timmy had been home on Thanksgiving weekend. Womack also elicited from Spencer's mother the information that half of those who attended the holiday meal were males who had a blood relationship with Timothy. In addition to several uncles and cousins, Spencer had three half brothers.

Karp immediately saw the implications of this information. There was a fifty-fifty chance that any one of the male relatives, especially the half brothers, could have a DNA pattern similar to that found at the crime scene.

The last of the seven defense witnesses was Timothy Wilson Spencer. Horgas watched as Spencer calmly and confidently strode to the stand, took his oath and sat down. Turning to Hill, who was sitting next to him, Horgas whispered, "We got him dead to rights and he's still one cocky son of a bitch! Look at him. Mr. Fucking Innocent!"

Clasping his hands piously in his lap, Spencer spoke in a soft voice that belied the evil of the crimes of which he stood accused. Helen Fahey was especially shocked by Spencer's nonthreatening demeanor. "He was . . . pleasant looking," she later commented. "There is a sense of disbelief that anyone who looks like a perfectly normal human being could have committed the crimes you knew he committed. . . . You have the feeling that you would . . . immediately recognize an evil person [but] that's not true. They look just like you or me or your next door neighbor."

Womack's examination was short and direct.

> Q: During the four days you were home for Thanksgiving did you ever go to 4801 S. 27th Road, the home of the victim in this case, Susan Tucker?
> A: No.
> Q: Never?
> A: No.
> Q: Did you break into Susan Tucker's home sometime during that four day period?
> A: No.
> Q: Did you rape her?"
> Q: No.

Q: Did you murder her?
A: No.
Q: No further questions, Your Honor.

Fahey declined to cross-examine. There was literally nothing she could gain from asking Spencer questions. Spencer
was not about to tumble off the witness stand and confess
his sins. But he didn't have to. His DNA had already done
the job for him.

As the attorneys were leaving the courtroom, Helen said
to Kelley slyly. "Have we got a surprise for you!"

"What do you mean, Helen?" Kelley asked.

"You'll see," she said with a smile.

Following the afternoon recess Arthur Karp rose, yellow
pad in hand.

There's a matter which needs to be taken up at this time
[outside the presence of the jury]. It relates to the defense
soliciting from various witnesses details on the size of the
defendant's family and where the half brothers lived. I can
assume they've done this for only one purpose—arguing
to the jury that the perpetrator of the crime that is on trial
now is one of the relatives. . . . Since they have raised the
question of identity in this fashion, they have said to the
jury in effect there is a pool of people that may have committed the crime. This puts the burden on the Commonwealth to eliminate those people and we can do it by
bringing in evidence of the two murders in Richmond.

Because a son has 50 percent of his mother's DNA, Womack and Kelley's strategy had been to suggest that any one
of Tim's three half brothers could be the killer. It was a desperate gamble that made a bad case worse.

During the guilt portion of a trial, the prosecution is typically prohibited from proving the existence of similar crimes
committed by the defendant. Such evidence is considered
incredibly prejudicial because it leads the jury to believe that
if the defendant committed these other crimes, he probably
committed the crime of which he stands accused. However,

there are exceptions. One such exception occurs when the defense raises the possibility that other people could have committed the crime. And it was for this reason that Judge Kendrick, ruling that he would allow such testimony, told Womack, "I think you walked out there on the gangplank and stepped right off the end."

The prosecution would have loved to bring in the Richmond murders, of course, but it would have been a very unusual step for the court to permit that. The defense sought a compromise.

"Would the prosecution agree to a stipulation wherein, in exchange for leaving out the prejudicial impact of the Richmond murders, the defense would agree to tell the judge that none of Spencer's relatives committed the crime?" Womack queried.

"We'll stipulate," Karp told Womack and Kelley, "but we want the language to be very clear." The judge allowed the attorneys until the next morning to work out the stipulation.

At eight the next morning Horgas reviewed the stipulation in Helen's office. As he worked through the document, he felt increasingly uncomfortable. How could the defendant say for certain that none of his blood relatives killed Susan Tucker? How could he know who killed Susan Tucker—unless he had done it himself? The stipulation was tantamount to a confession. A chill went through Horgas. One of his worse nightmares was the specter of Spencer's conviction being overturned because Womack and Kelley made a mistake in allowing the stipulation. Spencer would be released— free to go on torturing women to death. He had to intervene, and that meant going to the defense attorneys, since this ball was in their court. "I got to do something before we go in this morning, Helen," Joe called into her office. "I'll see you in court."

He ran downstairs to the law library where he knew Womack prepared each morning.

"Carl, you know what this stipulation does?" Joe cried.

"What are you talking about? I know what it says," replied Womack.

"No, you don't understand. If you read this to the jury

they'll convict him straight up. He's admitting his guilt. And the last thing I want is to have something like a fucked-up stipulation be the basis of reversible error," Joe insisted.

"How do you figure that?"

"Listen! How can Spencer know it wasn't any of his relatives unless he's the killer?"

Womack's jaw dropped. "God, you're exactly right!" As Womack later said, "We had a judge, two prosecuting attorneys, and two defense attorneys. Not one of us five lawyers caught that."

Later that morning, Judge Kendrick read the stipulation to the jury: "The person who murdered Susan Tucker was not the defendant's half brother Travis, one of the defendant's other half brothers, his father, one of his uncles, one of his cousins or any other blood relative of the defendant." Kendrick then read the Horgas language. "And in entering into this stipulation the defendant in no way admits his guilt."

Fahey's closing argument followed. It presented a chilling scenario of the death of Susan Tucker.

> It's Thanksgiving weekend, a quiet weekend. Many people are away. On this particular night I suspect Susan Tucker had gotten ready for bed and was sleeping quietly. She was in the security of her own home. The defendant on the other hand is out prowling, looking maybe just for some houses to burglarize but prepared with ropes, one of them already tied in a noose, looking very likely for a woman living alone. . . .

After five days of testimony, the jury retired to decide the fate of Timothy Spencer. They began at their deliberation at 12:10 P.M. and returned a verdict at 6:25 that evening. Horgas watched intently as the verdict slip was passed from the forewoman to the bailiff to the judge and back to the forewoman. The slender forty-five-year-old postal worker slowly opened and read the verdict: "We the jury find the defendant guilty of rape and capital murder."

Horgas did not smile or clap. He simply nodded his head in agreement.

Since the jury found Spencer guilty of capital murder they moved directly into the penalty phase to determine whether Spencer would die in the electric chair or spend the rest of his life in prison. Though Helen could not raise the Richmond murders in the trial, in the penalty phase she and Karp could bring out the deaths of Susan Hellams and Debbie Davis. These additional crimes helped raise the stakes in the Commonwealth's argument for death. Lifecodes representatives were on hand to testify that the DNA from semen stains found in the two Richmond woman's bodies matched Spencer's DNA.

Reggie Tucker refused to testify in the penalty phase because he was against the death penalty. However, Debbie Davis's father, William Dudley, was willing. As one of the Commonwealth's first witnesses, the seventy-year-old retiree told the jury that that day was Debbie's birthday. She would have been thirty-five.

The prosecution finished by 2 P.M. on Saturday July 16.

To persuade the jury to save Spencer's life, his attorneys called six witnesses, most of whom knew him as a youngster.

John Robinson, director of the community center where Spencer played as a youth, testified that he knew Spencer and his family for over twenty years. "I've never seen him aggressive [but] he was a loner. He didn't hang with a lot of guys like most of the teenagers today do." Wayne Snider, Spencer's junior high school teacher, similarly testified that Spencer was "pretty much alone a lot of the time." Snider also told the jury that he particularly remembered that twelve-year-old Spencer resented always having to baby-sit his younger brother because it prevented him from playing in after-school activities.

The portrait of Spencer that Snider painted was that of a quiet, fatherless boy who had no self-confidence, a theme that was repeated by most of the others. As a teenager Spencer had several scrapes with the law, but he'd been known in the neighborhood as a nonviolent person. There was no one, however, who testified positively about Timothy Spencer, the adult.

Thelma Spencer loved her son but shed no tears for him when she testified.

"Can you think of anything you could have done or would have done that might have made it all turn out different?" Tom Kelley asked, referring to how she raised Spencer.

"Yes," she answered despondently.

"What's that?"

"I shouldn't have called him and invited him here for Thanksgiving."

"[It] was just a totally useless answer," Carl Womack later commented.

The last witness to plead for Spencer's life was Spencer himself.

After a few questions about his family, Womack said, "Tim, this jury has convicted you of the capital murder of Susan Tucker and they have heard evidence that you also killed Susan Hellams and Debbie Davis. Now I ask you again, as I asked you before, did you kill any of those three ladies?"

"No I didn't," Spencer immediately responded.

"Do you have anything to tell the jury that's going to decide whether you live or die?" Womack then asked.

"I didn't kill those ladies and I feel sorry for their families. I ask you not to sentence me to death," Spencer quietly said.

Shortly after Spencer's testimony, Helen Fahey rose to give her closing argument. She looked each juror in the eye as she spoke.

The thought of sentencing anyone to death is horrible to all of us. It is unfortunate that there are situations in which such considerations have ever to come up. The murder of Susan Tucker shows a depravity of mind and an evil that is difficult, if not impossible for any of us to comprehend. It was not only the crimes he committed and how he committed them, but I would suggest that you think about his demeanor and conduct during the course of this trial. None of you, none of us in this courtroom can look at those pictures of the victims without sorrow, without a certain horror, without revulsion. If you will recall when Officer Schoembs stood in front of you and showed you the pictures of Susan Tucker, did the defendant look away? No. He wanted to get a good look at those pictures because he wanted to see what his handiwork looked like three or four days later. He also looked at the pictures of Debbie Davis and Susan Hellams. Something is terribly, terribly wrong with Timothy Spencer . . . and there can be no question that if he is ever released, that he will once again be looking for women to rape and murder. That is a risk that society and the people of this Commonwealth should not be asked to take.

In his closing argument, Carl Womack offered a theory for the murders. Horgas found this irritating. He had never been interested in why Spencer brutalized and murdered five helpless women. Womack, though, was hoping if he gave the jury a reason they might spare his client's life.

He never got any attention [from his mother]. I can't say she's a horrible mother and it's her that should be punished. I think she probably did what she had to do. But for Timmy it wasn't enough. He kept growing angrier, kept getting into trouble [as he grew up]. Finally he starts doing burglaries. He gets out in 1987 and if you believe the Commonwealth he's raped and murdered three women. And the question is still why. He hates his mother. . . . Every time, Tim's killing his mother, but his mother is black. You're supposed to love your mother. And you can't show that you hate your mother. And if you kill a black woman then you almost have to acknowledge that you hate your mother. So you kill somebody who is other than black. He's not killing white women—he's killing women who are not black.

"I just thought he was a mean scumbag," Horgas whispered to Hill. "Now I know he's a mean scumbag who doesn't like his mother. Ain't nothing wrong with Mrs. Spencer! She's a hardworking lady that had nothing to do with what Spencer did. I mean look at Travis—star basketball player, good stu-

dent. I don't see him raping and killing nobody!" Hill nodded in agreement.

But did Spencer really have a "normal" childhood? Was
there really nothing in his life that indicated he might end up
here convicted of a series of gruesome murders and begging a
jury to spare his life?

Clearly, his first arrest at the age of nine for setting a fire
in school and the string of burglaries that followed indicated
something was wrong. But what was it?

The defense actually presented very little about Spencer's
background aside from the few witnesses who had known
him as a youth, and Spencer himself never testified about
his family history. A portrait did emerge, however, from his
school records and a psychological assessment done in connection with an arrest in 1983 for trespassing and burglary.
He was twenty-one at the time the report was drafted.

Both of Spencer's parents were hardworking people. His
father, a postal worker, had no criminal record and completed two years of college; his mother, a bookkeeper, completed three years of college and she too had no criminal
record. They divorced after ten years of marriage, when Tim
was seven years old. The oldest of two children, Tim was
raised primarily by his mother and grandmother.

Spencer's very early childhood was unremarkable—he sat
up at five months and took his first steps at nine months. His
problems, however, began soon after he started grade school.

A September 19, 1973, school psychological report
summed up the eleven-year-old's very troubled history.

> Tim has a history of disruptive and maladaptive behav-
> ior. Records indicate that [when he was nine years old]
> ... he was suspended [and brought before the juvenile
> authorities] for starting a fire in the boys' bathroom. Since
> he has been attending Abingdon Elementary he has dis-
> played the same behavior. Reports from the staff refer to
> setting off the fire alarm, stealing a tape recorder and nu-
> merous articles from other students, defecating on the floor
> of the boys' rest room, and urinating on the steps and the
> landing area of his class group. On May 22, 1973, Tim was

placed on probation. . . . He [has] been referred to the mental health clinic but there is no record in his file indicating that he has attended any sessions there . . . Tim's mother has been involved in numerous conferences with school personnel regarding Tim's problems. . . .

Tim is . . . a boy who is performing academically on a second grade level in reading, spelling, and arithmetic. When required to participate in [remedial help groups] he displays anger and hostility.

A psychological assessment in April of 1973 found that "Tim's figure drawings [that of a person and his own family] look like puppets, reflecting feelings of ineffectualness and of impotence, in the sense of being manipulated by the forces over which he had no control. They almost reflect the defeatist attitude of 'what's the use? what do I have to lose?' . . . This defeatist attitude could account . . . for triggering the negative and aggressive reactions to [what he perceives as an] overcontrolling environment. He protests too much and seems determined to prove that he is the one in charge of the situation and not the environment."

As Spencer got older, his adjustment problems only got worse. In junior high he was placed in classes for learning-disabled children. Because of low grades he was left back in eighth grade.

Over the years, Spencer's mother spent many hours with school counselors. In 1976 one of these counselors noted that Mrs. Spencer "[saw] Tim as withdrawing, having a poor self-concept, was immature [and had] no motivation. [She also] said that Tim recognizes he is not accepted by his peers."

Things changed little over the next seven years. A psychological assessment, done after he was convicted of a burglary in 1983, noted that "[Spencer] withdrew from school in the tenth grade. . . . Vocationally he has been employed as a brick-layer and janitor. The longest job he held on a continuous basis was for six months and he has never been fired from any jobs. . . . He denied a prior psychiatric or suicidal history and no such self-destructive ideation was noted. He denied ever having experienced an hallucinatory or delusional ideation and none were noted at this time. He denied ever having been involved in a sexual relationship with another man. The revised BETA [a psychological test] indicated that this man is functioning in the low-average range of intelligence and that he has a tendency to disregard rules, is uninhibited and is easily led. . . . [In fact] he is very uninhibited and tends to set his own limits as compared to following those that are set by others."

In connection with this last observation the report noted that "prior to coming to the [reception center] he received numerous charges such as possession of contraband, delaying and hindering, setting a fire, abusing telephone privileges, etc."

After his next arrest on January 29, 1984, for burglarizing an Alexandria home where he stole specially minted coins, a pre-sentencing report revealed little had changed since his prior arrest. "Subject does not accept culpability for his action," the report noted, "but rationalizes his behavior and blames others for his involvement in the instant offenses."

While it is impossible to predict who will become a serial rape-murderer, research conducted in the mid-1980s by the FBI's Behavioral Science Unit in concert with nationally known rape expert Dr. Ann Burgess did identify certain behavioral characteristics shared by many of these offenders, including Timothy Spencer. The study focused on thirty-six males, many of whom were the eldest sons.

They were of good intelligence and over 80% described their family socioeconomic levels as average or better. In 47% of the cases, the father left home before the subject was 12 and [t]he loss of the father required many of the offenders to adjust to a new male caretaker during childhood and adolescent years. Examination of performance behaviors revealed that despite their intelligence and potential . . . performance in academics, employment and military was often poor. Only one third did average or better in school with 68% receiving a fair to poor academic rating. The majority did not finish school. Thus although these men were intellectually bright, they did not perform to their abilities. Interviews with the murderers in our study revealed that their internal world is often preoccupied with troublesome, joyless thoughts of dominance over others. In childhood these [thoughts expressed themselves through] cruelty toward animals, abuse of other children, negative play patterns, disregard for others, firesetting, stealing and destroying property. In adolescence and adulthood, the murderer's actions became more violent: assaultive behaviors, burglary, arson, abduction, rape, nonsexual murder and finally murder involving rape, torture, mutilation and necrophilia. . . . The early violent acts are reinforced, as the murderers . . . are able to express rage without experiencing negative consequences. . . . [Moreover] impulsive and erratic behaviors discourage friendships. The failure to make friends leads to isolation and interferes with the ability to resolve conflicts, to develop positive empathy and to control impulses. The men either as children or adolescents feel estranged from people . . . they are loners and self-preoccupied. Either by daydreaming or fantasies, they become self-absorbed in their own thoughts. . . . One of the primary functions of family life is to develop a child who has a positive bonding with his social environment. In our population of murderers this social bonding fails or becomes narrow and selective. Caretakers either ignore, rationalize or normalize various behaviors in the developing boy. . . . People significant to the boy did not provide nurture and protection; rather, they impose adult expectations on the boy ("Boys should be strong and take care of themselves."). This is the child who does not listen or respond to any limit setting and who often is described as aloof, cold and uncaring.

[T]his increased social isolation encourages a reliance on fantasy as a substitute for human encounter. In turn individual personality development becomes dependent on fantasy life and its dominant themes, rather than on social interaction. Without human encounters and negotiations, there is failure to develop the corresponding social values, such as respect for others' lives and property. The personal traits critical to the development of the murderers in our study include a sense of social isolation, preferences for autoerotic activities and fetishes, rebelliousness, aggression, chronic lying and a sense of entitlement.... Their social isolation and aggression interact, restricting sexual development based on caring, pleasure and companionship. Because they are so isolated, the men have little opportunity for interpersonal experiences that might modify their misconceptions about themselves and others. In turn, fantasy becomes the primary source of emotional arousal and that emotion is a confused mixture of sex and aggression.

It is clear from the research that Spencer demonstrated many of the behaviors the researchers found in their study of serial killers. With regard to Spencer's childhood, FBI Agent Stephen Mardigian commented, "Spencer's early maladaptive history of fire-setting and stealing are consistent with what we have seen in our interviews with serial offenders. It must be stressed, however, that not all young children who exhibit such bizarre behaviors will be serial killers." Mardigian found the public defecation and urination behavior especially significant. "These behaviors at such a very young age are clear indications of a very angry young person. They are the ultimate aggressive and defiant acts against society and specifically against those he perceived as controlling his environment. It's one thing to tell someone, "I 'shit' on your rules and authority, but it's a much more disturbing sign to actually perform those acts in public."

"Finally," Mardigian said, "it is interesting to note that the observations made by the school counselor in 1973 concerning young Spencer's need to control his environment were graphically played out in each of the rape-murders."

But the jury didn't need to know any of these reasons. It was enough for them that he had killed Susan Tucker and at least three other women.

And at 6:45 P.M., after three hours of deliberation, the jury announced it had reached its decision. Horgas watched a stone-faced Spencer rise and face the jury.

We the jury, having unanimously found that the defendant's conduct in committing the offense is outrageously
. . . vile, horrible and inhumane in that it involved torture,
depravity of mind . . . unanimously fix his punishment
at death.

Following these words, Judge Kendrick thanked the jury
for their service and they were escorted from the courtroom.
With two deputies at his sides, Spencer rose from his chair
and strode slowly to the door leading to the jail. As the door
opened, Spencer looked back over his right shoulder in Horgas's direction. And with a slight smirk on his face, he raised
his middle finger to the man who was responsible for his
arrest. "What an asshole," Horgas said to Mike Hill, who was
sitting next to him. "What a fucking asshole."

Tears welling in his eyes, a doleful Reggie Tucker spoke
to the group of reporters gathered outside the courthouse.
"[The verdict] was right. But there's no satisfaction in it because I'll never get my Suzy back." The same sentiments
were expressed by Susan Hellams's parents. However, William Dudley, Debbie Davis's father, felt very differently.

"We are very happy that it turned out the way it did. . . .
I hope the same thing [happens] in Richmond. You can't kill
a man but one time, but it will prove the man is a vicious
killer."

Helen, Arthur, and Joe had just obtained the first murder/
rape conviction in the United States using DNA fingerprinting. The Spencer case was also the first one in which DNA
fingerprinting was used to send a man to the electric chair.
Though the papers and television reporters hailed it as a
landmark victory, Horgas was not yet ready to celebrate.

His job was not done.

The next morning Joe sat patiently in the waiting room of
Helen's office. He paged through accounts of his weekend
triumph.

"We got the conviction, now what about Vasquez?" Joe
asked.

"I just got the name of an assistant AG. I'll call him right
now."

Helen provided the assistant attorney general a brief history of the situation. "So you see we may have an innocent guy in prison. What do we do?" Helen asked.

To her surprise Helen was told that if Vasquez had just been recently sentenced he would still be under the Arlington County court's jurisdiction and it would have been fairly simple to get him back. The judge could have ordered his return, held a new hearing, and he'd have been out. "But," the AG said, "sounds like Corrections has control over your guy. The local court has relinquished custody. I'm sorry. I've really never seen a situation like this. I can't give you any advice on what to do, but I know it won't be easy."

"You mean you've never had this happen before? You really can't tell me how to get an innocent man out of prison?"

In her enthusiasm to see an injustice righted, Helen had overlooked the messy details. Once an inmate is remanded to the Department of Corrections, from the court's point of view the case is over. The court no longer has jurisdiction over the matter and new evidence is immaterial. For the court to reconsider his case, Vasquez's defense attorneys would have to file a habeas corpus. This proceeding would drag on for years.

Helen knew this, but she thought that once she explained the situation to the Attorney General's office they'd find a way around these obstacles. Unfortunately, certain aspects of the scenario made this impossible. It was a capital murder case. Though the defendant entered an Alford plea, it had the same effect as if Vasquez pleaded guilty. And the new evidence had appeared long after the court had lost jurisdiction.

Helen's shocked expression made Joe extremely nervous. When he heard her next words he knew getting David out was going to take a lot longer than a half hour.

"Pardon's the only way? Are you sure? Really? You've never had a request like this before? OK. Thanks."

Helen put the phone back in its cradle and stared somberly at Joe.

"We have a problem. Though Spencer has been convicted and we have good reason to believe he killed Hamm, there's still no absolute evidence to show that Vasquez was not in Arlington, at the crime scene, that night. We have no way forensically to eliminate him. The Hamm semen sample was so degraded there was no way to extract sufficient DNA from it. And there's a technical problem. We generally assume that people who enter guilty pleas, even Alford pleas, are admitting something. It wasn't like he pleaded not guilty and was convicted by a jury. To get a pardon we're not only going to have to explain his confession, we're going to need some greater proof than just your theory that Spencer killed Hamm. I'm sorry, Joe. I know you were expecting to see me get him out today. But to do that it seems that I am going to need a really strong hook to hang my hat on."

Horgas easily read between the lines. It was more than mere legal technicalities that concerned Helen. A pardon application meant that she believed a mistake had been made not only by the police department. A pardon application would also imply that the most senior Arlington County superior court judge, William Winston, and the former Commonwealth Attorney, Henry Hudson, now the United States Attorney for the Eastern District of Virginia, had erred.

"You know me, Joe, I try not to make decisions based on my gut reaction. I want absolute proof. No matter what you think, Vasquez's mere statement that he wasn't there that night will not be absolute proof. It will be seen as self-serving testimony. DNA is evidence. A fingerprint is evidence."

"Listen, Helen, I've done everything I can do on my end. There's not gonna be any scientific test that says Vasquez wasn't there. But we have some other proof."

Helen's eyes went wide. "What do you mean?"

"It's not exactly proof, but it might work. The FBI. Ask them if they would give you a formal opinion on whether Vasquez or Spencer killed Hamm. They already know the case. They already helped me identify Spencer, now they just have to put their opinion in writing. And you know as well as I do that the FBI's word's gonna carry a lot of weight."

That afternoon Helen formally requested the FBI's assistance. It was the first request the Behavioral Science Unit

had ever received to help prove a man innocent and they
readily agreed to assist.

Within two weeks of Spencer's conviction, word of the
reinvestigation and FBI request was reported to the media.
In an article captioned, "Spencer cases cloud earlier conviction," Shelton told the *Arlington Journal*, "We felt from the
beginning that he did not do it. We always felt that he was
there with someone else. The problem was that nothing
turned up to eliminate him."

"U.S. Attorney Henry Hudson," the article continued,
"who as the Commonwealth's Attorney prosecuted Vasquez,
said the guilty plea dispelled any doubts he had about the
case."

Horgas read the quotes with dismay. The reinvestigation
had changed nothing in Shelton's mind except that Spencer
might have been Vasquez's accomplice—an alliance Horgas
felt was impossible. Hudson's position was even worse—it
could seriously jeopardize the pardon effort.

Horgas had hoped desperately that further DNA testing
might prove that the semen found at the Carolyn Hamm
scene was not David Vasquez's. But of course that semen had
proved untestable. There was just no evidence that excluded
David from the scene. And dammit, he had confessed, and
pleaded guilty.

Still, Shelton's and Hudson's comments in the *Journal* did
prompt the first public criticism of the Vasquez affair. It came
in the form of a stinging editorial in the same paper.

> What used to be the prosecution in the disturbing case
> of David Vasquez is now the defense. Detectives and
> prosecutors, including former Commonwealth's Attor-
> ney Henry Hudson, are trying to explain why they dis-
> carded contradictory evidence and pressed their case on
> the basis of a weak confession from this weak-minded
> young man. . . . Investigators coaxed three confessions
> out of him, only one of which was ruled admissible, but
> the facts of the case [cloud] the reality of the confession.
> Now DNA testing, the newest courthouse tool, is ex-
> pected to show that Vasquez is innocent of the crime

for which he served four years in prison. Suddenly the
police and prosecutors are recalling their earlier doubts
and expressing them publicly for the first time. They
seem to have pursued a conviction more diligently than
they pursued justice.

Hudson responded to the editorial with an op-ed piece of
his own two weeks later.

With all due respect to your fine newspaper I must take
exception to your editorial analysis of the David Vasquez case. . . . The Vasquez case was uniquely complex.
I personally spent several hundred hours examining the
crime scene, interviewing witnesses and reviewing evidence. . . . Everyone involved in the investigation agreed
that the crime probably had been committed by two individuals, and that Vasquez was probably the more pas-
sive of the two. However under Virginia law, an aider
and abettor shares equal culpability with his cohorts. . . .
[His] confession was admittedly less than textbook quality . . . but at no time was he abused or treated
rudely. . . . The decisions made daily in the criminal
justice system are gut wrenching. Lawyers, prosecutors
and police officers are called upon to make decisions in
the heat of the day which others casually review in the
cool of the evening. The decision to accept Mr. Vasquez's plea of guilty was based on all the evidence available after an exhaustive investigation. And it is
important to remember that if every case prosecuted
were required to be free of all doubt few people would
ever be convicted. . . . On the morning David Vasquez
pleaded guilty to murder, his own lawyers, the police
and I were convinced that a jury would find him guilty
beyond a reasonable doubt. Given that much what
would the informed conscience of the community—indeed, what would your editorial page have said had I
simply dismissed the charges and released David Vasquez back on to the streets?

One hundred miles away in his cramped office in the basement of the eleven-story FBI Academy, Steve Mardigian was drafting an answer to that very question. In a very real sense Mardigian was conducting his own reinvestigation of Vasquez, using much of what he had learned during his marathon meeting with Horgas on that snowy December day in 1987.

Following Fahey's request, Mardigian had begun an exhaustive computerized analysis comparing each of the five homicides and every rape attributed to the masked rapist. The final product was a thirty-four-page document, which broke down the five murders and twelve rapes into fifty-two categories. In addition to the victim's and suspect's age, sex, and race, the date and time of the offense, Mardigian evaluated for each crime the duration of attack; type of residence; point of entry and mode of entry; location of assault; whether and how the suspect moved the victim through residence or other place of attack; ransacking of victim's residence; type of weapon used to threaten the victim; victim's injuries; type of bindings; type of gag; sexual acts; whether the suspect ejaculated; clothes worn by the suspect; what the suspect said and when; and finally, forensic findings such as blood type and DNA.

Except for the computerized format, it was essentially the identical information Horgas had developed during the Tucker investigation. The purpose of the document, which ultimately accompanied a formal letter, was to illustrate the remarkable similarities between the rapes and the Tucker and Richmond homicides. And since Hamm had all the markers of the rapes and other murders, Mardigian concluded that whoever committed the 1987 murders also killed Carolyn Hamm.

On October 16, 1988, Helen Fahey received the letter. In addition to Mardigian, the letter was signed by FBI Agent John Douglas, the founder and director of the Behavioral Science Unit.

Per your request, case materials relative to the Carolyn Jean Hamm and Susan M. Tucker homicides have been extensively reviewed. The purpose of this review was to determine if the separate cases could have been perpetrated by the same person. . . . It is important to understand that over a period of time an offender will generally modify or alter certain aspects regarding his modus operandi based upon his experience, gaining confidence and learning from mistakes. While the M.O. may change due to learned behavior, the ritual performed by the offender will remain the same. This ritual reflects the things in the offender's fantasy, his personal needs that will never change. . . . After a careful examination of the Hamm and Tucker homicides, it is our professional opinion that the same perpetrator was responsible for both and he acted alone. . . . Not only was the same M.O. utilized in these cases but the same ritual was observed. . . . He enjoyed tying his victims, it furthered his feelings of dominance and control over them. It was the assailant's intention to keep the victim alive for a period of time [thereby] expressing his own virility through dominance, power, control and manipulation of the victims. . . . To do what was done to the victims the assailant would have had to have spent a considerable amount of time with them. . . . The fact that methods used by the assailant in the Hamm homicide were so elaborate strongly supports our conclusion that this was not the first time this assailant had been involved in a sexual assault. . . .

The five-page letter went on to describe the specific similarities between the two cases. The FBI's conclusion contained the language critical to Vasquez's release.

It is also important to note that these homicides were not perpetrated by someone who was mentally deficient, disabled or handicapped. A person so impaired would not have spent the amount of time at the scene as demonstrated in these killings. He would not have waited to confront the victims face to face, but would have been more secretive in his approach and interaction with [them] and would not have engaged in the sexual assault exhibited in these cases. An impaired personality who commits a violent crime will demonstrate through his behavior disorderly, haphazard and chaotic crime scenes. The Hamm and Tucker cases do not reflect an assailant of this type. To the contrary these assaults were perpetrated by an organized type personality of prior criminal sophistication who acted alone when he perpetrated these killings. We hope this analysis is of some benefit to you, the appropriate judicial authority and defense counsel.

Following the receipt of the FBI letter Helen approached her predecessor, Henry Hudson, to inform him of her intent to seek a pardon and to obtain his approval. Though not a legally required step, it was politically necessary. And the governor's decision on whether or not to grant a pardon would be a deeply political one.

Hudson told her that if she felt confident that a mistake had been made then he would endorse her actions. Not that another answer would have changed her mind—and not that she expected him to say anything else. The pardon train now was moving very fast and everyone seemed to be jumping on board.

Fahey worked hard on the pardon petition after Joe wrote a first draft. She forwarded the petition to Governor Baliles four days after receiving the FBI letter.

Dear Governor Baliles:

In accordance with Article V Section 12 of the Constitution of Virginia, I hereby request that executive clemency be granted to David Vasquez who is now incarcerated in the Buckingham Correctional Institute. Executive clemency is requested because the conclusion has been reached that another individual is responsible for the murder and burglary for which David Vasquez now stands convicted. . . .

Helen explained why it was believed that Timothy Spencer had killed Carolyn Hamm. But then Fahey parted company with Hudson and went on to publicly admit that Vasquez's arrest had been a mistake.

> Approximately 75% of [Vasquez's] statements were suppressed by the court because [he] had not been given his Miranda warnings earlier in the interrogation.... Even taken as a whole, however, the statements were of limited evidentiary value due to Vasquez's low intelligence level (IQ 75–85 borderline retarded/low normal) and his susceptibility to suggestion by the police during the interrogation.

The letter also highlighted several facts of Spencer's 1984 burglary arrest that circumstantially connected him to the Hamm murder.

Back in 1984, three days after Carolyn Hamm was murdered on January 29, Spencer was arrested for burglary. He was actually caught inside a home at 1508 Mt. Eagle Place. A neighbor saw him walk up to the rear patio door at that address, and she called another neighbor to tell her she saw a strange man standing outside the back door a few houses away. Then she heard a tapping sound. She told her neighbor she was hanging up and calling the police.

While the first neighbor dialed the ACPD, the second neighbor ran to her bedroom window and watched as the young man broke the window and vanished into the dwelling. When police arrived they saw him through the window; a K-9 officer commanded him to come out, and he was placed under arrest without incident. He had collector's coins in his pocket, which were to link him definitively to another burglary, earlier that evening, in which those coins had been taken.

Spencer's possession of stolen coins was the first point Fahey used in her petition to tie him to the 1983 rapes (and to the admittedly linked murder of Carolyn Hamm); the rapist on at least two occasions had had property on him from other, recent burglaries. She also pointed out that when he was arrested at 1508 Mt. Eagle Place Timothy Spencer wore a tan jacket and Puma sneakers, had a small flashlight in his pocket, and wore socks on his hands. Several rape victims had described a tan jacket and the socks on the hands. A Puma footprint was discovered at the point of entry of one rape. Multiple victims said the rapist used a small flashlight. And then there were the forensics; Spencer's hair matched the hair found at the first rape and his blood type and DNA matched each murder.

Finally, there was, as Joe called it, "the icing on the cake." Though there was no usable DNA from the Hamm semen samples that could be compared to Spencer's DNA, Lifecodes had obtained a match between Spencer's DNA and the fifth victim of the masked rapist. This evidence fairly conclusively proved Joe's initial theory that the masked rapist was the one who had killed Hamm. But had Joe not asked Chapman at the beginning of the investigation to retrieve all the evidence in the masked rapist case, it would have later been impossible to make the comparison to Spencer, for just before Chapman retrieved the evidence from the property room, it had been slated for destruction.

Then Helen invoked the mantra of the FBI National Center for the Analysis of Violent Crime—the formal name of the program under which the Behavioral Science Unit operated. And she attached the FBI's letter.

The pardon process took much longer than Joe and Helen expected. First, the governor was obliged to turn the matter over to the Board of Pardon and Parole, and they in turn had to conduct a formal reinvestigation. At a minimum this meant reviewing every allegation made in the pardon petition, and a full psychiatric evaluation. Once the parole board had approved everything, the governor conducted his own investigation, which included not only a review of all facts and evidence but a careful weighing of the political implications of his decision.

On January 4, 1989, David Vasquez was released—almost a year to the day after Joe had come up with the name of Timothy Spencer. Governor Baliles had granted him an absolute pardon, in a formal document that said that "reason and justice required the use of executive clemency."

On that day, as reported in a retrospective July 17, 1989, article in *The Washington Post,*

As [Vasquez] was eating a cheeseburger in the mess hall at Buckingham, a guard tapped him on the shoulder and told him to pack and call his attorney. He didn't move. While other inmates at the table cheered, Vasquez sat calmly and finished his dinner. Then he walked outside, across "the boulevard" and into his cell-block, where he found his friend Charles Young. Young suggested he call his attorney before he did anything else.

"He was just stiff, kind of stunned, because he hadn't really heard it yet," Young said. "He got on the phone and called his lawyer, then he kind of looked at the phone and said, 'A full pardon?' and the next words were 'Tonight?' And he hung up the phone and he walked halfway to the stairs and then he leaped about four feet into the air. He didn't say anything, but he screamed."

Vasquez's mother, Imelda Shapiro, had kept her Christmas decorations up for her son. In the front yard were big red bows, plastic Christmas holly and little yellow ribbons. Shapiro was on the phone with a reporter when her son walked up the yard carrying a television set and a fan. She gasped and dropped the receiver. They embraced.

Still, there were those with mixed feelings.

As Carrig later commented, "I probably would have felt one hundred percent better about the whole thing if Ansari or Ranser admitted that they lied or were mistaken, but they didn't. . . . No matter what the hell we do we still can't prove that Vasquez didn't do it and prove that Spencer did do it. It's still the same thing as it was the day that we found Hamm." Carrig continued to believe that Vasquez had been present, if only as a peeper.

Hudson also continued to believe that there was legally admissible evidence against Vasquez. Soon after the pardon he was asked to comment on it. As a U.S. attorney he worked closely with the FBI and had to walk a very fine line—after all, the FBI's opinion had been that Spencer murdered Hamm.

"[I]t was very, very important to weigh the existing legally competent evidence in the case because you have to remember that while the FBI agents and [scientists] in the Behavioral Sciences laboratory are very, very bright, talented people, that their educated assessment is not competent evidence. That's a well-thought-out guess," he said. "There is no competent, legally admissible evidence at this point that is exculpatory of David Vasquez. On the other side of the ledger, you have the evidence which we would have introduced against him in the trial in Arlington County which may or may not have been sufficient to convict him. . . . There is, from that evidence, a more than fifty percent chance that he could have been convicted of capital murder."

In other interviews, Hudson later commented that he believed Horgas was "a solid, grade B detective. . . . He's a very good detective. Very good. Don't take anything away from him. He's a topnotch investigator. But he was not the most brilliant investigator in the robbery-homicide section. He was not the kind of person that the sergeant would turn to in the most difficult case. . . . Solid grade B detective. Which isn't bad. I give my grade very, very judiciously. But he was not the superstar. He wouldn't be the man who would carry the ball on the one yardline."

Hudson continued to insist that, had it not been for the plea bargain, "the chances were ninety percent I would have tried that case. If I had walked into court and nol prossed [dismissed charges on] that case, I would probably have been confronted with a recall move in Arlington County. You had a very serious homicide, you had enough evidence to get it through preliminary hearing, the judge had no problem. . . . It's the type of case that just lent itself to a trial by jury."

Horgas, though, could have cared less what Hudson thought. Spencer had been captured and convicted. He wasn't going to hurt any more women.

Now, on the evening of January 4, 1989, he watched the news footage of David Vasquez walking in the door of his mother's home after being released from Buckingham earlier that day.

The television camera zoomed in on a heartfelt embrace

between Vasquez and his mother. Sitting on his mother's couch surrounded by yellow ribbons and Christmas presents Vasquez said, "All I kept dreaming was that they would catch the real guy. I prayed a lot that they'd find him."

Horgas picked up the remote and clicked off the set.

"Come on, David!" he roared, good-naturedly.

"Huh?" His son looked up from his book.

"Think you can pin me?" He grinned.

David grinned back, and ran into his father's arms.

EPILOGUE

MARCH 1994

FOLLOWING HIS CONVICTION IN ARLINGTON, SPENCER WAS TRIED and convicted in Richmond in October of 1988 for the murder of Debbie Davis and was convicted of the murder of Susan Hellams in January of 1989. At the close of the Davis case, Ray Williams somberly told a reporter, "This one's for Glenn. I wish he had been sitting next to me because I know how hard he worked on it." After Glenn died, Ray Williams hung a photo of his partner over his desk. He continues to visit Glenn's grave every month.

Five months later in June of 1989, Spencer was convicted in Chesterfield of the murder of Diane Cho.

The Cho prosecution was not based solely on DNA. Because the DNA in crime scene samples had been degraded and bacterially contaminated by vaginal blood and yeast, Lifecodes was unable to do the testing. The samples were then sent to Dr. Edward Blake in California—the same scientist who examined the Hamm crime scene hairs. The PCR test developed by Blake however, was not nearly as definitive as the restriction length polymorphism or RFLP test used by Lifecodes. All Blake could conclude was that the Spencer's

DNA was consistent with the Cho semen samples and that this genotype occurred in about five percent of the population—a number not nearly as impressive as 1 in 135 million.

Because of the inability to obtain a more definitive DNA match, Warren von Shuch, the assistant Chesterfield County prosecutor, tried the case as "signature crime." Typically, evidence of the defendant's other crimes is inadmissible in the guilt portion of a trial if it is used merely to prove the likelihood that the accused committed the crime with which he was charged. A very narrow exception to this rule is that prior crimes may be introduced if they are so similar as to indicate the identity of the accused. The law requires, "Where evidence of a separate crime is used to establish the identity of the accused, more is required than merely proving the repeated commission of crimes of the same class. Generally, the device used to commit the crime, or the manner in which the crime was committed, must be so distinctive as to indicate a modus operandi or to act as a signature [of the accused]." Using this strategy, von Shuch introduced all three previous convictions along with their DNA results and then set forth for the jury the thirteen ways in which Cho was similar to each of them. In all three cases the jury sentenced Timothy Wilson Spencer to die in Virginia's electric chair.

Though Spencer was silent when the death sentence was imposed in Tucker, Davis, and Cho, he was moved to speak after the Hellams jury returned its verdict.

Now I am not going to take my life and you are not going to take my life. And I'm going to prove Mr. Davis [referring to the Commonwealth Attorney] and your sidekick there Detective Horgas set me up. . . . You watch, Your Honor. All this little DNA stuff you all brought up here, I'm going to show you how low-life these people, come up here, call me a murderer. . . . These people come in here, try to play God, but God doesn't call for me yet.

Unmoved by this clearly unrepentant plea, Judge James Wilkinson formally sentenced Spencer to death.

* * *

•Following Spencer's convictions, a complete review was conducted of why Spencer was placed in a halfway house and how he could have committed those crimes while supposedly under the jurisdiction of the Department of Corrections. The findings were tragic but unfortunately not surprising. On October 1, 1988, the *Richmond Times-Dispatch* reported,

> Had a Virginia Parole Board recommendation been followed, Timothy W. Spencer—the "South Side Strangler"—wouldn't have been able to wander the streets at night, a parole official says. . . . "If he had been put in work-release, he would have had supervision at all times and would not have been allowed to wander around all hours of the night," said Lewis W. Hurst, the parole board's vice-chairman.
>
> When the board denied Spencer parole in June 1987, it recommended he be considered for work-release, Hurst said. That would have meant Spencer's confinement in prison or jail when he was not at work.
>
> [However] in the pre-release program that put Spencer in the halfway house, Spencer was allowed to leave the facility at night and on the weekends. . . . Also he was not supervised by a state probation and parole officer or by a corrections officer. . . . A case-worker in the [Corrections] division's classification and records [who] made the decision to release Spencer to the South Richmond halfway house said . . . "There was nothing about [Spencer] that would have triggered a special review for me."

In addition, according to a report issued by a Richmond grand jury, Hospitality House failed "to follow with any degree of diligence the rules, regulations it agreed to enforce before it [was] awarded its contract by the Department of Corrections and the Bureau of Prisons." The report found among other things that the house was not secure. Though exit doors were equipped with alarms, the system could easily be disabled by removing a fuse from the breaker panel.

In addition, the report noted, "the room assigned to Spencer was situated [so that] he could step out of the window on to the fire escape and witnesses presented evidence of seeing Spencer step out of the window, go out, secure beer and return the same way. . . . Witnesses also indicated that oftentimes the prisoners would leave without signing out or in with no action taken against them. . . . Witnesses also stated to foul the required nightly bed checks, they would arrange pillows to give the appearance of being in bed, while [actually they were] absent from the house."

In 1989, William and Josephine Dudley, the parents of Debbie Davis, filed a $9 million civil suit against Offender Aid and Restoration, the agency overseeing the halfway house where Spencer lived, for not adhering to the security measures dictated by Spencer's "prerelase" status. The suit was settled out of court in 1991.

•Agents Stephen Mardigian and Judson Ray look back on their participation in the case with pride. It was the first time the FBI's Behavioral Science Unit had had a role in freeing an innocent man from incarceration. "The truth was served here," Mardigian later said. And it was a substantial effort. Between the investigation of Spencer and Vasquez's pardon, the BSU put in more time than on any other matter in the history of the unit—more than on Wayne Williams, the Atlanta Child Murderer, and more than on the case of the Green River Killer, a case that is still unsolved. But not everyone was happy with the FBI's performance.

Long after Spencer's convictions, some in the Richmond law enforcement community strenuously asserted that it was the FBI's fault they hadn't caught Spencer sooner. They argued that because the FBI had led them away from focusing on black males, Spencer was ignored.

Though these persons never made this charge directly to the FBI, it was a well-known fact among Richmond and Arlington officers, especially Horgas. The FBI never formally responded to the complaint, but in an interview for this book they simply said that they never told Richmond to focus exclusively on whites. (At least one Richmond officer supported the FBI on this version of events.) The FBI maintained that they merely informed Richmond that, absent any contrary evidence, there was a statistical probability the man they were looking for was a white male.

The arrest of Spencer didn't formally change FBI policy but it did make them stress to law enforcement agencies that their predictions were qualified ones. After Spencer, the FBI emphasized exploration of *all* theories concerning race. As one of the agents later commented, "Each one is a lesson."

•Two months after Vasquez was released, the Arlington Police Department presented Joe Horgas with a $500 bonus. He was honored by the local American Legion and then received the American Legion's Law Officer of the Year award. At that ceremony, Joe's son, David, came up to present the award to his dad. David still had not been told the details of the case. Still, he was immensely proud of his father, and kept the award plaque in his room.

Joe also received many heartfelt letters of thanks. One was written by Carl Womack—and this was unprecedented, since he was Spencer's defense attorney. Writing to Arlington Police Chief Smokey Stover, Womack wrote, "I am writing to commend Detective Joseph Horgas for the finest police work I have seen in my thirteen years as a criminal defense attorney. . . . Joe's intellect benefited our community immeasurably. Without it a number of murders might still be unsolved and David Vasquez could still be in prison."

Paul Ferrara, director of the Virginia Bureau of Forensic Science, also wrote to the chief. "In the many speeches I have made regarding DNA analysis and the Spencer case, I emphasize the dependence of this technique upon the investigator to identify a suspect with which to compare DNA found at the crime scene. . . . For after all is said and done, if Joe Horgas had not applied his own power of deductive reasoning and perception . . . Timothy Spencer would never have been developed as a suspect. How many lives Joe Horgas has saved by his extraordinary police work will never be known."

Still another letter written to Chief Stover came from Marcie Sanders, the woman who had been raped and stabbed but had fought back and escaped when Spencer tried to tie her up. "My experience leaves me with the impression of a dedicated, tenacious professional with great concern for the work he does and the people who he deals with," she wrote. "He is to me a thinking man with a heart. It gives me peace of mind to have a resolution of my case, to have the question of [who raped me] brought to an end."

•Vasquez, upon his release, pondered a lawsuit against the Arlington County Police Department and his defense attorneys. Vasquez retained one of the most experienced civil liberties litigators in the nation, Phil Hirschkopf. Hirschkopf, who practiced in the D.C. area, found Vasquez's original defense attorneys to be extremely open and willing to share their files. After carefully reviewing their files, Hirschkopf concluded that the lawyers hadn't done anything wrong, and that a lawsuit against them didn't have a chance.

"It was a horrendous murder," Hirschkopf later explained. "Once David denied being there after two independent IDs, it's not unreasonable for cops to say, this might be the guy. Cops have tunnel vision. And then they told him little lies to get him to confess, like about having his fingerprints. It's something they're trained at police academy to do. They didn't physically brutalize him. They did emotionally brutalize him. But all that's fair play."

Hirschkopf also pointed out that it didn't help, of course, that Vasquez's mother had tried through one of her son's friends to get a bartender to lie about her son's whereabouts on the night of Carolyn Hamm's death. Things did not look good. The family went to several other attorneys, and all rejected the civil case.

"I knew all along," Rich McCue said, ". . . that if the pardon was granted, someone was going to come out and say, 'Why did you let this innocent man plead guilty?' Number one, I didn't let him plead guilty. It was his decision and given what he was facing it was a good decision." McCue also felt that given the evidence, Henry Hudson really had no choice. "I think that he would have been lynched if he hadn't gone ahead with the prosecution."

Despite the criticism of the Hamm investigation and Vasquez's pardon, Henry Hudson will never agree that he or anybody else did anything improper. "I don't see where anyone made a mistake. People have criticized Chuck Shelton and Bob Carrig for doing a tough job. They had a difficult homicide here. They used proper interrogation techniques. There may have been high pressure, but when you deal with a homicide case, there are high-pressure stakes. Their confession was reviewed by a judge and the court authorized our use of a portion of it. . . . Can I warrant beyond a reasonable doubt he was guilty of capital murder? I'm not sure. It would have been up to twelve citizens to sort this case and that's what the U.S. Constitution mandates. . . ."

Though he never sued Arlington County, David Vasquez nevertheless did receive a monetary award. In February of 1990, Vasquez's plight came to the attention of Virginia state senators Clive Duval and Charles Colgan. The senators introduced special compensatory legislation and in August of that year, a state law was passed, and David Vasquez was awarded $117,000. With interest, Vasquez will receive about $1,000 per month for nineteen years.

Upon receiving news of the award Vasquez told the *Arlington Journal* that he deserved a $500,000 award. "I'm not happy at all. They're getting away with everything. They're getting away with murder. . . . It's ridiculous. The system stinks," he said. Vasquez was last reported to be working as a janitor.

It was painful for Horgas and Helen Fahey, who had worked so hard to get Vasquez out, to see a lawsuit even contemplated. Anyway, they knew it was impossible to blame any one person or agency. Some had a different opinion. *The Washington Post*, in a July 17, 1989, article called it a "system failure."

The reality is that our system of justice is not a perfect system. It is a system where the acceptable risks are that sometimes the guilty go free and the innocent are incarcerated. But, even though our system of justice grinds its gears, belches smoke, and often stalls, it works most of the time.

•What is unique about the story of David Vasquez is that the people who put him behind bars were also the ones who set him free. No family member, crusading journalist, or civil libertarian banged the drum for David's release. Police and prosecutors did so. Ironically, it was Susan Tucker's horrific demise that ultimately became David Vasquez's salvation; if she had not died, he would still be in prison.

The advent of DNA fingerprinting, meanwhile, is gradually changing the geometry of justice as surely as did fingerprints more than 100 years ago. Prosecutors hail it as revolutionary. The defense bar cautions that it may be a threat to civil liberties.

The primary defense challenges have focused on the procedures used to determine a match and on the reliability of calculating the odds of a match. The vast majority of courts who have reviewed DNA fingerprinting have found it to be scientifically reliable. In fact, following Spencer's conviction, Virginia became the first state in the nation to have its own DNA analysis facility, and by 1994 twenty-eight states and the federal government had permitted the use of DNA in their courts. Other courts, however, such as those in California, have limited the admissibility of DNA fingerprinting. Regardless of how heated the battle has become, it is safe to say that DNA fingerprinting is here to stay.

Detectives like Joe, however, point out that it will never replace the human cop, for "you still have to come up with suspects, and somebody's got to be there to answer the phone when an informant calls."

POSTSCRIPT

ALL FOUR OF TIMOTHY SPENCER'S DEATH SENTENCES WERE INITIALLY affirmed by the Virginia Supreme Court and the United States Supreme Court. But then, as in all death penalty cases, the long and tedious process of additional federal and state challenges began. No one expected Spencer to be executed for at least ten years, if indeed he was to be executed at all.

Yet after less than six years, on March 7, 1994, Richmond Circuit Court Judge James B. Wilkinson made the following ruling:

It is hereby ordered that the date of execution for Timothy Wilson Spencer is set on April 27, 1994. . . . It is further ordered that the . . . defendant is to be conveyed from his present place of incarceration to the state correctional facility housing the death chamber and there on April 27, 1994, be put to death in the manner prescribed by law, by being electrocuted until he is dead, unless a suspension of execution be ordered by the Governor or some other Court of competent jurisdiction.

Though Spencer was first charged and convicted for the murder of Susan Tucker, because of procedural delays in that appeal, the scheduled execution was for the murder of Debbie Davis. Moreover, everyone was astonished at how quickly the process moved, especially Spencer and his lawyer, Barry Weinstein. In his seventeen years as a death penalty lawyer, Weinstein had never seen a case moved so furiously through the system. "The only explanation I can think of," he later said, "is that the South Side Strangler wreaked havoc in Richmond so everybody concerned wanted Tim dead. The Attorney General's office very aggressively pursued this case, much more than other case I've seen."

Donald Curry, the assistant Attorney General who fought Spencer's appeals, responded to Weinstein's allegations. "To assert . . . that Timothy Spencer was singled out for particularly aggressive conduct by our office is incorrect," he said. "If Spencer's case proceeded through the system faster than others, it was only because the lack of merit to his claims was so clear and the evidence of his guilt so overwhelming."

Once the execution date had been set, Spencer's defense attorneys moved into high gear for their last assault. This final set of appeals challenged the validity of the original DNA tests linking Spencer to the crimes.

Bill Linka, one of Spencer's appellate attorneys, argued in his brief, "Mr. Spencer, who has steadfastly maintained his innocence, contends that Lifecodes may have engaged in some of the same deceptive or faulty practices with respect to the testing and computing in his case that the court identified in *People v. Castro.*"

Following Spencer's conviction, Bronx, New York, janitor Joseph Castro was charged with murdering a woman and her two-year-old daughter. A bloodstain found on Castro's watch was analyzed by Lifecodes and found to match the blood of the young woman. Barry Sheck and Peter Neufield, the two New York attorneys who represented Castro and had in fact been at the forefront of the assault on DNA testing, argued to the trial court that the evidence should not be admitted because Lifecodes did not follow its protocols for extracting and analyzing the DNA. The judge agreed with Sheck and

Neufield and excluded the bloodstain on the watch. Interestingly, however, Mr. Castro eventually pleaded guilty.

The thrust of Linka's argument was that because Lifecodes had not followed its own rules and protocols for measuring and calculating the size of the autorad bands in *Castro*, it was likely Lifecodes committed the same error in Spencer. Seeking to prove this theory the defense asked to analyze Lifecodes' original work on all four cases—the laboratory workbooks, computer printouts, and other original documents.

The appeal also complained that Spencer's original defense attorneys were remiss in not having undertaken such an analysis—thus providing him ineffective legal representation.

Dave Johnson and Jeff Everhart, Spencer's defense attorneys in Davis, responded to this accusation with an affidavit revealing that they had secretly had Spencer's DNA tested.

[W]e sought to independently test the reliability and accuracy of the Lifecodes DNA testing which had inculpated Spencer. We knew that such testing had inculpated Spencer in both Richmond offenses, as well as the Arlington offense. We also knew that the Lifecodes test in the Arlington case had been corroborated by the independent test conducted by Cellmark (another DNA lab). Nevertheless Spencer adamantly maintained his innocence. Therefore, prior to the first Richmond trial and without notice to either the trial court or the prosecution, we obtained a fresh sample of Spencer's blood and took it to Dr, James Geyer, the Director of Disputed Paternity testing at Genetic's Design Incorporated in Greensboro, North Carolina. . . . Dr. Geyer sent the fresh sample of Spencer's blood to Lifecodes for DNA testing under a fictitious name and in the guise of a fictitious paternity case. . . . The results of this "blind" testing only confirmed Lifecodes' previous conclusion that the DNA pattern from Spencer's blood matched the DNA pattern from the DNA found in the body fluids at the crime scene.

The court was convinced that the defense had in fact made a sufficient effort to challenge Lifecodes' findings. New requests for further DNA tests were firmly rejected. Oddly, though, Spencer seemed to remain optimistic. As his scheduled execution approached, he believed that some court would finally recognize his right to a new DNA test.

As the day came closer, Spencer spent most of his time by himself, watching a little television but mostly sleeping long hours.

The final flurry of attempts to save Spencer's life began on Thursday, April 21. While Spencer's attorneys were before Judge Wilkinson seeking a reconsideration of their request for a new DNA test, FBI agent Steve Mardigian arrived at Greenville penitentiary in Jarratt, Virginia, with the hope that Spencer, knowing the end was near, would finally bare his soul. Such an effort had worked with other convicted serial killers like Ted Bundy. The information gleaned was enormously valuable in building the FBI's understanding of serial killers.

Within moments of being introduced, Spencer said emphatically, "I have nothing to say to you. I didn't kill anybody. I was framed." That was the end of the interview.

The response—"I was framed"—was not new. Spencer had steadfastly and defiantly maintained the same position all along.

According to Weinstein, Spencer was plagued by one question: How did Horgas get an indictment? Weinstein later commented that each time Spencer asked him that question, Weinstein replied, "I can't answer you. I don't know myself."

On Tuesday, April 26, the United States District Court for the Southern District of Virginia rejected Spencer's appeal. The next morning, April 27, the United States Court of Appeals for the Fourth Circuit affirmed this lower court ruling. While Weinstein hurriedly assembled his final appeal to the United States Supreme Court, Virginia prison authorities made the final preparations for Timothy Wilson Spencer to die. The execution time was set for 11 P.M.

Several hours before Spencer was scheduled to die, I called Horgas at work to ask if he had any second thoughts about Spencer's guilt. "Silence speaks louder than words," he announced. "If Spencer was innocent he'd have been screaming and crying, 'I never did this. I'm innocent! Help me. Please help me.' He wouldn't be lying around sleeping, just waiting to die for something he didn't do." I then asked Horgas if he was going to attend the execution.

"My job is done. I identified Spencer and arrested him. I wanted to see him tried for Tucker's murder and he was. I don't need to see him die. My ego's not that big."

After spending a little over an hour with his mother, grandmother, brother, and other relatives, Spencer was given his last meal at about 4 P.M. He specifically requested prison authorities not to disclose the contents of the last meal to the media.

At about 10:45 P.M., fifteen minutes before he was to die, Spencer lost his last legal battle when the United States Supreme Court rejected his request for a new DNA test.

A few minutes later, Spencer strode into the silver gray death chamber. According to eyewitness accounts,

> [H]e rubbed his newly shaven scalp and stared straight up at the clock over the electric chair. . . . He [wore] gray shoes, a powder blue shirt and jeans cut off at the right knee—to improve the flow of current. . . . The warden asked Spencer if he had any last words. "Yeah, I think . . ." Spencer then fell silent, blinked and looked around. After about 20 seconds he nodded firmly for the officers to proceed. The leather death mask was strapped on his head.
>
> A chaplain rubbed Spencer's back, then stepped into the witness booth and softly recited the Lord's Prayer as the executioner—hidden behind a one way mirror—pushed the green execution button. Spencer received 1825 volts at 7.5 amps for 30 seconds, then 250 volts for 60 seconds. Then the jolts were repeated. After the third jolt, drool ran down a face strap onto Spencer's shirt. His left arm slipped off the arm rest. Smoke rose from the contact attached to his right leg.

Timothy Wilson Spencer was pronounced dead at 11:13 P.M.

Though the murders of Susan Tucker, Debbie Davis, Susan

Hellams, and Diane Cho were reported only in Virginia, newspapers around the country reported Spencer's execution. The *New York Times* headline read, "First U.S. Execution Based on DNA Evidence," while the *Los Angeles Times* reported, "Virginia Serial Killer Convicted by DNA Evidence Is Executed." It was DNA fingerprinting, not Spencer's death, which was the focus of one debate in *The New York Times*.

> "It's peace of mind for the prosecution," said Virginia's Attorney General, James S. Gilmore 3d, who argued that DNA matching minimizes the likelihood that innocent people will be executed. . . . "DNA is a deadly weapon," said Steven E. Feldman, a defense attorney in San Diego. "Where the defense is funded on a shoestring, we're being out-gunned. The biostatistician comes into court and says, 'There's a one in 10 billion likelihood that someone other than the suspect placed that specimen there.' But nobody really knows how good the labs are."

Unlike the national papers, the *Richmond Times-Dispatch* focused on the execution itself. "Unbowed . . . to the end," reported the local paper. "Described by those who knew him inside and outside of prison as something of a loner," the story continued, "Spencer largely remains a puzzle, a sometimes pleasant looking and easy-going man capable of savage torture. . . . As if to haunt his accusers, a killer synonymous with sadistic rage took his secrets with him. 'This is Timothy Spencer's revenge,' said Detective W. Ray Williams."

Horgas, for one, was not haunted by Spencer's refusal to talk. He would have liked to have had Spencer admit that he had killed Hamm, though. "Not for me," he said after the execution, "but for others around here." Horgas refused to elaborate but it was clear he was referring to those in the police department who still believed that Spencer might not have killed Carolyn Hamm. And Horgas wasn't the only one who wanted a deathbed confession from Spencer.

On the previous Friday, April 22, Horgas received a handwritten note from Vasquez's family attorney asking Horgas to try, in the last few days before the execution, to obtain Spencer's written confession to the Hamm murder. After everything that had happened, including the pardon and the monetary award, Vasquez's attorney still hoped for final closure in the form of Spencer's confession.

Yet even if Spencer had given a deathbed confession, it is unlikely it would have satisfied David Vasquez. "It's over for him, but it's not over for me," Vasquez told the *Arlington Journal* the day after Spencer died. "It's still very hard to put this behind me," added Vasquez's mother. "I really wanted to witness the execution. It sounds terrible . . . but all those years my son was suffering Spencer was probably laughing that someone was taking the rap for him."

Vasquez's bitterness ran so deep, in fact, that he never publicly acknowledged or let alone thanked the man who was responsible for his freedom.

"This was not just about David Vasquez," Horgas said soon after the execution. "I met the man only once for a few minutes but he represented the difference between right and wrong. We're supposed to have a justice system where there are safeguards against an innocent guy going to prison—you know the expression, 'Better ten guilty people go free than one innocent person go to jail.'

"And you really believe that?" I asked.

"What do you mean?" Joe retorted. "Of course I do. It's the only game in town."

With those bolts of electricity on April 27, 1994, Timothy Wilson Spencer became the first person in history to be executed on the basis of DNA fingerprinting. At the Tucker sentencing hearing, Travis, Spencer's younger brother, put it more succinctly when he testified, "DNA took my brother."

But it must be remembered that DNA didn't bring Spencer in.

Joe Horgas did.

364.1523 Mones, Paul A.
M
          Stalking justice.